ORALITY AND LANGUAGE

Part of the series Key Concepts in Indigenous Studies, this book focuses on the concepts that recur in any discussion of the society, culture and literature among indigenous peoples.

This book, the fourth in a five-volume series, deals with the two key concepts of language and orality of indigenous peoples from Asia, Australia, North America and South America. With contributions from renowned scholars, activists and experts from across the globe, it looks at the intricacies of oral transmission of memory and culture, literary production and transmission, and the nature of creativity among indigenous communities. It also discusses the risk of a complete decline of the languages of indigenous peoples, as well as the attempts being made to conserve these languages.

Bringing together academic insights and experiences from the ground, this unique book, with its wide coverage, will serve as a comprehensive guide for students, teachers and scholars of indigenous studies. It will be essential reading for those in social and cultural anthropology, tribal studies, sociology and social exclusion studies, politics, religion and theology, cultural studies, literary and postcolonial studies, and Third World and Global South studies, as well as activists working with indigenous communities.

G. N. Devy is Honorary Professor, Centre for Multidisciplinary Development Research, Dharwad, India, and Chairman, People's Linguistic Survey of India. An award-winning writer and cultural activist, he is known for his 50-volume language survey. He is Founder Director of the Adivasi Academy at Tejgadh in Gujarat, India, and was formerly Professor of English at M. S. University of Baroda. He is the recipient of the Sahitya Akademi Award, Linguapax Prize, Prince Claus Award and Padma Shri. With several books in English, Marathi and Gujarati, he has co-edited (with Geoffrey V. Davis and K. K. Chakravarty) *Narrating Nomadism: Tales of Recovery and Resistance* (2012); *Knowing Differently: The Challenge of the*

Indigenous (2013); *Performing Identities: Celebrating Indigeneity in the Arts* (2014); and *The Language Loss of the Indigenous* (2016), published by Routledge.

Geoffrey V. Davis was Professor of Commonwealth and Postcolonial Literatures at the University of Aachen, Germany. He was international chair of the Association for Commonwealth Literature and Language Studies (ACLALS) and chair of the European branch (EACLALS). He co-edited *Cross/Cultures: Readings in the Post/Colonial Literatures and Cultures in English* and the African studies series *Matatu*. His publications include *Staging New Britain: Aspects of Black and South Asian British Theatre Practice* (2006) and *African Literatures, Postcolonial Literatures in English: Sources and Resources* (2013).

Key Concepts in Indigenous Studies

Series Editors: G. N. Devy

Honorary Professor, Centre for Multidisciplinary Development Research, Dharwad, India, and Chairman, People's Linguistic Survey of India

Geoffrey V. Davis

Former Professor of Commonwealth and Postcolonial Literatures, University of Aachen, Germany

This series of volumes offers the most systematic and foundational literature available to date for use by undergraduate and postgraduate students of indigenous studies. It brings together essays by experts from across the globe on concepts forming the bedrock of this rapidly growing field in five focused volumes: *Environment and Belief Systems* (Vol. 1); *Gender and Rights* (Vol. 2); *Indigeneity and Nation* (Vol. 3); *Orality and Language* (Vol. 4); and *Performance and Knowledge* (Vol. 5). These contain short, informative and easily accessible essays on the perspectives of indigenous communities from all continents of the world. The essays are written specifically for an international audience. They thus allow drawing of transnational and cross-cultural parallels, and form useful material as textbooks as well as texts for general readership. Introducing a new orientation to traditional anthropology with comprehensive and in-depth studies, the volumes foreground knowledge traditions and praxis of indigenous communities.

Environment and Belief Systems
Edited by G. N. Devy and Geoffrey V. Davis

Gender and Rights
Edited by G. N. Devy and Geoffrey V. Davis

Indigeneity and Nation
Edited by G. N. Devy and Geoffrey V. Davis

Orality and Language
Edited by G. N. Devy and Geoffrey V. Davis

Performance and Knowledge
Edited by G. N. Devy and Geoffrey V. Davis

For more information about this series, please visit: www.routledge.com/ Key-Concepts-in-Indigenous-Studies/book-series/KCIS

ORALITY AND LANGUAGE

Edited by G. N. Devy and Geoffrey V. Davis

Routledge
Taylor & Francis Group

LONDON AND NEW YORK

First published 2021
by Routledge
2 Park Square, Milton Park, Abingdon, Oxon OX14 4RN

and by Routledge
52 Vanderbilt Avenue, New York, NY 10017

Routledge is an imprint of the Taylor & Francis Group, an informa business

© 2021 selection and editorial matter, G. N. Devy and Geoffrey V. Davis; individual chapters, the contributors

British Library Cataloguing-in-Publication Data
A catalogue record for this book is available from the British Library

Library of Congress Cataloging-in-Publication Data
A catalog record for this book has been requested

ISBN: 978-0-367-24536-8 (hbk)
ISBN: 978-0-367-60937-5 (pbk)
ISBN: 978-1-003-10259-5 (ebk)

Typeset in Bembo
by Apex CoVantage, LLC

CONTENTS

FIGURES

TABLES

MAPS

CONTRIBUTORS

Dany Adone is Chair of Applied English Linguistics at the University of Cologne, Germany. In Australia, she is also University Professorial Fellow at Northern Institute/Charles Darwin University, Visiting Professor at AIATSIS and Visiting Scholar at the Mirima Dawang Woorlab-gerring Centre in Kununurra. Her research focuses on language endangerment and contact in indigenous Australia. She has conducted field work in Australia since 1992 and works mostly with several indigenous communities in Arnhem Land.

Geoffrey V. Davis, to whom the five volumes in this series are dedicated, was to be the joint editor for the series but could not be since he passed away after a short illness in November 2018. He studied at Oxford and taught at the RWTH, Aachen in Germany. He was Chairperson of the Association for Commonwealth Literature and Language Study (ACLALS), the international body, as well as its European wing, EACLALS. He was a prolific editor and writer and during his life published articles and books on African literature, Canadian literature and indigenous studies. He co-edited, with G. N. Devy and K.K. Chakravarty, *Narrating Nomadism, Knowing Differently, Performing Freedom* and *The Language of the Indigenous* (Routledge).

Aone Van Engelenhoven lectures on Southeast Asian linguistics at Leiden University, the Netherlands. He received his PhD degree on a description of Leti, an endangered minority language in Indonesia, in 1995. His research focuses on, among other things, linguistic anthropology, specifically its verbal folklore and the semiotics of storytelling. Topics of his interest are lexical parallelism, oral poetry and the use of Indonesian and indigenous languages for the transfer of ritual knowledge.

Darin Flynn is Associate Professor and Chair of Linguistics at the University of Calgary, Canada, in the Treaty 7 territory of the Blackfoot, Tsuut'ina and Îyethka

Nakoda. He teaches and researches mainly on Algonquian, Dene and Wakashan languages. He also helps to train indigenous language teachers, community linguists and other professionals at the Canadian Indigenous Languages and Literacy Development Institute at the University of Alberta since 2004, and in the First Nations and Endangered Languages Program at the University of British Columbia since 2010.

Bentley James is a linguist and anthropologist who has lived and worked in North-East Arnhem Land, Australia, for over 20 years. His research interests include sign, ritual, social organization and marine archaeology. In 1993, he began work in the Crocodile Islands. Collaborations with senior people created a family of interrelated projects on the islands, ranger and heritage programs, language nests, a dictionary and an atlas, and language resources in support of bilingual education and linguistic, cultural and biological diversity.

Elaine L. Maypilama is an honorary research fellow at Charles Darwin University, Australia, and is employed by Menzies. She has been involved in participatory and action research projects on indigenous health, education, community development and indigenous languages. Since her involvement with the Graduate School for Health Practice, and now Research Centre for Health and Wellbeing, she has been involved in ARC-funded, FACSIA-funded and ESS-funded projects.

Roberto Viereck Salinas is Associate Professor at Concordia University, Montreal, Canada. He earned his PhD (2003) in Hispanic philology from Universidad Complutense de Madrid, Spain. He has published several articles and chapters on translation and Spanish American colonial literature, and also has two books on current indigenous Spanish American poetry: *La voz letrada. Escritura, oralidad y traducción: diálogos con seis poetas amerindios contemporáneos* (Abya Yala, 2012) and *Poéticas mapuche(s)* (Askasis, 2018). He also co-coordinated the colonial section of the *Diccionario de la traducción en Hispanoamérica* (Iberoamericana/ Vervuert, 2013), and participated as a contributor for *On Words to that Effect: Orality and the Writing of Literary History* (John Benjamins, 2016) and *A History of Chilean Literature* (Cambridge University Press, forthcoming).

PREFACE

The volumes in this series have long been in making. The idea came up in 2011 in a conversation between Prof. Geoffrey Davis and me. The two of us had by then worked on six anthologies related to indigenous studies to which scholars from all continents had contributed. Two of these are published by Orient BlackSwan (*Indigeneity*, 2009 and *Voice and Memory*, 2011) and four by Routledge between 2012 and 2016 (*Narrating Nomadism*, *Knowing Differently*, *Performing Identities* and *The Language Loss of the Indigenous*). However, we felt that we needed to do more, a lot more, in order to firmly establish this newly emerging field. Shashank Sinha and Shoma Choudhury of Routledge showed a keen interest in our proposal. Enthused by the idea of bringing out a set of volumes dealing with some of the definitive themes of the field and assured by the possibility of publication of the volumes, we started our work. Of course, it was not entirely easy going for us. The challenges were many and the scale in which we wanted to cast the volumes was not easy to handle. Despite the difficulties and setbacks expected in such an intellectual venture, we kept up. Most of the editorial work was completed by early 2018. As we were getting ready to send the typescripts, alas, Prof. Geoffrey Davis died in a short internment in an Aachen hospital. His last mail came to me a day before he was to be admitted. The loss was a big blow to me. His friends and colleagues spread over all continents mourned his death deeply. For me, the most civilized way of mourning was to ensure that the volumes to which he had contributed so much care and toil got published. Who was Geoffrey Davis and why was he interested in the indigenous? Perhaps the best way for me to explain this is to repeat here the response I sent to two questions from Prof. Janet Wilson (hereafter JW) of Southampton University.

JW: What were the points of synergy (ideological, intellectual, political activist) that brought you and Geoff together, and when and how did this happen, i.e., what were the particular contexts/motivations? I remember I think Geoff had just retired and was possibly looking for a new project? And might have been inspired through his involvement with ACLALS.

DEVY: I think I met him the first time in 1984 at the EACLALS conference at Sitges, Spain. During the 1980s, I was a "regular" at the EACLALS since India did not have an active Commonwealth Literature culture as yet. But, my memory of that meeting is not very clear. In 1988, Geoff had convened a conference at Aachen, Germany, where Geoff spent most of his academic life. I was invited to it for a plenary. This experience left me impressed by his organizational ability. In between, we had met at other places too – Austria, Hungary, Singapore. But all these meetings were casual; and I do not recall any memorable conversation having taken place between us during these conferences. During the 1990s, Geoff hosted a conference on literature and activism. I left my professorship at Baroda, India, in 1996. Geoff had heard about this move from friends. He asked me to lecture at the conference. I did. It was during this conference I noticed that he was deeply respectful of activism; that his empathy for the dispossessed was genuinely deep. I also noticed that he was extremely wary of using clichéd and fashionable jargon. The impression these qualities made on me was strong. A few years later, he was to attend the ACLALS Triennial in Hyderabad, India. He wrote to me asking if he could visit me after the Hyderabad conference. He knew that I had stopped attending academic conferences and there was no chance of our meeting in Hyderabad. So, I invited him to Baroda, 1500 km north of Hyderabad.

I am not sure if he enjoyed his visit to Baroda. On the day he was to arrive, for reasons difficult for to me know, I altogether forgot about his arrival. I was to meet him at the airport. Baroda in those days was a very small airport and every day only three or four flights arrived there. And overseas visitors were not a common sight. Geoff waited there till almost the last co-traveller had left the meeting area. The last one to leave happened to be an architect named Karan Grover, who is a living legend in the field of architecture. Grover asked Geoff if he was expecting anyone. Geoff mentioned my name. This worked. Karan Grover and I had been friends for decades, and Geoff was made to feel welcome on my behalf, brought to his lodgings and, the forgetting and forgiving over, we met over dinner. The next day, I drove him in my car to the location of the Adivasi Academy (the Tribal University) that I was trying to establish in those years. This location was 90 km east of Baroda. On the way, I talked with passion all about my plans, my dreams. He listened. He spent another day in Baroda meeting Karan and enjoyed the famous Grover wine. I was busy in my work with the tribal academy. The next morning, I drove Geoff to the airport as he was leaving for Bombay and then to Aachen. At the airport, he asked me if I could have him visit the Adivasi Academy again for a longer time, a week or so. I said, "Why do you not stay for a semester?" He was a bit puzzled by my offer, made in such a casual manner. So, I added, "Be a Fellow with us." He took that offer and returned to Baroda the following year, but for a short time. I think it was after two more brief trips that he agreed to spend six months in Baroda.

I must explain that the Adivasi Academy is not like a university. It is a community workstation at best, with really very minimum facilities that makes for most of us what we call "civilization." The "Fellowship" had no set rules. They were made looking at the individual's ability and desire to contribute what one had promised to contribute. . . . The "projects" ranged from writing a book or an article, teaching music or language to children, keeping the library or museum in good order, tending a piece of agricultural land, setting up a community micro-credit group or just documenting any of these activities. When Geoff became a fellow of the Adivasi Academy, there were three others, Brian and Eileen Coates from Limerick, Ireland and Lachman Khubchandani, a linguist from Pune, India. Eileen had accepted to help us with the museum and Lachman was to write a book in linguistics. I was more ambitious with Geoff. I said to him, "If you do not mind, please do nothing, only watch what goes on here and when it pleases you discuss ideas with me." He agreed. The facilities given to the fellows included housing in Baroda and meals when they visited the Academy, 90 km away from Baroda. All my meetings with tribals were transacted in their languages. English words were rarely heard. Only occasionally, some visitors helped Geoff with English interpretations. Geoff, I must say, braved all of this discomfort without a murmur. The impression I had formed about his deep empathy for the dispossessed became firmer. In the fifth month of his stay, I sent a word to him asking if he was available for a serious conversation. He obliged. We met in my Baroda office – the Bhasha Centre – at 2 PM. I asked him if he would join me in imagining an international "non-conference" for looking at the world through the perspective of the indigenous. He said, "I cannot promise, but I will try." Our conversation continued for several hours and, probably, both of us had a reasonably good idea of what all must be avoided in making our idea of conference a completely rooted to the ground. I proposed the name "chotro" (a shared platform); he consented to it with great enthusiasm. Next morning, I found him at Bhasha. He had a "Call for Chotro" ready with him. I made several calls to various offices and individuals in Delhi to finalize the material arrangements for the First Chotro. That afternoon, Geoff sat at the computer and sent out close to 150 mails. Before he left Baroda, we were fully involved in putting together the unusual conference. He made one visit to India before the conference was held in Delhi in January 2008. We met in Delhi. I had to combine some of my other works with the work related to Chotro. One of these involved a visit to the prime minister's office. He was a bit shocked when I told him that after sorting out the conference related arrangements for stay and local transportation, I would be going to the PM's office and he was welcome to join me. Years later, I have heard him narrating this anecdote to friends over a glass of wine. The Delhi Chotro was the first one. We put together several more in subsequent years and worked on the conference volumes, meeting in several countries. Geoff became a frequent visitor to India to Baroda, and also to my home and family. I am not aware if we shared an ideology. In a way, all of us in the field of literature have a varying degree of progressive outlook on life and society. But, what clicked between Geoff and me is something else, and that is his immense patience with me and his ability to cope with surprises and shocks, which could not be avoided considering my involvement in several social causes. John Keats, speaking of William Shakespeare's "genius," had used the term "negative capability" – the ability to live amidst uncertainties. The mutual recognition of this negative capability brought us together for under-taking unconventional kind of work, serious though not strictly academic.

JW: What roles/or positions did Geoff take as collaborator, e.g., in co-organizing Chotro and in working with the Adivasis/Bhasha more generally?

DEVY: When we thought of creating the Chotro non-conferences, we had no funding support. We had no sponsors, no funds for international travel. Bhasha Centre was not a full-scale "institution" till then. Besides, "Indigenous Stud-ies" was not any accepted field of academic work. We were not sure if any self-respecting publisher would accept to publish the proceedings. Therefore, in all of these matters, we shared responsibility. But, generally speaking, he dealt with the overseas participants and I handled the Indian issues, material and academic. I accepted to identify publishers, negotiate with them, do the nec-essary correspondence; Geoff focused on copy editing of the texts. But, this division of work was not sanctimonious. Either of us was free to cross over and even required to do so looking at each other's convenience. Never forget that Geoff had his other major obligations and academic projects, and I had mine. We had no desire to claim credit for the work we were doing. It was born out of our desire to create a legitimate space for the voice of the indigenous.

I hope my response to Janet Wilson will have made it clear why I enjoyed working with Geoffrey Davis on so many intellectual projects. In India's intellectual history, there have been glorious examples of intellectual collaboration between Indian thinkers and scholars and writers and scholars from other countries. W.B. Yeats and Purohit Swamy, Yeats and Tagore, Tolstoy and Gandhi developed their ideas through such collaborations. In our time, with the rising tide of the "Right" politi-cal parties, a narrow idea of nationalism is gaining a greater currency, making such collaborations difficult to carry through. I am pleased that this series of volumes is seeing the light of the day, bringing my work together with Geoffrey Davis to a successful conclusion.

ACKNOWLEDGEMENTS

The initial idea of this volume and the series to which it belongs came up in 2012. Since then, Prof. Geoffrey Davis, who was to be the co-editor, corresponded with several scholars from the field of Commonwealth literature from other academic disciplines. These scholars from various disciplines and several continents gave their advice and suggestions for identifying scholars to be involved in the project. They are too numerous to be mentioned individually. I would like to record my gratitude to them. The scholars and activists who consented to contribute, and the majority of them who kept their promise, made the putting together of the volumes possible. Their participation in the most tangible way calls for my thanks. Several organizations and institutions offered Prof. Geoffrey Davis and me opportunities of meeting and taking our plans for these volumes forward. They include the Association for Commonwealth Literature and Language Studies, for a conference in Cyprus; Bhasha Research and Publication Centre, Baroda, for various events through these years; the Kiel Voche, organized by Kiel City Council in Germany; the German Academy, for convening a conference at Hamburg; Aide et Action, for convening a meeting in Geneva; and several Indian colleges and universities, for creating spaces on the sidelines of conferences – I thank all of them. I wonder if without these meetings the project would have moved forward at all.

I would like to thank Ingrid, Prof. Davis's wife, for ungrudgingly encouraging him to spend his funds and time on travels to India to work on this project. Surekha, my life partner, has most generously supported the project throughout its years of slow progress by providing ideas, hospitality and courage. I cannot thank her enough.

The publication of these volumes would not have been at all possible had it not been for the abiding friendship and support of Dr. Shashank Shekhar Sinha, Publishing Director, and his inspiring colleague Shoma Choudhury at Routledge. I carry in my heart the comfort drawn from their genuine friendship.

INTRODUCTION

G. N. Devy

Over the last two decades, scientists have come up with mathematical models for predicting the life of languages (Braggs and Freedman, 1993). These predictions have invariably indicated that the human species is moving rapidly close to the extinction of a large part of its linguistic heritage. These predictions do not agree on the exact magnitude of the impending disaster, but they all agree on the fact that close to three-quarters or more of all existing natural human languages are half in the grave. There are, on the other hand, advocates of linguistic globalization. The processes of globalization have found it necessary to promote homogenized cultures. The idea has found support among the classes that stand to benefit by the globalization of economies. They would prefer the spread of one or only a few languages all over the world so that communication across national boundaries becomes the easiest ever. Obviously, the nations and communities that have learned to live within only a single language, whose economic well-being is not dependent on knowing languages other than their own and whose knowledge systems are well-secure within their own languages will not experience the stress of language loss, at least not immediately, though the loss of the world's total language heritage which will weaken the global stock of human intellect and civilizations will have numerous indirect enfeebling effects on them, too (Dalby, 2003). Since it is language, first of all things, that makes us human and distinguishes us from other species and animate nature (Blench and Spriggs, 2012), and since the human consciousness can only function given the ability for linguistic expression, it becomes necessary to recognize language as the most crucial aspect of the cultural capital. It has taken human beings the continuous work of about half a million years to accumulate this valuable capital (Corballis, 2011). In our time, we have come close to the point of losing most of it. Historians of civilization tell us that a comparable, though not exactly similar, situation had probably arisen in the past, some seven or eight thousand years ago (Crystal, 2000). This was when human beings discovered the magic of nature that are seeds. When the shift from entirely hunting-gathering or pastoralist economies to early agrarian economies started taking place, we are told, the language diversity of the world was severely affected (Corballis, 2011; Blench and Spriggs, 2012). It may not be wrong to surmise that the current crisis in human languages is also triggered by the fundamental economic shift that has enveloped the entire world, north or south, west or east. This time, though, the crisis has an added layer, as a lot of human activity is now dominated by human-made intelligence. The technologies aligned with artificial intelligence are all heavily dependent on modelling the activity of the human mind during linguistic transactions. Language-based technologies are now well entrenched partners in the semantic universe(s) that bind human communities together (Gillespie, 2007). Therefore, that universe is being re-shaped. Language today is as much a system of meaning in cyberspace affecting communication between a machine and another machine as it has been a system of meaning in the social space achieving communication between a human being and another human being. Amidst these unprecedented global-cultural changes, languages of the indigenous are being reduced to pale shadows of their old self (Cru, 2010). Many of them have been around for centuries and, in some cases, such as Munda and Satal, for over a millennium. The six in-depth essays included in this volume bring out the complex process of the loss of orality and the loss of the indigenous languages. Aone Van Engelenhoven ("Orality in Southeast Asia") and Roberto Viereck Salinas ("Orality and writing in Spanish America") show how foundational orality has been in the cultural transactions of Southeast Asia and Latin America, respectively. Complementary to these two insightful essays are the two essays dealing with the languages of the indigenous, one jointly written by Dany Adone, Bentley James and Elaine L. Maypilama ("Indigenous languages of Arnhem Land") and one by Darin Flynn ("Indigenous languages in Canada"). They present objective status reports of numerous indigenous languages from two different continents. Read together, these four essays present an acute cultural pathology of the global situation of the oral heritage of humanity and the indigenous communities that have thus far preserved them. The essay by Geoffrey V. Davis ("How to Write an Oral Culture") shows how several Canadian poets have engaged with rapidly disappearing indigenous languages and their oral traditions, and how they have found literary strategies to shore up what still can be salvaged (Florey, 2010). My essay ("The languages in India and a movement in retrospect") is designed to complement his. It reports on the situation of the languages of the adivasis in India, and how a people's movement emerged to document and empower them (Devy, 2014). The six essays deal with different geographical zones, languages and writers, but they are all together in providing a kaleidoscopic view of the woeful plight of oral traditions and speech communities. These six essays are a common meditation on a global issue that needs everybody's immediate attention. Language and orality are two major fronts of the existential struggle that the indigenous peoples of the world have to face. Language, orality, identity, environment, gender, belief systems, performance traditions and rights are the issues relating to the struggles and the survival of the indigenous all over the world. Their local features vary from community to community and from country to country. However, the general narrative is fairly common. Quintessentially, this narrative refers to a colonial experience that hammered a break in the long-standing traditions of the indigenous, and yet they kept close to their traditions and nature while losing control over natural resources, land, rivers and forests in the process and clashing with a radically different framework of justice, ethics and spirituality (Bragg, 2003). For the indigenous, invariably, there are two points in time marking their emergence: one that is traced back to a mythological time enshrined in their collective memory and expressed in their community's "story of origin," and the other that is synchronous with a Columbus or a Vasco da Gama setting foot on the land that was once their dominion. It is true that no established research or theory in archaeology, anthropology, genetics, cultural geography, historical linguistics, agriculture and forestry goes to show that any or all of the indigenous people have been inhabitants of the land where they were when colonialism was inaugurated or that a very small portion of them have been associated with their present habitat since the time the homo sapiens have inhabited the Earth. There were migrations from place to place and from continent to continent during the pre-historic times as well. Yet, despite pre-historic migrations, it is true that indigenous communities have been associated with their habitats for a considerably long time. The European colonial quest, the territorial and cultural invasion associated with it, and the interference of alien political, ecological and theological paradigms brought a threat to the traditions that the indigenous had developed. The absence of desire on their part to accept and internalize the new paradigms made them stand out, be marked as "others," interpreted as "primitive" and represented as "indigenous." It is common sense that term "indigenous" as a part of a binary can only have meaning when there are other terms such as "alien," "outsiders," "non-native" and "colonialists." The one without the other would cease to have the meaning that it now has.

Though census exercises in different countries do not use a uniform framework, methodology and orientation (Bianco, 2012), the data available through the censuses carried out by different nations shows that approximately 370 million people in the world's population are indigenous. The communities identified as indigenous on the basis of their location, uniqueness of tradition, social structures and community law number close to 5,000 and are spread over 90 countries. Several different terms are used for describing them in different continents: "Aborigine" "Janjati," "Indigenous," "First Nations," "Natives," "Indian" and "Tribe." In most countries, the identification and listing of such communities is, by no means, complete and has remained, over the last seven decades since the United Nations organization was set up, an unfinished process. Despite the inadequacy in the world's knowledge about the indigenous, it is clear that their existence, environment, cultural ethos, lifestyles and values have been under a relentless assault by the practices, culture and value of the rest of the world. In recognition of the threat to indigenous cultures and knowledge systems, to their land and environment, languages, livelihood and law, the United Nations came out with a Declaration on the Rights of Indigenous People, accepted by the UN General Assembly in September 2007. The following three Articles of the Declaration address the most fundamental issues involved in the genocidal threat to their survival and their unique cultures:

Article 25:

Indigenous peoples have the right to maintain and strengthen their distinctive spiritual relationship with their traditionally owned or otherwise occupied and used lands, territories, waters and coastal seas and other resources and to uphold their responsibilities to future generations in this regard.

Article 26:

1   Indigenous peoples have the right to the lands, territories and resources which they have traditionally owned, occupied or otherwise used or acquired.
2   Indigenous peoples have the right to own, use, develop and control the lands, territories and resources that they possess by reason of traditional ownership or other traditional occupation or use, as well as those which they have otherwise acquired.
3   States shall give legal recognition and protection to these lands, territories and resources. Such recognition shall be conducted with due respect to the customs, traditions and land tenure systems of the indigenous peoples concerned.

Article 27:

States shall establish and implement, in conjunction with indigenous peoples concerned, a fair, independent, impartial, open and transparent process, giving due recognition to indigenous peoples' laws, traditions, customs and land tenure systems, to recognize and adjudicate the rights of indigenous peoples pertaining to their lands, territories and resources, including those which were traditionally owned or otherwise occupied or used. Indigenous peoples shall have the right to participate in this process.

Given that the population of the indigenous is less than 5% of the world's total population, and also that they are sharply divided in terms of tribe and community within a given country, every indigenous community exists as a minuscule minority within its political nation. To be indigenous is, in our time, to be severely marginalized in economy, politics, institutionalized knowledge and institutionalized religion. The space for the indigenous is rapidly shrinking. The year 2019 has been declared by UNESCO as the Year of the Indigenous Languages. There have been official celebrations and academic conference to "celebrate" the year. However, it is a fact that several thousand of the languages still kept alive by communities are close to extinction (Fishman, 2001). A comprehensive survey of languages that I had conducted of the 780 living languages in India in 2010 showed that nearly 300 languages, all of these spoken by the indigenous peoples, may disappear in the next few decades. In India, the national government passed a law in 2008 requiring the return of tribal community land ownership. However, nearly half of the claims have yet to be settled and the Supreme Court of India has already asked the families whose land title claims not been accepted to evacuate them. This situation is not only in India. It is also so in Thailand, where the tribals in the Chang Mai area have been fighting a bitter battle for land ownership. In Mexico, they are struggling to keep their languages alive; in Australia, despite the best efforts by the government, the status of the aborigines in professions and educational institutions remains far from what was visualized; in New Zealand, they had been facing social discrimination and continue to do so; and in Africa, their plight still deserves the description "a genocidal neglect." Despite legal provisions aimed at safeguarding the communities and their cultures, they are diminishing and suffering an undeserving obsolescence in a world that is considering when to officially announce that the Anthropocene, the epoch of unprecedented interference with nature fundamentally altering the Earth, has commenced.

Rarely do the indigenous succeed in getting their voice heard and respected. From Paraguay to Malaysia and from Canada to Australia – west, east, north, south – the story of the conquest of the natural resources of the indigenous peoples by the "civilized," read exploitative economies and industrial technologies, has been with us as commonplace for the last few decades. An unending environmental degradation of habitats of the indigenous has been the norm, not an exception, implied in the massive movement of capital across countries. Exploitation of natural resources has left the traditional habitats of the indigenous people devastated. This situation is not peculiar to any single country or continent; it is the general condition of the indigenous all over the world. The exploitation of natural resources in indigenous habitats has implications far more profound than either anthropologist or ecologists like to accept. European countries engaged in the hugely exploitative project of colonialism proposed an idea of the "savage" as a descriptive category for the ancient surviving civilizations in distant continents. Initially, the "savage," as in William Shakespeare's *The Tempest*, was a mindless brute, more mindless perhaps than brute. Later, during the 18th century, the "savage" became an object of the colonial curiosity, and because genocide of the ancient surviving peoples was a raging priority in the colonies, a great amount of "literature of curiosity" emerged in European languages. Though Rousseau's "noble savage" was not exactly drawn upon the dispatches about the indigenous sent back home by the colonial administrators and adventurists, the need to weave the indigenous in the grand theory of "society" was beginning to be felt. The three decades after the 1820s were of crucial importance in this direction. On the one hand, the regulations related to land, land measurement, land ownership and forest land were being formulated in Britain, France and Germany with a great gusto during these decades, and on the other, the ideas of citizenship had started taking into account land and forests as inescapable factors. The result of these legal, economic and political shifts within Europe had an irreversible impact on the destinies of the indigenous on all continents. For instance, in India, the entire forest cover in the sub-continent was passed on to the British sovereign as a "non-civil domain." This was precisely where the indigenous communities in India had been living for several thousand years. The transfer of their land at once made them "a little less than the subject citizens." They became isolated from history and reduced to the status of anthropology's laboratory objects. This process has not been, nor could not have been, exactly identical on all continents, Africa, North and South America, Australia and the Pacific; but the general trajectory of the process on these continents was fairly similar. It began with curiosity, passed through confrontation and ended with a unilateral imposition of sovereignty of the colonial state. When countries in these continents acquired self-rule, in most cases during the first half of the 20th century, the colonially produced "state" had come to be an antagonist for the indigenous "nation."

Readers of the volume need to bear in mind that this collection of essays is not an exercise in academic cultural theory. This and the other volumes in the five-volume series are intended as a "position" by activists who are also scholars, and by scholars who in no mean measure have been activists.

The five-volume series being brought to the readers is intended to comment on the processes through which the clash of civilizations has played out and is impacting society, culture, belief-systems and languages. Each of the volumes deals with a related set of two key issues crucial to understanding the indigenous and thinking about the processes affecting their culture and life. These are: *Environment and Belief Systems*, Volume 1; *Gender and Rights*, Volume 2; *Indigeneity and Nation*, Volume 3; *Orality and Language*, Volume 4; and *Performance and Knowledge*, Volume 5. These key concerns were selected for discussion based on my three decades of experience living amidst and working with some of the indigenous communities in western India. A large number of consultations, discussions, workshops and field visits have led me to believe that at this juncture of history, these ten form the "key concepts" that one must understand in order to imagine and understand indigenous peoples. The volumes present in-depth studies in the form of long essays, ranging from 8,000 to 10,000 words, and useful bibliographies. However, these essays are not exactly purely academic studies. Their reference is not so much to the previously accumulated knowledge in the fields of anthropology, linguistics, literature, social sciences, law and art criticism. The essays focus on the lived life more than on any field of knowledge. They relate to the prevailing contexts surrounding the communities discussed, without, however, lacking in academic rigour. Many of the contributors have been activists in addition to being scholars. Besides, they are drawn from all continents, in most cases from the communities themselves, and they bring to these volumes their valuable experience of the indigenous from all of those continents. Thus, the five volumes, focusing on ten key concepts, effectively speak about the indigenous peoples in Australia, New Zealand and the Pacific region; in India and East Asia; in Africa and in the Americas. Each of the volumes has seven or eight intensive essays which open up a range of themes and questions related to the specific key terms discussed. It is hoped that these volumes will form valuable reading for students, researchers and academics interested in knowing what the indigenous communities think about themselves and about the contemporary world.

The publication of this series of volumes brings me a great personal satisfaction. I was trained in literary studies in an era when "excellence" in literature was ascribed to works in the main European languages alone. In my early years as a professor at an Indian university, I started noticing that the rich and unique culture of the indigenous communities was at that time like a continent about to be submerged under the ferocious cultural assault of the urban–industrial values and materials. My unease increased so much that I felt compelled to drop out of academic life and to move to a tiny village where the Rathwa indigenous community lived. That opened a new universe for me. There was so much to experience, see and learn from them, most of all how limited what I had till then imagined as "knowledge." Throughout my years spent with them, it was never my intention to "represent" them to the rest of the world that was on a path of ecological destruction. My task was to let the indigenous express themselves, to create spaces for their voice and to facilitate that expression. I realized that the gap between the indigenous and the universe of formal knowledge, labour and economy was unbridgeable. During the last three decades, all of my intellectual and activist work has remained devoted to bridging this abysmal gap. The publication of this series, Key Concepts in Indigenous Studies, is a small step in that direction. I would like to hope in all humility that it will achieve what it aims to, and will remind the readers that the Earth does not belong to us, we belong to it.

References

Bianco, Joseph Lo, 2012, 'National Language Revival Movements: Reflections from India, Israel, Indonesia and Ireland', in *The Cambridge Handbook of Language Policy*, Bernard Spolsky (ed.), Cambridge: Cambridge University Press, pp. 501–522.

Blench, Roger and Mathew Spriggs (eds.), 1999–2012, *Archaeology and Language: Theoretical and Methodological Orientations*. 4 vols, London and New York: Routledge.

Bragg, Melvyn, 2003, *The Adventure of English: The Biography of a Language*, London: Hodder & Stoughton.

Braggs, I. and H. I. Freedman, September 1993, 'Can the Speakers of a Dominated Language Survive as Unilinguals? A Mathematical Model of Bilingualism', in *Mathematical and Computer Modeling*, Vol. 18 (6), Oxford: Pergamon Press, pp. 9–18.

Corballis, Michael, 2011, *The Recursive Mind: The Origins of Human Language, Thought and Civilization*, Princeton, NJ: Princeton University Press.

Cru, Josep (ed.), 2010, *The Management of Linguistic Diversity and Peace Processes*, Barcelona: UNESCOCAT.

Crystal, David, 2000, *Language Death,* Cambridge: Cambridge University Press.

Dalby, Andrew, 2003, *Language in Danger,* New York: Columbia University Press.

Devy, G. N., 2014, *The Being of Bhasha: General Introduction to the People's Linguistic Survey of India*, New Delhi: Orient Blackswan.

Fishman, Joshua A. (ed.), 2001, *Can Threatened Languages be Saved?* Clevedon and Sydney: Multilingual Matters.

Florey, Margaret (ed.), 2010, *Endangered Languages of Australia*, New York: Oxford University Press.

Gillespie, Tarleton, 2007, *Wired Shut: Copyright and the Shape of Digital Culture*, Cambridge, MA: The MIT Press.

World Bank, 'Indigenous Peoples', www.worldbank.org/en/topic/indigenouspeoples (accessed 29 May 2019).

1

ORALITY IN SOUTHEAST ASIA

Aone Van Engelenhoven

1 Introduction to the linguistic and cultural diversity of Southeast Asia[1]

Southeast Asia can be divided into two principal regions: mainland Southeast Asia, comprising Myanmar, Thailand, Laos, Cambodia and Vietnam; and Insular Southeast Asia, covering Indonesia, the Philippines and the tiny nations of Singapore, Brunei Darussalam on the island of Borneo and Timor-Leste on the island of Timor. Malaysia is found both on the mainland and on Borneo Island, and is considered to be part of Insular Southeast Asia in this chapter. Both regions are very complex linguistically. Mainland Southeast Asia lodges about 500 languages in at least five different language families. Insular Southeast Asia, in fact, mainly lodges three language families. The largest one is the Austronesian family with about 1,200 languages. The tiny West Papua and Timor-Alor-Pantar families are represented by 26 languages whose genetic relatives are all found in New Guinea, outside of Insular Southeast Asia.

Large parts of Southeast Asia lodge literate cultures in principle. All national languages, as for example Thai on the mainland and Malay in the archipelago, have a literary tradition that dates back at least to the 15th century CE. Literary traditions of local languages like Cham in Cambodia and Javanese in Indonesia can be dated back to an even earlier time. Consequently, many oral traditions found in both regions are intimately linked to a parallel literary tradition.

In other words, in the context of Southeast Asia the characteristics of orality itself depend on whether the society has a literary tradition or not. The tradition of Buddhist monks in Laos and Northeast Thailand to elucidate their sermons by means of oral folktales is obviously oral, but nevertheless closely connected to the literary religious texts in Pali that they recite from (McDonald 2006: 64–66; Souvanxay 2005). The 6,000 folio pages in the 12 volumes of the *La Galigo* epic at

Leiden University's Library that are inscribed on the Memory of the World List at UNESCO obviously confirm the literary and thus erudite character of the Bugis society (Sulawesi Island, Indonesia). Nevertheless, its stories are preferably told orally and recitation from a manuscript is confined to instances when a specific reference is required (Koolhof 1999).

Ivanoff (2013: 200) rightly warns against the literate prejudice of denying the erudition in oral compositions in illiterate societies, for example the Moken sea nomads off the coast of Myanmar and Thailand. An oral epic like *Biag ni Lam-ang* of the Ilokano (Luzon Island, Philippines) would, according to such thinking, be necessarily inferior to a literary epic like the Thai *Ramakien*, although both epics display a similarly complex and elaborate composition (Flores 2016; Waradet 2014).

To bypass the complex linguistic and cultural diversity in both literate and illiterate dimensions, this contribution intends to elaborate on orality in insular Southeast Asia in the neighbouring districts of Southwest Maluku (Indonesia) and Lautém (Timor-Leste). Southwest Maluku is a regency of 16 islands in the east of Indonesia. It lodges 22 languages that are all Austronesian, except for Oirata on Kisar Island, which belongs to the Timor-Alor-Pantar family. A local variant of Indonesian functions as the main *lingua franca*. To the south, the area borders on Lautém, which is the easternmost municipality of Timor-Leste. In five of its administrative posts, Fataluku – another Timor-Alor-Pantar language – is spoken. In Tutuala, the easternmost administrative post, an additional secretive language called Makuva, which is Austronesian, is used. Here, Indonesian functions as the contact language with people from outside the municipality, albeit this language is replaced more and more often by Tetum, one of the official languages of Timor-Leste (Da Conceição Savio 2016). Notwithstanding this linguistic and sometimes cultural diversity, the oral traditions in both areas appear to be broadly similar.

Orality is defined in this contribution as the exclusively oral transfer of cultural knowledge. Section 2 discusses the phenomenon of storytelling and addresses in subsequent paragraphs the storytelling setting, narrative topology, and lexical and canonical parallelism. The final paragraph elaborates on "story stealing" and narrative annexation in storytelling pragmatics. Section 3 links storytelling to the practice of singing. Section 3.1 elaborates on Fataluku polyphony in Lautém and Section 3.2 describes the traditional singing practice in the Babar archipelago in Southwest Maluku. The next section provides a discussion on "literary fraud" and mystique in the pragmatics of singing. Section 4 contains a conclusion and addresses the endangerment of oral traditions.

2 Storytelling in Lautém and Southwest Maluku

Just as it is impossible to cover all ethnolinguistic groups in Southeast Asia in this contribution, it is also not possible to extensively discuss all the diverse narrative genres and performance types that are found in this part of the world. In his analysis of Malay oral narratives, Sweeney (1987: 165) defined a narrative as a combination of fixed storylines or plot patterns, which he dubbed "narrative chunks." These invariable narrative chunks can be recombined into an endless row of new stories. In this contribution, then, a "story" or a narrative is seen as a set of person and location names that interrelate separate plot patterns within a single narrated frame of reference.

2.1 Storytelling setting

Each storytelling performance requires its own setting. The genre determines where the story is told, what kind of performer is needed and what kind of audience is expected. This is exemplified in Figure 1.1.

Figure 1.1 shows the storytelling setting as it has been demonstrated in Southwest Maluku and Lautém. The setting as it is described here, however, may apply throughout eastern insular Southeast Asia and, with some minor adaptations, may be found everywhere in insular and mainland Southeast Asia. The outer box with the dotted line in the figure represents the private space where the audience is confined to either one person or a few people, and has established a direct and exclusive discourse relationship with the storyteller. The inner box featuring a continuous line represents the public space. Here – depending on the physical reach of the storyteller's voice – the audience is significantly larger, but lacks the intimate discourse relationship that the storyteller and the audience have in the private space. Both boxes are cut across by a grey bar that represents the scale of sacredness of the stories told, with the most profane stories at the extreme right and stories that are most sacred at the extreme left.

Due to its two-dimensional limitations, the figure is best interpreted as a pyramid seen from the top. The public space is at the top and is the most accessible for outsiders. The private space lies below the public space, and is only accessible for insiders. As a consequence, researchers can study oral traditions in the public space of a community, but usually are locked out from performances in the underlying private space. The performance of an extremely sacred story is normally exactly the same as a storytelling performance of an extremely profane story. The highly sacred end of the scale, therefore, interlocks with the fully profane end, which makes the scale in fact circular.

The default performer in public space is a man, whether it concerns a sacred narrative or a profane story. The reason for this can differ per ethnolinguistic group.

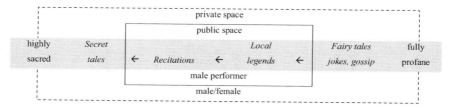

FIGURE 1.1   Storytelling setting in Southwest Maluku and Lautém

Among Fataluku speakers in Lautém, for example, only men are considered to be able to handle the words that are seen as dangerous weapons in the sacred *no lolo* performance which recounts the itinerary of the ancestors (Van Engelenhoven 2010a). In the matrilineal communities of Leti Island in Southwest Maluku, the explanation would be that women are the keepers of ancestral knowledge. The women speaking in public would severely endanger the audience's well-being. Because of this, women are better represented by either their husband, brothers or sons.

In the private space, the choice of performer very much depends on who is available and on what the audience is like. In a setting with a children's audience, women – prototypically sisters, mothers or grandmothers – may function as storytellers of profane fairy tales and jokes. The jokes for an adult audience obviously have more mature – often erotically laden – content that is considered to be either not suitable for children or simply beyond the comprehension of children. In the latter case, the story requires a special performance using, for example, different word choices or whispering that exclude the children as listeners. At the other end of the scale, where the secret tales are located, the storyteller will use similar strategies, but now they are used to emphasize the sacredness and secrecy of the story and to prevent it from being overheard by outsiders. The gender of the storyteller and the audience appears to not play a role here.

Although one can experience them privately, the genres at the extremes of the sacred–profane scale usually fall outside the abilities of the researcher because they lie outside the performance setting as it is sketched in Figure 1.1. The audiences in these contexts are confined to a single person. Whereas in the full profane register – for example "girl talk" about intimate hygiene – the message is conveyed by means of down-to-earth daily language. The highly sacred register very often makes use of a special language that is different from daily speech. This language can be either a genuine language, like Makuva in Lautém, or a constructed one, like the "Sung Language" on the Southwest Malukan islands (Van Engelenhoven 2010c, 2010d). On the Babar Islands in the extreme east of the regency, this language is usually referred to as "the language of the land" (Lewier 2016). Although not formalized traditionally, the gender of the storyteller and the audience at the fully profane end of the sacred–profane scale is obviously defined by the topic. A story about intimate hygiene with a female storyteller and audience would probably be broken off instantly if a male person suddenly joins the audience. On the sacred extreme of the scale, age appears to be the restriction in that certain secret stories will only be revealed if the audience has achieved a certain age.

Whereas private-space performances usually remain hidden from the researchers' attention, the public space is where they can gain access. Unlike performances in the private space, a performance in the public space requires a large audience. Sacred and profane genres in the public space are differentiated by means of the performance. A narrative can be recited as an epic poem, which requires the recitation of intricate formulae and extensive lexical parallelisms and prohibits any interference by the audience. The same narrative can be told much more "leisurely" – although not with less commitment – in prose, in which case, the audience can take the opportunity to intervene and adjust or redirect the story.

Although this may seem less obvious in the public space, it is always the audience that controls the performance. It is the audience that invites the performance and it is the audience that determines whether a performance is suitable or correct. Storytellers are in principle duty-bound to respond to a request. To evade a story request, a storyteller must either refer the intended audience to someone who is more qualified or entitled to the task, or explain that he feels inhibited by the inappropriateness of the context.

The storytelling setting determines the attitudinal expectations of both the storyteller and the audience. In a prose performance, the audience has the right to interrupt or correct the storyteller, while a storyteller can invite someone in the audience to continue a story. A principle of continuation applies to performances where songs or poetry are recited. The interruption of a recitation is expected to have a direct negative impact on the audience or the storyteller. To prevent this, each storytelling session usually has at least one, but usually three, attendees to guarantee the quality of the performance and can immediately take over if the performer cannot finish his recitation for some reason.

2.2 Narrative topology

Traditional audiences in Southwest Maluku and Lautém assess the quality of an oral narrative by three features that make up its topology: names, songs and so-called narrative artefacts, which are names are narrative chunks in the form of clichés that function as temporal landmarks in a story. As most languages in insular Southeast Asia lack tense markers on the verb, narrative time is usually signalled by means of names. Person names epitomize an action by the name-bearer that is very often a heroic deed in an epic setting somewhere in narrative time. Place names either epitomize an event at a certain location, or are epithets that describe the quality or function of that location. For the audience, they are clues with which they locate the narrated event in narrative time based on the narrative chunks of the names. This is exemplified in Figure 1.2 which displays the three names of the protagonist

FIGURE 1.2   Person and place names epitomizing consecutive stories in a metanarrative

in the creation myth of Leti Island (Southwest Maluku): Slerleti, alias Sieruliona and alias Sairmalai. Because each person name and its supplementary place name can be located in narrative time, the audience perceives the three epitomized events as consecutive stories in one meta-story (Van Engelenhoven 2010b).

Songs are distiches that summarize part of a tale and function as truth landmarks in a story. The truth value of stories without an ancillary song cannot be assessed by the audience and are generally dismissed. In a sacred context, a narrative without a song may be considered to be either stolen or completely made-up, and therefore will not be taken seriously by the audience. Even profane genres like fairy tales are often accompanied by a distich. "Serious" distiches, especially, cannot be sung randomly, but require a singer or storyteller who has the right and the qualities to perform them. In Southwest Malukan prose sessions, it is common for a performer to start to sing to overrule an unwanted interruption and then is overruled himself by another song from the audience, leading up to a chain of mutually contesting songs.

In both regions knowledge of these singing registers is confined to specialists. An enigmatic feature of the Lautém distiches is that they are sung in polyphony. Outside Lautém, Tanjung Bunga at the eastern end of the nearby island of Flores (Indonesia) is the only location where duets mixing drone polyphony and independent movement of the parts has been demonstrated in insular Southeast Asia (Rappoport 2015a; Yampolsky 2015).

In Lautém, the distiches are composed in a specific poetic Fataluku register. In Southwest Maluku, the song texts are composed of a limited lexicon of about 150 items. This lexicon belongs to a special register or jargon that is labelled "Sung Language" (Van Engelenhoven 2010c) or "Language of the Land" (Lewier 2016). Notwithstanding apparent differences found in texts from different islands, there is a general consensus in Southwest Maluku that the "Sung Language" is inherited from Luang Island, one of the mythical cultural centres of the regency.

Unlike the poetic Fataluku register, the "Sung Language" is characterized by vast homonymy and a simplified grammar. It shares the latter feature with the Makuva language in Tutuala. Whereas both poetic Fataluku and "Sung Language" may appear in both the private and public spaces, Makuva is confined to contexts of extreme secrecy.

Narrative artefacts are like theatrical properties in a play. Where names may provide a setting for a narrated event, narrative artefacts function as visual mnemonic instruments for both the storyteller and his audience.

Typical narrative artefacts are physical features in the environment – stones, mountains, islands and alike – whose existence are explained by a story. Additionally, they can also be manufactured as motifs on statues, ritual poles or cloth. On the Southwest Malukan islands these statues are normally stored in the attic of the clan house where only the storyteller can identify them. In their absence, other items like pebbles, table legs or even corners of a room may function as *ad hoc* narrative artefacts. Some artefacts – and their stories – are exclusive property of a clan, and their meanings are concealed to outsiders (Van Engelenhoven 2013).

The square *poko* and *faria* motifs in the cave paintings on Ilikerekere Mountain (Tutuala, Lautém), for example, are said to be interpretable only to members of the landowner clan.

Whereas men appear to be the default performers of storytelling in the public space, as the traditional manufacturers of cloth and thus of narrative artefact motifs, women are becoming more and more the exclusive custodians of narrative knowledge.

2.3 Lexical and canonical parallelism

An all-permeating feature of the verbal arts in Southeast Asia is the pairing of words in text, referred to in the literature as parallelism. In research on the oral traditions and languages of mainland Southeast Asia, this phenomenon is often referred to as "grammatical parallelism," as for example in Khmu (Lundström 2014), or "syntactic parallelism," as in Lahu (Matisoff 1991). This terminology stresses the creation of paired phrases or clauses with the same grammatical construction but with different lexical constituents. This is exemplified in the following by a quote from the *Lord of the Golden Cloth* poem in the Fataluku language in Timor-Leste.

(1)   A   *Ili* le-ara ocava,   "Lord of the **mountain** house,
         B   *mai* le-ara ocava!   lord of the **eagle** house!
         C   E *cala* kecule,   Your **ancestors** dispersed
         D   e *pala* kecule.   your **ancestors** dispersed.
         E   E *huru* navaren la'a nara,   As they came to know your **moon**,
         F   e *vacu* navaren la'a nara,   as they came to know your **sun**,
         G   *ira* ukun va'are,   they visited all **waters**,
         H   *pala* ukun va'are.   they visited all **gardens**."

                                                           (Meneses 1997: 36)

The segment "As they came to know your moon" (E) containing the construction "as they came to know" is generally recognized in oral tradition research as a formula: a set linguistic unit that functions as a mnemonic devise for the performer (Kuiper 2000). Segment E is mirrored or paralleled as formula F, which only differs in the choice of the noun, "sun." Similarly, segments A and B are parallel formulae that only differ in their possessor nouns "mountain" and "eagle." Clauses C and D are parallel formulae where the subjects differ: "(your) ancestors" versus "(your) fathers." Clauses G and H are parallel formulae where the objects differ: "waters" versus "gardens."

Oral tradition research in insular Southeast Asia usually favours the term "lexical parallelism" to refer to this phenomenon, focusing on the parallelism of the lexical items – in bold print in example 1 – rather than of the formula. The term "lexical" in linguistics more or less suggests that the performer pronounces fixed word combinations that are all defined in the lexicon. This may be the reason that the scholar who introduced parallelism research in insular Southeast Asian research, James J. Fox, prefers the label "semantic parallelism." This term stresses that it is the meanings of the words that are combined. However, some languages also feature parallel grammatical words, as for example conjunctions in Leti in Southwest Maluku and Fataluku in Lautém.

Based on his research on the language of Rote (Indonesia), Fox (2014: 4) introduced the term "canonical parallelism," with which he refers to the common use of recurrent, parallel phrasing of words that define which terms and phrases may form pairs. Unlike "lexical parallelism," this term postulates that the combination and order of the words are semantically motivated and, as such, may provide significant clues about the culture where an oral tradition is embedded.

Word pairs are motivated by cognitive schemas that are grounded in the performer's and audience's culturally specific or general knowledge of the world. Three pairs are given in Table 1.1 that ultimately derive from a culturally defined dualistic FORCE schema where entities that are smaller, younger or female are considered less powerful than the opposite bigger, older or male entities. As can be seen in Table 1.1, the parallels profile opposite extremes on a scale where the first-mentioned words relate to less powerful forces and always precede the latter-mentioned words that relate to more powerful forces.

In example 1, shown previously, the bold printed words are all lexical pairs, although they are not all canonical. The canonical character of the combination

TABLE 1.1 FORCE schema in Fataluku parallelism

FORCE SCHEMA	
SIZE PAIR: small // big	
pua // vata	"areca nut // coconut"
peleku // loiasu	"proa // boat"
iniku // horu	"sand // gravel"
ilahu // kalahu	"sweet potato // yam"
hikaru // hupila	"knife // sickle"
AGE PAIR: young // old	
vaianu // painu	"brother-in-law // parent-in-law"
noko // kaka	"younger sibling // older sibling"
calu // moco	"grandchild // child"
miri // matu	"new // old"
pupuke // lahute	"to bud // to grow"
GENDER PAIR: female // male	
tupuru // nami	"woman // man"
nalu // palu	"mother // father"
lerenu // noko	"sister // younger brother"
pua // maluhu	"areca // betel nut"
lau // malu	"cloth // loincloth"

"ancestors" and "fathers" in C and D is confirmed by the 34 instances attested in eight different sources in my Fataluku lexical parallelism database. The order of the words reflects the GENDER pair in Fataluku, where nouns with female referents precede male referents. Also, the canonical pair "moon" and "sun" in E and F, with 17 attested instances in nine different sources in the database, reflects the word order of the GENDER pair, since in Fataluku culture, the sun is classified as a masculine concept and the moon as a feminine concept.

While different languages may share the same cognitive schema, the word orders may be opposite. Rote, for example, which is spoken at the western end of Timor Island in Indonesia, uses the same GENDER pair as Fataluku, but with a reversed word order: "man // woman," "father // mother" and "sun // moon." The nearby Leti language off shore in Southwest Maluku uses the same GENDER pair and the same word order as Fataluku, but does not allow combinations with "moon." Instead, it uses "Pleiades," hence: "Pleiades // sun" (Van Engelenhoven 2010a).

Non-canonical pairs also adhere to these schematic word orders. The combination of "mountain" and "eagle" in A and B, for example, has been shown only four times in the database, in two poems of one specific clan. Example 2 shows that the words "mountain" and "eagle" combine into a genuine lexical pair in which the slots of both words are fixed. In other word combinations, "mountain" is always in first position and "eagle" is always in the final position.

(2) combinations with "mountain"

ili // apa	"mountain // mountain"	*ci-ara // mai*	"k.o. tree // eagle"
ili // calu	"mountain // ancestor"	*ili // mai*	"mountain // eagle"
ili // foe	"mountain // plain"	*pere // mai*	"k.o. snake // eagle"
ili // mai	"mountain // eagle"	*olo // mai*	"bird // eagle"
ili // pere	"mountain // ridge"	*kikinu // mai*	"mouse // eagle"

combinations with "eagle"

The same observation applies to the combination of "water" and "garden," which is not canonical either since it is confined in the database to a single instance in the *Lord of the Golden Cloth* poem. In other combinations, "water" usually occupies the first slot and "garden" always the final slot.

(3) combinations with "water"

ira // aca	"water // fire"	*hamua // pala*	"soil // garden"
ira // le	"water // house"	*ia-mari // pala*	"footprint // garden"
ira // pala	"water // garden"	*ira // pala*	"water // garden"
ira // tahi	"water // sea"	*lau // pala*	"cloth // garden"
ira // tua	"water // toddy palm"	*le // pala*	"house // garden"
ira // veru	"water // river"	*leku // pala*	"yard // garden"
aca // ira	"fire-wood // water"	*lipalu // pala caca'e*	"wedding // garden aid"
macenu // ira	"food // water"	*tua // pala*	"toddy palm // garden"
lakute // ira	"to drip // to water"		

combinations with "garden"

The final three "water" combinations show that conceptual considerations can overrule the seemingly fixed lexical order of the pair. The combinations "firewood // water" and "food // water" are obviously inspired by a FOOD PREPARATION pair where "water" must fill the final slot, whereas "to drip // to water" obeys to the SIZE pair mentioned in Table 1.1, where the word with the smaller referent ("to drip") must occur in initial position.

Besides near antonyms as described previously, parallelism also combines synonyms where one of the items is used in daily speech and the other one is exclusive to ritual speech. This is exemplified by the Fataluku nouns in Table 1.2.

The starred items occur exclusively in ritual speech. Although they may schematically constitute near antonymic pairs in Fataluku culture, comparable to the ones displayed in Table 1.1, "rattan // liana" and "table // bank" are difficult to recognize as such for the outsider. Interestingly, *falu* – the word for "rattan" in daily speech – may also combine with "liana." The archaic *pu*, however, occurs only in this parallel and in certain person and place names. The combination "table // bench" is interesting in that it refers to entities that are alien to Fataluku culture. Both words ultimately derive from Portuguese *mesa* "table" and *banco* "bench." The Fataluku derivative *paku* "bench," however, is confined to ritual speech and the Tetum derivative *banku* is preferred in daily speech. Whereas Fataluku-speaking Lautém is still very much monolingual, this borrowing from other languages is especially salient in Southwest Maluku, whose small islands and many languages automatically imply intense language contact (Van Engelenhoven 1997). Larger language communities like Termanu Rote to the west of Timor Island borrow their ritual words from other Rote dialects instead (Fox 1974).

In Fataluku synonymous pairs, as the last three mentioned in Table 1.2, word order seems unpredictable and, as such, is probably lexically determined. In some languages, for example Leti (Southwest Maluku), the order of the words in some pairs appears to be phonologically motivated. Words with stressed high vowels precede words with stressed non-high vowels and words with stressed front vowels precede words with non-front vowels. This is exemplified by the words "to see" and "to scratch" in Table 1.3, where the stressed vowel is indicated by means of an acute accent. Although this phenomenon has only been confirmed in bisyllabic words, the long vowel in *lléésa* "he reads", while its counterpart only features a short vowel, suggests that phonotactics or syllable weight does not seem to play here.

TABLE 1.2 Ritual speech nouns versus daily speech nouns in Fataluku speech

Ritual noun pairs		*Daily speech noun*	
*pu // taru	"rattan // liana"	*falu*	"rattan"
meza // *paku	"table // bench"	*banku*	"bench" (Tetum)
*huhu // hoku	"mud // mud"	*hoku*	"mud"
lulira // *lacia	"territory // territory"	*lulira*	"territory"
cicika // *fafaku	"shoulder // shoulder"	*cicika*	"shoulder"

TABLE 1.3 Stressed vowel hierarchy in Leti ritual speech (Van Engelenhoven 1997: 6)

Stressed vowel hierarchy: i < u < e < o < a			
-tóli "to see"		*-kéri* "to scratch"	
nkíli // ntóli	"he looks back // he sees"	*nkíkri // nkéri*	"he saws // he scratches"
ntóli // ntákra	"he sees // he looks (at)"	*nkéri // nkói*	"he scratches // he scrapes"
lléesa // ntóli	"he reads // he sees"	*nkói // nkártu*	"he scrapes // he scratches"

2.4 Storytelling pragmatics: "story stealing" and narrative annexation

A comparison of oral texts shows that storytelling is structured around two major pragmatic functions – confirmation of the narrator's erudition, and focus on the central message of the text – that are both profiled by means of lexical and canonical parallelism.

Since, as has been explained previously in Section 2.2, it is the audience that controls a storytelling performance, it is also the audience that needs to assess and ascertain the quality of the candidate performer. Although performance skills are surely acknowledged as assets, it is the narrator's proficiency in lexical and canonical parallelism that confirms his or her erudition to the audience in any storytelling setting in Lautém and Southwest Maluku. This is exemplified in Figure 1.3 which displays a graph of a 19th-century Leti speech.[2] This speech is built out of three main paragraphs: the opening, labelled A; the core message, labelled B; and a conclusion, labelled C, that are all shown on the A axis. The transitional sections from A to B and from B to C are labelled ab and bc, respectively. The word count is shown on the B axis.

A closer look shows that the opening and the core message share the same amount of parallels and that they decrease sharply in the subsequent transitional section after the core message B and in the conclusion. Traditional speeches are an intrinsic part of verbal artistry in both Southwest Maluku and Lautém. Consequently, the opening, in which the audience is welcomed and introduced to the topic of the speech, requires a high amount of parallels to demonstrate the erudition of the speaker. Similarly, the high amount of parallels in paragraph B highlights the importance of the core message.

The focus on the central message has two separate exponents: historiographic reliability and sacredness, the functions of which can co-occur in the same performance context, depending on the type of oral text.[3] As shown in Figure 1.3, the paragraph in speeches and sermons that contains the central message may contain a similar amount of parallels as the opening text. In other prose texts, paragraphs with historiographic value through which the audience can locate the narrated event described in their own "phenomenal world" (after Brandt and Brandt 2005) require that for each name – whether this be the name of a person, a place or a narrative artefact like a sword – at least one parallel equivalent be given. In poetic

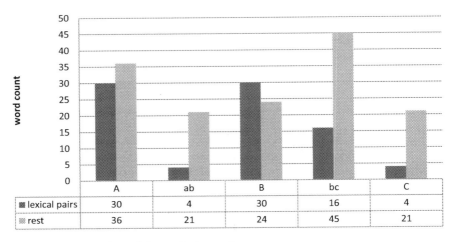

	A	ab	B	bc	C
lexical pairs	30	4	30	16	4
rest	36	21	24	45	21

FIGURE 1.3   Lexical parallels in a Leti speech

texts, like the *no lolo* in Fataluku in Lautém that recount the often mythical past, all couplets are built of parallel lines. This feature confirms the sacredness of the text and enhances its potentially lethal character, because of which it can only be recited by a trained performer and can sometimes only be received by a qualified audience. In Lospalos in Lautém, for example, certain texts can only be heard by adult men.

As it is essential to a proper performance, attempts to question the erudition of the performer, and consequently the historiographic reliability of the text, are quintessential to storytelling on the Southwest Malukan islands. Where in Lautém, the dangerous character of the text itself ensures that only qualified performers will narrate the text, on the Southwest Malukan islands a performer must constantly prove his or her quality.

One way to prove one's quality is by the phenomenon called "story stealing": the illegitimate telling of a story that is not owned by the performer or not has been authorized by the rightful owner. It is a dangerous act that can only be done by a very skilled narrator who can safely evade or curb all the possible retribution ascribed to it: insaneness, sometimes physical illness or even death of either the performer or people that in some way are related to the performer. Although one generally refuses to tell stories from other clans, "story stealing" is actually a story-telling skill that is much aspired to.

A much safer strategy for both the performer and the audience is what we have dubbed "narrative annexation": the appropriation of chronotopes or narrative units in time and space (Lawson 2011) from stories that are owned by people the performer does not affiliate with.

This is well exemplified in the oral narratives on the island of Kisar (South-west Maluku) which lodges two ethnolinguistic groups: the Austronesian-speaking Meher and the non-Austronesian-speaking Oirata (Van Engelenhoven and

Nazarudin 2016). The impact of the Dutch East India Company (VOC) in the 17th century on the local societies is central to all the narratives on the island. The arrival of the first Dutch captain in 1665 is therefore a chronotope that appears in many stories. As its narrative scene is located on a beach that lies in their territory, the Oirata are the logical owners of this specific narrative piece. Their ownership is emphasized, in their eyes, by a rock on the beach whose grooves are interpreted as Dutch writing that commemorates this particular event. In the Meher-speaking Abusur domain north of Oirata, the arrival of the Dutch captain is explained as a consequence of the Abusur chief meeting him at sea and inviting him to come to the island. In the rival domain of the Meher-speaking Wonreli west of Oirata and Abusur, the captain's arrival is rather explained as the result of the Wonreli chief going to the VOC quarters to ask for help against Portuguese invaders. In other words, although the landing story is acknowledged by both Meher-speaking domains, the arrival of the Dutch captain is annexed by adding a narrative chunk of events that logically precede the event on the Oirata beach.

3 Singing in Lautém and Southwest Maluku

Whereas the storytelling traditions in Lautém and Southwest Maluku appear to be quite similar, the singing traditions are less comparable. As already noted in Section 2.2, one major difference between both regions is that singing distiches in Fataluku in Lautém is done polyphonically, unlike in Southwest Maluku, that only knows monophony.

3.1 Singing in Lautém: vaihoho

Fataluku distiches can either be chanted or sung. Chanting is done by individuals whereas singing is done in polyphonic duets in which the second voice adds a drone to the melody sung by the first voice (Rappoport 2015b). This is exemplified in the Figures 4a–d, which follow.

The metrical units in Fataluku distiches are double trochees, spondees or dactyls. The perfect distich consists of two lines, preferably containing four double trochees, of which the fourth is separated from the others by a spondee. Alternatively, the final metre can also be a dactyl (Yampolsky 2012). An example of a scansion is given in example 4 where the final metre is a double trochee in (a), but a dactyl in (b).[4]

	/ x /x / x / x /x /x // / / x xx
4(a)	*Nelu hia	Sina timi |rika Mua| na lou |k' ana nie?*
	"From the Heaven the tin of Sina has jumped onto Earth, has it?"
	/x /x / x /x / x / x // / x x
(b)	*Ica aci| ica kama| aci i po	laue| losire*
	"Some they told, some they didn't, but it was spread" (Yampolsky 2012).

FIGURE 1.4A Tinolo introduction

FIGURE 1.4B Tinolo second musical sentence

FIGURE 1.4C Tinolo third musical sentence

FIGURE 1.4D Tinolo conclusion

Yampolsky (2014a) suggests there may be between 15 and 30 different melodies in which to sing a distich. Melodies are formulae of set musical lines with fixed vocable sequences that sometimes have lexical meaning – for example, *olo* "to tell" and *aniri* "me" – and sometimes are meaningless. This is exemplified in 4(c) by the *Tinolo* or *Tihinolo* formula whose name is derived from *tu i hin olo* "that you tell it'" (Valentim 2002: 100).

4(c)   *Tinolo i olo | | F1 i olo F2 olo | | i anire F3 pele | | i olo elo.*
         "That you tell it, tell this, tell F1 tell F2 it is me F3 then, tell this *elo*" (Yampolsky 2014a).

The *Tinolo* formula has four musical sentences, each with its own vocables. Figures 1.4a–d show that, except in the final sentence, the vocables *olo* "to tell" all more or less share the same musical motif: A–E–D. The first sentence is the introduction that contains the vocables the melody is named after.

The second and third musical sentence contain three empty metrical slots, labelled F1, F2 and F3 in 5(c). Each slot can lodge a double trochee and, by filling its first three metrical units in these slots, the distich's line is merged with this specific formula. The second musical sentence is the longest in that it lodges two metrical slots. A comparison between 5(a) and Figure 1.4b reveals the mismatch between the text and the formula. Since they belong to a different metrical unit, the last two syllables of the word *timirika* "tin" are clipped and shifted into F3 in the third musical sentence.

Similarly, the third musical sentence only features one empty slot, where the final two syllables of *timirika* "tin" and the word *Mua* "Earth" are inserted. The final spondee and double trochee *na louk' ana nie* "has jumped from, has it?" in the distich are thus omitted, as can be seen in Figure 1.4c. This sentence is marked by an abrupt stop at the end.

The final musical sentence concludes with both singers singing the final syllable of *elo* in unison in F. The second duo then repeats the entire formula, referred to in Fataluku as *aca vate* "echoing."

After the final sentence has finished, the first duo sings the second line of the distich, which is then repeated by the second duo. The final two metrical units in the second line of the distich, *laue* and *losire*, literally mean "to dissolve" and "to loosen," respectively. They are a spondee and a dactyl that form a lexical pair that in this context means "to divulge." Since the third musical sentence only has room for one double trochee, these two metrical units are clipped in the same way as the final two metrical units in the first line.

Section 2.4 discussed that focusing on the central message is one of the main pragmatic functions of lexical parallelism. However, because of the compulsory omissions from the poem's text to fit the melody formula, there is no longer a lexical pair in the song to emphasize the central message: the dissemination of the information about the burial.

In itself, the distich is already quite obscure. The original text of this poem relates the story of a baby that died on the same day as it was born and was buried without the family being informed (Yampolsky 2012). The baby and its birth are metaphorically referred to as "tin of Sina" and "jumping from Heaven onto Earth," respectively. The reference to the burial is even more hidden in that it is only hinted at by the word "tin," which literally means "leaden" (*timir*) "dibber" (*ika*). The division of this word into the two meaningless segments *timi* and *rika* over two musical sentences precludes any possible recognition by someone who does not know the distich.

Vaihoho are normally sung during daily activities like planting and fishing, and as such do not have an audience as in storytelling performances. Often, a *vaihoho* song is confined to a single distich, which then can be repeated on and on as long as there are two duos to perform. Alternatively, more distiches can be added, which can be originally made or taken from existing distiches. The length of these songs enables a more narrative character, to which the performers can apply the same strategies as in storytelling.

In Section 2.4, narrative annexation was explained as the appropriation of chronotopes from stories owned by people the performer does not affiliate with. A comparable practice also occurs in *vaihoho* by adopting a line from an outsider's distich. This is exemplified by the distiches in examples 5 and 6, which belong to a longer *vaihoho* of eight distiches about a shipwreck on Leti Island.

5(a)	*Uhulapa Taitoli,*	"Uhulapa (and) Taitoli,
	Ma'aleki-Maho Home Ratu	Ma'aleki-Maho (and) Home Ratu
(b)	*Lanu horu Savirara mara*	With their friends went to Savirara
	hinu loi-loi nehere.'	to embark on their boats" (Valentim 2004: 39).
6(a)	*Uhulapa Taitoli,*	"Uhulapa and Taitoli,
	Romonapa Naja Ratu	Romonapa and Naja Ratu
(b)	*Lanu horu Savirara maran*	With their friends went to Savirara
	hinu lai-lai nehere.'	to play their Knucklebones game" (Yampolsky 2014b).

The texts in 5 and 6 display a typical case of the appropriation of chronotopes. The variant in example 5 was recorded in Loikere territory and mentions the clans the singers are affiliated with: Ma'aleki-Maho and Home Ratu. The variant in example 6 was recorded in a territory that lies outside Ma'aleki-Maho authority. Here, the singers replaced the names of Ma'aleki-Maho and its ally Home Ratu with the names of two other clans: Romonapa and Naja Ratu.

The text in 5(b) narrates how these four clans embark at Savirara Beach – a beach that is owned by a fellow sub-clan of Ma'aleki-Maho. As such, this line fits the shipwreck theme of the song. The text in 6(b), however, appears to be completely out of context. Here, the clans go to Savirara Beach not to embark on their boats, but rather to play a game of Knuckles bones, a metaphor for ritually dividing land. In other words, whereas the singers of variant 5 profile their clans as actors in a chronotope in which they embark on a beach, the singers in 6 reformulate that same chronotope into a scene in which the clans they affiliate with are rather the agents in the ritual division of the land.

Uhulapa and Taitoli in 5(a) and 6(a) are the names of mountains that metonymically refer to the Tana Ratu clan. Romonapa in 6(b) is also the name of a mountain whose owners are a sub clan of Naja Ratu. The reference to these mountains seems unrelated to the shipwreck theme of the song and is probably itself annexed from a different distich (examples 7[a] and [b]) that narrates the dispersal of the ancestors of the Tana clan to the Uhulapa and Romonapa mountains (Gomes 1972: 21).

7(a)   *Afi calu tali-tali vakile nu,*   "Our ancestors by turns dived and,
       aie, palise.   hey, swam.

(b)   *Ica ta la'a Uhulapa Taitoli,*   Some went to Uhulapa (and) Taitoli (and)
       Naja Romonapa.   to Naja (and) Romonapa" (Gomes 1972: 21).

This suggests that the singers of version 5 "borrowed" line 7(b) into their own version and adapted it to fit the narrative context and the authority of the local clans. The singers of version in 6 "repaired" the line, but by doing so, destroyed the narrative coherence of the text.

3.2 Singing in Southwest Maluku: the "Sung Language"

The Babar archipelago at the eastern end of the Southwest Maluku Regency is, in a way, the opposite of Lautém in Timor-Leste. Where Fataluku-speaking Lautém acknowledges only one cultural framework, the inhabitants of the Babar archipelago group their villages into a western and eastern traditional territory, of which the boundary runs through the middle of the main island of Babar (Lewier 2016: 35). The western territory is in fact part of a larger cultural region that encompasses most islands to the west of the Babar archipelago up to Timor-Leste.

The archipelago's ethnolinguistic composition is very complex, with about eight indigenous languages that all belong to the Austronesian language family. They are all under severe threat from the national language, Indonesian, of which a local variant functions as the *lingua franca* on all five islands. Both territories apply a special linguistic register for singing – referred to in the Babar archipelago as "language of the land" – which is composed of words from different languages in the region and is used throughout the archipelago. Throughout the regency, variants of this "singing language" that share the same simplified grammar and most of its lexicon of about 150 items are found (Van Engelenhoven 2010c).

One type of song that is used throughout the Babar archipelago is labelled *tyarka* by Lewier (2016: 2). This song functions as a formal expression by a single performer in ritual and official contexts. It features a single basic melody that allows for minimal variation per location or performer. This is exemplified in Figure 1.5.

The smallest text in a *tyarka* is a distich composed of lexical parallels. A text can be expanded by as many distiches as deemed necessary by the performer. The multilingual setting of the archipelago adds a unique feature to its traditional singing that

FIGURE 1.5   Basic Tyarka melody

has not been demonstrated elsewhere in the regency. To meet the fixed melody of the song, the performer may incorporate words from different local languages. This is exemplified in the song text in example 8, taken from Lewier (2016: 132).

	Song text	Literal translation	Interpretative translation
8(a)	*Rweruro yane moruri.*	"Noisy people, don't be noisy.	"Don't be emotional.
(b)	*Umene yane sis wek.*	Mine, don't, don't shout.	Don't be angry.
(c)	*Mkiane lire Ul Ray.*	Use the talk of the Commandments.	Embrace the Commandments.
(d)	*U otye ulye Lir Ray.*	I carry and lift the Commandments.	Uphold the Commandments.
(e)	*Rayo nemetetety.*	The world is solid.	We live in one environment.
(f)	*Rune kolye namileteter.*	Village life is as a family."[5]	We live together" (Lewier 2016: 132).

This text is composed out of at least four different languages. Three words are from Western Babar: *rweruro* "they are noisy" in 8(a), *yane* "don't" in lines 8(a) and (b), and *namileteter* "as a family" in line (f). Three words are taken from the Masela language: *moruri* "you are noisy" in line 8(a), *umene* "mine" in line (b) and *rune* "village" in line (f). Lines (d) and (e) are completely in Southeastern Babar, the language of the composer. Two words, *sis* "don't" and *wek* "shout," in line (b) are taken from the Dawelor language. All the remaining words are generally known throughout the archipelago and not acknowledged as coming from one specific language.

A quick comparison between the literal and interpretative translations shows that, in fact, the meaning of the loaned word is rather broadly interpreted. The interpretative text displays three distiches that are built around a set of near synonyms: (a) "emotional" – (b) "angry," (c) "embrace" – (d) "uphold" and (e) "one environment" – (f) "together." Table 1.4 shows that all concepts except "embrace" are represented by a word or a phrase from a specific language.

TABLE 1.4 Representation of synonymic paired concepts in Babar song text

Concept	Song word	Language
"emotional"	"you (singular) are noisy"	Masela
"angry"	"shout"	Dawelor
"embrace"	"you (plural) use"	--
"uphold"	"I carry and lift"	Southeast Babar
"one environment"	"solid"	Southeast Babar
"together"	"as a family"	Masela

Very often, a performer or composer appears to not be able to parse or segment the song text into lines. Rather, they see the whole text as a single unit (Van Engelenhoven and Nazarudin 2016: 196).[6] This is confirmed by the obsolescence of person and number inflection, which is compulsory in all spoken languages in the region (Van Engelenhoven 2010c). Whereas it is a salient feature of "Sung Language" in general, it can be explained here as a consequence of the multilingual context the song text is composed in. The Southeastern Babar clause *U otye ulye Lir Ray* in line (d), for example, literally means "I carry and lift the Commandments," but is intended as the imperative "Uphold the Commandments." The Western Babar word *rweruro* in (8a) literally means "they are noisy," but in this specific context, it is intended as a noun referring to "noisy people." Similarly, the literal meaning of the word *kolye* in line (f) is "we (inclusive) dwell," but is used here in the meaning of "life."

In the past, to learn the song one needed to memorize the entire text as a whole. The introduction of literacy in the region has changed the way song texts are learned and memorized. Whereas there is no tradition of literacy in the local languages of the Babar archipelago, *tyarka* texts are learned and transferred between performers in writing. Nevertheless, they are exclusively performed in singing. A *tyarka* song may only contain one distich, which is referred to as "trunk." A standard *tyarka* preferably contains two parts. Because of this, at least one distich is added that is generally referred to as "tip." This is exemplified in example 9.

	Song text	Toolbox translation[7]	Interpretative translation
9(a)	*U meseno lira malilipo,*	"I'm alone with a calm voice,	"We have agreed
(b)	*Up Raye yati mayo.*	Lord King, badness comes.	to end the issue.
(c)	*Ik ru suly kote ito,*	We two carry one word,	Let's live together,
(d)	*Ik ru kwawe lane ito.*	We two carry one name."	in peace and tranquillity" (Lewier 2016: 216).

The text in 9 is entirely in "Sung Language," but only the last distich is composed out of lexical pairs: *suly* and *kwawe* – both meaning "to carry" – and *kote* "word" and *lane* "name."[8] First, the "trunk" (9a)–(b) is sung twice and then the "tip" (c)–(d) is sung twice. Next, the first and third lines are combined – 9(a) and (c) – followed by a combination of the second and fourth lines – (b) and (d). The song is closed off by a repetition of the "trunk": 9(a)–(b).

Whereas the interpretative translation was not too far from the literal translation in 8, the interpretative translation in 9 diverges sharply from the literal Toolbox translation. This confirms the idea that the composer does not translate text from one language into "Sung Language," but rather combines "Sung Language" phrases that are supposed to reflect a certain idea. In the ritual registers of most languages in the west of the regency, the parallel words "word" and "name" combine into the new meaning "clan." The concept of "clan" is aptly described in the interpretative translation as "living together" in (c), while the phrase "in peace and tranquillity" probably expresses how this should ideally be done. Similarly, a "calm voice" in 9(a) may be construed as "agreeing" with discarding pronominal particularities: "I" in the literal translation versus "we" in the interpretative translation. "Issue" in the interpretative translation is the only word that concurs with "badness" in the literal translation.

3.3 Singing pragmatics: "literary fraud" and the mystique of singing

Outside the Babar archipelago, the counterparts of the *tyarka* genre are sung in daily speech rather than in "Sung Language." Their function as evidence in traditional lawsuits requires that they be immediately understood. From Section 2.4, it can be concluded that in insular Southeast Asia, as probably everywhere in Southeast Asia, the historiographic reliability and sacredness of an oral text are closely linked to its authenticity and related relative age, which are implicitly challenged if the evidence is provided by a song text in daily speech.

Safeguarding the audience's consent of the performance is done by aging one's text by means of "literary fraud" (Van Engelenhoven 2010c). This is specifically salient in Southwest Malukan distiches that function as truth landmarks in a story. Example 10 provides a Leti distich, and its manipulated counterpart is given in example 11.

10(a)	*Lanti mpupnuale rai,*	11(a)	*Lanikye pupinyale raye,*	"The sky covers the land,
(b)	*mpupnuale nus paikrane.*	(b)	*pupinyala noha paikrane.*	and covers the ordered islands.
(c)	*Yaari nkadvetu sletnane,*	(c)	*Yoirye kadvekye letnane,*	And the billow shuts off the sea,
(d)	*Nkadvetu rapiatatrane.*	(d)	*Kadvekye ryaye pyatatrane.*	and shuts the arranged land" (Van Engelenhoven 2010c).

A typical strategy to make the words sound older is shown by the change of the word *nkadvetu* "he shuts off" into *kadvekye* "shut off" in 10(d) and 11(d). First the final back high vowel <u> is replaced by its front high vowel counterpart <i>: *nkadvetu – nkadveti.* Next, the dental consonant <t> before <i> is replaced by its velar counterpart <k>: *nkadveti – nkadveki.* Subsequently, an echo vowel <e> is added to the final <i> to yield <ye>: *nkadveki – nkadvekye.* Finally, the person prefix <n> is deleted: *nkadvekye – kadvekye.* Additionally, words are replaced by a counterpart from another dialect, as for example Leti *nus* "island" in 10(b) that is replaced by the etymon from the Western Moa dialect *noha* in 11(b).

In a context in which the performer is aware that among the audience there may be alternative stories – whether they be myths, oral histories, fairy tales or even Biblical stories – that may compete with the performed version, "literary fraud" in sung texts is a frequently used strategy to prevent unwanted interruptions.

Although storytelling and singing are clearly interrelated, their performances are very different. Southwest Malukan singing is closely connected to the rhetoric of storytelling and the example of "literary fraud" shows that it can function as a strategy for the performer to continue his performance. However, where a prose text in storytelling needs to guarantee its historiographic reliability and the erudition of its performer by means of lexical parallelism, a *vaihoho* or *tyarka* text is intrinsically obscure.

Texts in "Sung Language" focus on authenticity and are always multi-interpretable; it is the social status of the performers rather than their capacities as singers that is subject to scrutiny. Particularly in the Babar archipelago, composers need to be of the right clan and have a good understanding of the local traditions. They are usually around their fifties or older, and as a consequence of the imposed restriction, *tyarka* singing is more and more becoming a highly endangered verbal art (Lewier 2016: 178). Whereas *vaihoho* singing in Lautém takes place in a more leisurely context, it is in a comparable condition of endangerment, although there is no social restriction. A changing of aesthetics in favour of present-day popular and church music means that the necessary singing techniques are no longer transferred. The performers who are still capable of singing *vaihoho* were mostly born before 1970 (Yampolsky 2012).

In Section 2.1, it was explained that names specify narrative time and, as such, link the narrating event to the narrated event for the audience. Songs have a comparable function as landmarks of narrative truth: if a story contains a distich, then the story must be true. In the semiosis of storytelling, songs are meant to link the narrated event back to the narrating event. Due to the typically obscure character of *vaihoho* and *tyarka* texts, however, this intended link is unsuccessful and remains suspended, as it were. It is this phenomenon that creates the mystique of traditional singing and turns it into the most appreciated intangible heritage in the eyes of the local communities in Lautém and Southwest Maluku (Lewier and Van Engelenhoven 2013).

4 Conclusion: oral traditions in jeopardy versus orality

Orality is defined in this contribution as the exclusive oral transfer of cultural knowledge. Mainland and insular Southeast Asia are complex multilingual zones that lodge a myriad of different oral and literate traditions. To provide an overall picture of these regions would be impossible due to the immense cultural, religious and historical differences that exist between and inside them. Except for Laos and Cambodia, all of the nations in the region are acknowledged as literate societies and many of them have a long literary tradition.

Orality without literary influences must thus be found in remote territories that are not yet under the influence of modernity. Therefore, this contribution intended to exemplify orality by focusing on storytelling and singing – two interrelated oral traditions in Lautém (Timor-Leste) and Southwest Maluku (Indonesia). Notwithstanding their remoteness, modernity and its implicit accomplice globalization have also begun to affect these two regions. The introduction of literacy and schooling connects remote societies to the modern world on the one hand, but on the other hand may cause an irrevocable decline of an oral tradition, as happened in the east of Flores Island (Indonesia), where oral texts were written down and subsequently lost their authority (Lewis 1998).

The awareness that oral traditions are fragile and contain unique cultural information boosted all kinds of national and international programs to save them in this rapidly changing world. An important Southeast Asian example is the multimedia Philippine Epics and Ballads Archive that is lodged at the Ateneo de Manila University in Manila, the Philippines (Revel 2013) and can be accessed on the Internet. It contains sound files, video fragments and accompanying texts of 16 Philippine languages, with additional references to related academic publications.

A shining example of how the output of academic research on oral tradition can benefit the local community is Dana Rappoport's (2009) publication on the music of the Toraja (Sulawesi Island, Indonesia) that became available in French, English and Indonesian. It contains two volumes of ethnographic analysis and song texts, and an accompanying DVD that is an exquisite ethnomusicological tool that explains all the techniques, functions and rituals related to musical performances among the Toraja.

It should not be forgotten, however, that oral traditions are just an expression of the human quality called orality. As long as the characteristic orality of a people is maintained, its oral traditions will remain in some form.

Notes

1 Part of this chapter relates to ongoing research on singing in Timor-Leste by Philip Yampolsky. I want to thank him wholeheartedly for our many discussions on his research. Of course, I am the only one to blame for any shortcomings or misinterpretations.
2 Although this is the same speech as discussed in Van Engelenhoven (1997), the analysis has been slightly adapted to fit the present discussion. A fourth paragraph containing a Leti translation of the Christian "Our Father" prayer and the transitional section that precedes it have not been included.
3 Van Engelenhoven (1997) uses the term "historiographic truth." We prefer to use "historiographic reliability" here to stress that it is the use of parallelism that guarantees credibility of the oral text.
4 In the text examples, a slash (/) and an x mark stressed and unstressed vowels, respectively; a single vertical line (|) marks a metrical boundary in scansion and a double vertical line (| |) marks a musical sentence, which is indicated in the musical notations in Figures 4a–d with a double bar.
5 *Kolye* literally means "we (inclusive) dwell."
6 In a personal communication in May 2016, Mariana Lewier explained that the performers or composers never gave a line-by-line translation, but rather provided an interpretation

for the whole text. In fact, the synonymous pair "embrace" – "uphold" in lines (d) and (e) was devised for presentational purposes in this paper; the performer of the song himself gave one single interpretative translation for both lines together: "Though hold on to the Commandments."

7   Toolbox is a computer program devised by the Summer Institute of Linguistics for gloss-ing and analyzing texts.

8   *Kwawe* is inflected for the first person inclusive plural: "we carry." The preceding lexical parallel *suly* is not inflected.

References

Brandt, Line and Per Aage Brandt. 2005. 'Making Sense of a Blend: A Cognitive-semiotic Approach to Metaphor', *Annual Review of Cognitive Linguistics* 3: 216–249.

Da Conceição Savio, Edegar. 2016. *Studi sosolinguistik bahasa Fataluku di Lautém*. Unpub-lished Ph.D. dissertation, Leiden University.

Flores, Randolf C. 2016. 'Wrestling with God: Stories of Initiation in the Old Testament and Some Asian Parallels', *Orientis Aura: Macau Perspectives in Religious Studies* 1: 75–89, https://hub1.usj.edu.mo/index.php/orientisaura/article/view/7/7 (accessed on 18 January 2017).

Fox, James. J. 1974. 'Our Ancestors Spoke in Pairs: Rotinese Views of Language, Dialect and Code'. Reprinted in James J. Fox, 1986. *Bahasa, sastra dan sejarah: Kumpulan karangan mengenai masyarakat pulau Roti*, pp. 144–199. Jakarta: Djambatan.

Fox, James J. 2014. *Explorations in Semantic Parallelism*. Canberra: ANU Press.

Gomes, Francisco de Azevedo.1972. *Os Fataluku*. Unpublished Ph.D. dissertation, Technical University of Lisbon.

Ivanoff, Jacques. 2013. 'From the Founding Epic to a Millenarian Unknown: Moken Answer to Contemporary History', in Nicole Revel (ed.) *Songs of Memory in Islands of Southeast Asia*, pp. 199–244. Newcastle upon Tyne: Cambridge Scholars Publishers.

Koolhof, Sirtjo. 1999. 'The "La Galigo", a Bugis Encyclopedia and its Growth', *Bijdragen voor Taal-, Land- en Volkenkunde* 155(3): 362–387.

Kuiper, Koenraad. 2000. 'On the Linguistic Properties of Formulaic Speech', *Oral Tradi-tion* 15(2): 279–305, http://journal.oraltradition.org/issues/15ii/kuiper (accessed on 2 February 2017)

Lawson, James. 2011. 'Chronotope, Story and Historical Geography; Mikhail Bakhtin and the Space-time of Narratives', *Antipode* 43(2): 384–412.

Leids La Galigo-manuscript opgenomen in UNESCO's Werelderfgoedlijst. www.bibliotheek. universiteitleiden.nl/nieuws/2012/09/leids-la-galigo-manuscript-opgenomen-in-unesco%E2%80%99s-werelderfgoedlijst (accessed on 17 January 2017).

Lewier, Mariana. 2016. *Kesintasan Tradisi Lisan Tyarka di Kepulauan Babar Maluku Barat Daya.* Unpublished Ph.D. dissertation, University of Indonesia.

Lewier, Mariana and Aone van Engelenhoven. 2013. 'Sung Memories: Composing and Performing Traditional Songs in Southwest Maluku'. Paper presented at the Semiot-ics of Parallelism in Southeast Asia Panel at the 7th European Association for Southeast Asian Studies Conference, held at the School of Social and Political Sciences, Technical University of Lisbon, 3 July.

Lewis, E.D. 1998. 'The Tyranny of the Text. Oral Tradition and the Power of Writing in Sikka and Tana ʔAi, Flores', *Bijdragen tot de taal-, land- en volkenkunde* 154 (3): 457–477.

Lundström, Håkan. 2014. 'Beautifying Techniques in Kammu Vocal Genres', in Jeffrey P. Williams (ed.) *The Aesthetics of Grammar. Sound and Meaning in the Languages of Mainland Southeast Asia*, pp. 118–132. Cambridge: Cambridge University Press.

Matisoff, James A. 1991. 'Syntactic Parallelism and Morphological Elaboration in Lahu Religious Poetry', in Sandra Chung and Joge Hankamer (eds.) *A Festschrift for William F. Shipley*, pp. 61–76. Santa Cruz, CA: Syntax Research Center.

McDonald, Margaret Read. 2006. *Ten Traditional Tellers*. Urbana/Chicago: University of Illinois Press.

Meneses, Filipe da Costa. 1997. *Sastra Lisan No Lolo Kabupaten Lospalos: terbitan teks, analisis struktur dan fungsi*. Unpublished BA Thesis, University of East Timor.

Rappoport, Dana. 2009. *Songs of the Thrice-Blooded Land. Ritual Music of the Toraja (Sulawesi, Indonesia)*. Paris: Éditions de la Maison des Sciences de l'Homme/Éditions Épistèmes.

Rappoport, Dana. 2015a. 'Music as Evidence of Settlement: The Case of Diphonic Singing in Eastern Indonesia (Eastern Flores, Eastern Timor)', in I. Wayan Arka et al. (eds.) *Language Documentation and Cultural Practices in the Austronesian World. Papers from 12-ICAL, Volume 4*. Asia – Pacific linguistics 019 / Studies on Austronesian languages 005, pp. 135–148. Canberra: Asia-Pacific Linguistics, http://hdl.handle.net/1885/13514 (accessed on 31 January 2017).

Rappoport, Dana. 2015b. 'Music et ritual dans l'Est insulindien (Indonésie orientale et Timor-Leste): premiers jalons', *Archipel* 90: 275–305.

Revel, Nicole. 2013. 'The Philippine Epics and Ballads Archive', *Oral Tradition* 28(8): 371–378. http://journal.oraltradition.org/files/articles/28ii/23_28.2.pdf (accessed on 6 April 2017).

Souvanxay Phetchanpheng. 2005. 'L'usage des texts dans les monastères tai lue du Laos', *Moussons* 25: 57–77.

Sweeney, Amin. 1987. *A Full Hearing: Orality and Literacy in the Malay World*. Berkeley, CA: University of California Press.

Valentim, Justino. 2002. *Fata-lukunu i Disionariu*. Dili: Timor-Lorosa'e-Nippon Culture Center.

Valentim, Justino. 2004. *Fataluku Waihohonu 828*. Dili: Timor-Lorosa'e-Nippon Culture Center.

Van Engelenhoven, Aone. 1997. 'Words and Expressions: Notes on Parallelism in Leti', *Cakalele, Jurnal Ilmu Pengetahuan Budaya* 8: 1–25.

Van Engelenhoven, Aone. 2010a. 'The War of the Words: Lexical Parallelism in Fataluku Discourse', in Clara Sarmento (ed.) *From Here to Diversity: Globalization and Intercultural Dialogues*, pp. 241–252. Newcastle upon Tyne: Cambridge Scholars Publishers.

Van Engelenhoven, Aone. 2010b. 'Living the Never-Ending Story: On Story-telling in Tutuala (East Timor) and Southwest Maluku (Indonesia)', in Castro Seixas P. (ed.) *Translation, Society and Politics in Timor-Leste*, pp. 61–76. Porto: Fernando Pessoa University Press.

Van Engelenhoven, Aone. 2010c. 'Lirasniara, the Sung Language of Southwest Maluku', *Wacana, Jurnal Ilmu Pengetahuan Budaya* 12(1): 143–161.

Van Engelenhoven, Aone. 2010d. 'The Makuva Enigma: Locating a Hidden Language in East-Timor', *Revue Roumaine de linguistique* 80(2): 161–181.

Van Engelenhoven, Aone. 2013. 'The Spoor of the Mythical Sailfish: Narrative Topology and Narrative Artefacts in Southwest Maluku (Indonesia) and Tutuala (East Timor)', in Nicole Revel (ed.) *Songs of Memory in Islands of Southeast Asia*, pp. 251–286. Newcastle upon Tyne: Cambridge Scholars Publishing.

Van Engelenhoven, Aone van and Nazarudin. 2016. 'A Tale of Narrative Annexation: Stories from Kisar Island (Soutwest Maluku, Indonesia)', *Wacana, Jurnal Ilmu Pengetahuan Budaya* 17(2): 191–231.

Waradet Mesangrutdharakul. 2014. 'A Comparative Study of Thai and Indian Cultures Influences by the Phra Rama Stories', *Review of Integrative Business and Economics Research* 3: 101–106. http://sibresearch.org/uploads/3/4/0/9/34097180/riber_h14-134_101-106.pdf (accessed on 18 January 2017).

Yampolsky, Philip. 2012. 'Intangible Cultural Heritage in Nino Konis Santana National Park, Distrito Lautem, Timor-Leste'. Unpublished report to ONGD Cives Mundi, Soria. Spanish translation of the adapted English text plus sound files at www.ninokonis nationalpark.com/vaihoho/ (accessed on 25 March 2017).

Yampolsky, Philip. 2014a. 'Variation of Melody and Form in *vaihoho*, the Sung Duets of Fataluku-speakers (East Timor)'. Invited presentation at the Third International Conference on Analytical Approaches to World Music, held at the School of Oriental and African Studies, London, 1–4 July.

Yampolsky, Philip. 2014b. 'Tutuala 5 – Cailoro 4.x'. Manuscript.

Yampolsky, Philip. 2015. 'Is Eastern Insulindia A Distinct Musical Area?' *Archipel* 90: 153–187.

2

THE LANGUAGES IN INDIA AND A MOVEMENT IN RETROSPECT

G. N. Devy

Colonialism and the indigenous

The term "indigenous" holds within it a tragic and an unending saga, an unceasing epic of "othering," "alienation," "alterity," "exclusion" and people being pushed out. One does not notice the term being commonly used in any part of the world before the emergence of colonialism. The indigenous communities that had been in self-command at the beginning of colonialism were reduced to minorities in their respective lands during the colonial era. The present global population of the indigenous is estimated at about 390 million out of the total 8 billion human population. Before colonialism, in the Americas, their population was 100%. In the wake of the "discovery" of the Americas came new diseases, armed attacks, expulsion and the extermination of the indigenous. The population of the indigenous in North America is currently only 1% of its total population. It is the same story in Australia and the Pacific. Everywhere, the indigenous are now miniscule minorities. When one thinks of the languages of indigenous peoples, one notices that only in exceptional cases are their languages associated with knowledge production and knowledge transactions in the contemporary world. Most of these communities have been living in their habitats over an enormously long time, probably for thousands of years. Though the pre-colonial world changed altogether during colonial times, there is no point in imagining that everything before colonialism was perfect. There were numerous instances of social exclusion in that past, and they, too, contributed to exclusionary notions of "indigenity." There have been migrations all throughout human history, and many native matters in which large sections of populations were "indigenously" turned indigenous. There is also no point in imagining that everything that Europe spread out into the world was socially perilous. That would be an extreme historical over-simplification. Thinking of the indigenous in terms of binaries is of no use to either the indigenous or the non-indigenous. Therefore, it is desirable to look at the exchanges between the indigenous and non-indigenous, particularly during colonial times.

The colonial taxonomies

Colonialism brought four great ideas to the rest of the world: freedom, reason, equality and individualism. For the traditional societies, freedom became an attractive idea. The kind of freedom that a phenomenon like the French Revolution seemed to offer was very attractive for many other continents. The idea of individualism was of great interest for a society such as India or Nigeria, which had been long saddled with caste and feudal orders. It was a potential mode of escape from the prevailing kinds of oppressions. The idea of equality, particularly legal equality, was a great European invention. Finally, reason, which helped organize knowledge in a systematic way, was found desirable by societies which had thought of knowledge as rooted in a mix of nature and the supernatural. Quite naturally, the ideas that Europe was developing during the colonial times attracted the rest of the world. Momentarily leaving aside the utter cruelty and brutality that Europeans displayed in exterminating the indigenous, these four ideas appear to have complemented something previously missing in the indigenous cultures.

However, the contact with these ideas resulted in a greater loss than gain for the indigenous communities. The losses included the loss of traditional cultural memory. The colonial impact affected the indigenous notions of love, affinity, affection, and their ability to relate to their community and the rest of the world. Similarly, the asymmetrical power equation in the colonial context led to a severely diminished self-image and low self-esteem in indigenous communities. These communities started thinking of themselves as inherently inferior, necessarily lagging behind and essentially underdeveloped; and that discourse has continued on both sides, bolstered by the self-assertion of Europe and deepened by the timidity of the rest of the world in thinking that the indigenous belong to the past and not the present. That was a great loss affected by colonial impact. The loss of cultural memory, the loss of self-esteem, the loss of the ability to relate to nature and society, and the pervasive domination of the twin gods of reason and individualism brought in by the Europeans resulted in such a great loss for the indigenous that they started losing their languages altogether. As in other former colonies, this has happened in India, too.

Archaeological and historical researches during the last two centuries have made it possible for us to know something about the complex linguistic transitions and migrations that took place over the last five millennia, roughly from the early Harappan times to our time (Blench and Spriggs, 1999–2012). During this long period, the Indian subcontinent accepted language legacies as distinct as the Avestan of the Zoroastrians, the Austro-Asiatic of the Pacific and the Tibeto-Burman of the East and Northeast Asia (Anthony, 2007). The Indic (or the Indo-Aryan) languages in the northern states, together with the Dravidic languages in the south and the Tibeto-Burman languages in the Northeast, each with a great variety of sub-branches, make for the large bulk of Indian languages. Throughout the known history of the subcontinent, there has been an active exchange and cultural osmosis between the indigenous languages and the migratory languages, producing great literature in many tongues.

In the pre-colonial epistemologies of language, hierarchy in terms of a "standard" and a "dialect" was not common. Language diversity was an accepted fact of life. Literary artists could use several languages within a single composition, and their audience accepted the practice as normal. Great works like the epic *Mahabharata* continued to exist in several versions handed down through a number of different languages until almost the beginning of the 20th century (Deshpande, 1979). When literary critics theorized, they took into account literature in numerous languages. Matanga's medieval compendium of styles, *Brihad-deshi* (Jiarazbhoy, 1975), is an outstanding example of criticism arising out of the principle that language diversity is normal. During the colonial times, many of India's languages were brought into the print medium. It is not that writing was not known previously. Scripts were already used; paper, too, was used as a means for reproducing written texts. However, despite being "written," texts had been mainly circulating through the oral means. Print technology diminished the existing oral traditions. New norms of literature were introduced, privileging the written over the oral, which brought in the idea that a literary text needs to be essentially monolingual. These ideas, and the power relation prevailing in the colonial context, started affecting the stock of languages in India. The languages that had not been placed within the print technology came to be seen as "inferior" languages. After independence, the Indian states were created on the basis of languages. If a language had a script, and if the language had *printed* literature in it, it was given a separate state within the Union of India. Languages that did not have printed literature, even though they had rich tradition of oral literature, were not considered. Further, the official state language was used as a medium of primary and high school education within a given state. A special Schedule of Languages (The Eighth Schedule) was created within the Indian Constitution. In the beginning, it had a list of 14 languages; at present, the list has 22 languages. The "Margins" of the Indian language spectrum, constituted by the indigenous peoples and the nomadic communities, are thus marginalized mainly due to the "aphasia" being systemically imposed on them.

Prior to the hierarchy of languages determined in terms of languages being printed, written but not in print and merely spoken without having any script came into vogue, the Indian states had almost never been "linguistic states." They had been predominantly poly-lingual or multi-lingual. Therefore, when the spirit of nationalism started developing in India, the idea of forming a single-language nation never crept into the thinking of any of the Indian nationalists, despite the differences between the ideological positions of the leaders during the freedom struggle. India, to them, was already a single nation with many languages and was going to continue being one. The long and involved discussions in the Constituent

Assembly from 1946 to 1949 provide ample testimony to the general acceptance of the idea of India as a nation with many languages. However, the Constituent Assembly had to resolve the contradiction between the astronomically large numbers of languages – which it knew through Grierson's Survey – and the need for a nationally shared language of communication. The Constituent Assembly's debates on this issue remained fairly inconclusive, resulting in the adoption of the special Schedule of Languages, the Eighth Schedule of the Constitution. (Sarangi, 2009).

It is generally believed by post-independence generations that the formation of the Eighth Schedule contributed towards the restructuring of Indian provinces into linguistic states. This popular perception has no basis in the history of the state formation in India. It was Sir Herbert Risley, then the home secretary, who wrote to the Bengal government in 1903 and brought in language as the divisive principle. As a result, Bengal was proposed to be partitioned in 1905 into East Bengal and West Bengal. When the idea of using language as the defining principle for demarcating provinces appeared in the Congress Session of 1917, Annie Besant strongly opposed it. A decade later, in its Nagpur Session in 1927, the Congress accepted the idea of linguistic distribution of the states. After independence, while Jawaharlal Nehru accepted the principle and the Linguistic Provinces Commission was set up in 1948, he cautioned against language becoming a threat to India's national unity. During the early 1950s, Andhra Pradesh became the first such Linguistic State to be created in the wake of a violent popular agitation. In 1953, the State Reorganization Commission was set up; however, two years later, Nehru was still trying to understand how the USSR had implemented this principle, and thus S.G. Barve was assigned to the USSR to study the Russian experience. That year, assured by the USSR experience, 14 states and nine Union Territories were created. In the 1960s, Punjab was created as a result of the agitation led by Sant Fateh and Singh Master Tara Sing. During the 1970s, the North Eastern States were created. The process of creation of smaller states, making language as the central part of the arguments for creating them, has continued in India ever since independence. However, though the Constituent Assembly debates displayed abundant respect for the idea of India as "a linguistically plural nation," language identity has played an important role in shaping the process of restructuring states (Schwartzberg, 2009). Implicit in the process is the flawed logic that every language that has a script, or has entered print technology and has therefore produced some of its literature in print, is required to assert its identity through aspiring to form a state within the "nation as a language plural." This insistence will probably continue to create political upheavals and mass movements till we understand that the hierarchy of languages based on the idea of writing as inherently superior to speech is neither linguistically scientific nor historically valid. I therefore felt very strongly that a fresh enumeration of Indian languages and their proper sociological description involving not the government machinery but rather the people of India is necessary for reversing the linguistic Balkanization of India. This, too, would be a way of decolonizing knowledge and recovering the self.

George Grierson's linguistic survey

The last large-scale survey was carried out by George Abraham Grierson. My first acquaintance with Grierson's *Survey* dates back to the 1970s. As a young reader of his monumental work, what struck me most was not the amazing range of his knowledge of India's language situation, nor his determination to complete the task in the face of enormous challenges. These, it is needless to say, will leave no reader unimpressed. The most striking feature of Grierson's *Survey* that I noticed was the silent spaces. Even at the beginning of the 20th century, which was Grierson's time, through his account one notices the beginning of a slow death spelt for nearly a 165 out of the 179 languages – the languages not in print in his time – that he documented and described (Grierson, 1905–28/2006). I am not aware of any full-scale comparison between Grierson's "linguistic discoveries of India" with a similar discovery by his eminent predecessor Sir William Jones. Jones was *excited* about the presence of "different" languages in India, though of course he had no way to know how many of them existed in his time. In contrast, Grierson's description had no such "eureka" about it. When one wades through the Grierson volumes, one returns home with the impression that the languages reported in them are, in most part, the rustic varieties, fit only for housing childish songs and materials good enough for folklorists subservient to anthropology. Against the fewer than 200 languages that he described, he described over 500 dialects. The arithmetic of the great work is indicative of its essential bias. Perhaps the beginning of it was embedded in the work of William Jones and the other scholars of his generation who collectively created Indology as a field of knowledge, despite their apparent euphoria in discovering India as an unknown continent of civilization.

Indian languages in the 21st century

Despite the vast range of the existing linguistic diversity in India, and the official support that is being given to a relatively large number of languages, the language stock in the country has started showing signs of a rapid decline (Sengupta, 2005). Several historical factors appear to be responsible for the decline. Print technology impacted Indian languages profoundly during the 19th century. The languages that were printed acquired importance (Austen, 2009); the ones that remained untouched by it came to be seen more as dialects than as languages, though that was not the case in every instance. Subsequently, the process of state reorganization in the country invoked the principle that a language is a language only if it has printed literature. The reorganization of Indian states as mainly linguistic states turned the already marginalized and "non-printed" languages into "minority" languages. Thus, Bhili, a major language in itself with over 20 million speakers, got divided into four states and became a minority language in all of them – Maharashtra, Madhya Pradesh, Gujarat and Rajasthan. The list of "Mother Tongues" reported by the 1961 Census had 1,652 names. Beginning with the 1971 census, the government decided to only include the languages that had more than 10,000 speakers on the list. The list of 1971 had a total of 108 names, with a 109th entry of "all others" (Nigam, 1971). The policy of using a cut-off figure further eliminated the already marginalized and minor languages. They started becoming increasingly invisible in social practice or political discourse. The relative lack of livelihood possibilities in the areas where the minor and marginalized languages are spoken has led to an exodus to areas where major and mainstream languages are spoken. This, too, has accelerated the rate at which Indian language diversity is shrinking. The number of languages that may have disappeared during the last 50 years was estimated to be 250 by the *People's Linguistic Survey*. India seems to have lost nearly a quarter of its "world views" since independence. The grave crisis is not confined to India alone. A similar situation of language loss is being experienced by most countries and in all continents. The global languages, or "mega-languages," have become or are being perceived as a threat to the local languages (Lukanovic, 2010; Meierkord, 2012). Besides, the idea of nation state, within which is implicit the idea of a language or languages for preserving national unity, has put stress on sub-national languages for a somewhat forced alignment. The sub-national languages, or the "regional languages," have learnt to expect the migration of yet smaller language communities within their fold as a natural result of "development" and "education," while they themselves feel uneasy in the face of the increasing influence of the "mega-languages' and the "national languages" (Schreier et al., 2010). Thus, quite a hierarchy of fears and anxieties seems to have besieged languages all over the world (Bianco, 2012). The fear and anxiety have even taken the mega-languages in their grips, for distinct continental varieties of these languages are emerging and beginning to become increasingly dissimilar (Barber et al., 1993; Bragg, 2003). It is argued that while languages always go through the "natural cycle" of rise and decline, in our time the incidence of a very rapid decline of natural languages has assumed worrisome proportions (Crystal, 2000; Nettle, 2000; Florey, 2010). In recent years, as never before in the history of the discipline of language study and linguistics, books on language endangerment and language decline have been appearing in a rapid succession (e.g., Fishman, 2001; Dalby, 2003; Janse and Tol, 2003; Harrison, 2007; Austin, 2008; Asp and De Villiers, 2010). The discussion on language endangerment and the conservation of threatened languages has received endorsement from UNESCO, too (Wurn, 2005; Mosley, 2010). Over the last two decades, scientists have come up with mathematical models for predicting the life of languages (Braggs and Freedman, 1993). These predictions have invariably indicated that the human species is moving rapidly close to extinction of a large part of its linguistic heritage. Since it is language, mainly of all things, that makes us human and distinguishes us from other species and animate nature (Blench and Spriggs, 2012), and since the human consciousness can but only function given the ability for linguistic expression, it becomes necessary to recognize language as the most crucial aspect of cultural capital. It has taken human beings continuous work of about half a million years to accumulate this valuable capital (Corballis, 2011). In our time, we have come close to the point of losing most of it.

Historians of civilization tell us that a comparable, though not exactly similar, situation had probably arisen in the past, some 7,000–8,000 years ago (Crystal, 2000). This time, though, the crisis has an added theme, as a lot of human activity is now dominated by manmade intelligence. Language-based technologies are now well entrenched partners in the semantic universe(s) that bind human communities together (Gillespie, 2007). Language today is as much a system of meaning in the cyberspace affecting communication between a machine and another machine as it has been a system of meaning in the social space achieving communication between a human being and another human being. In the new experience of the world waiting for all of us, memory as we have so far used it (Rossi, 2006) is expected to be of little use, and imagination as we have so far exercised it is predicted to be entirely transformed. The homo-sapiens, it is believed, are moving out of memory, imagination and even language, and are poised to enter a post-human phase of natural evolution (McMohan, A. and R. McMohan, 2013). However, language is not only a social system of verbal icons, arbitrarily assembled through ages; it is also a "means" of carrying forward the cumulative human experience of millennia to the future generations. When language trajectories are snapped, the accumulated wisdom in those languages gets submerged and continues to survive in severely truncated, irreparable and insensible forms (Cru, 2010). It is in the context of this rapid language decline that I decided to undertake a social experiment closely involving the indigenous communities in India. It eventually turned into a people's movement and resulted in what is now known as the *People's Linguistic Survey of India.*

The genesis of the people's language movement

In 1972, The Publication Division of the government of India brought out R.C. Nigam's compilation of the census data on Indian languages under the title *Language Handbook on Mother Tongues in Census*. This work, like hundreds of other uninspiring titles brought out by the Publication Division, would have deserved no mention, except in arcane academic works, had it not become one of the causes to trigger a very unique language movement a quarter century later. The book contained no profound analysis, nor any emotive appeal for preservation of languages. All that it presented was tables and statistics on mother tongues in India. The term "mother tongue" has been used during various census exercises with a variety of meaning ranging from "the language spoken in the locality" and "the language of the parents" to "the language claimed by a person as the first language." Nigam did not contest any of these definitions. However, what his cold statistics pointed out was that more than 1,500 of the mother tongues listed in the 1961 Census had been all bundled up under a single label "all others" in the 1971 census. The reason for hacking such a large number of "mother tongues" to death was that an arbitrary "cut-off" figure of 10,000 speakers was introduced by the census for legitimizing the existence of a mother tongue. I had seen this volume of work as a young researcher in my university library, and casually noted in my mind the mysterious label "all others," probably forgotten it altogether and continued with my academic pursuits.

About a decade later, as a young lecturer at the Maharaja Sayajirao University of Baroda, I started making weekly forays into the indigenous underbelly of the rapidly industrializing, and therefore urbanizing, Gujarat. During the 1980s, the agrarian distress had started its early signs in the eastern parts of the state; and one could notice hordes of tribals pouring into the cities as construction labourers. As I travelled through the villages in eastern Gujarat and started conversing with the villagers, one thing that struck me was that their speech was remarkably different from the Gujarati language that I heard spoken in Baroda and Surat. This led to my rather nascent perception that the economic deprivation of the indigenous may perhaps be related to the denial of their languages in schools and offices. Back home, in my studies, I started quietly plotting indigenous areas against the main languages on the map of India, till then known to me as "the languages of India" (which did not even cover the entire spectrum of the scheduled languages). What emerged out of this haphazard exercise was a serious question. It was: "Was not the indigenous belt in central India responsible for keeping the Dravidian languages distinct from the Indo-Aryan languages for nearly three millennia?" I felt that this mystery had to be unravelled. There were no academic works known to me that provided any clues. And, therefore, I decided to leave my university job, carry a notebook and a pencil with me, and travel through the indigenous areas of central India examining folklore and language samples. Though I could not actually carry out my plans in the exact manner in which I had made them, my decision led me to a complete immersion in indigenous history, culture, arts and language. Through a series of events – not entirely planned or desired consciously – I hit upon the idea of establishing "Bhasha" (language or voice), a sort of a rustic research initiative.

In 1984 I had planned to set up a school in an adivasi village, but I could not. In 1987–88 I took up relief work in drought-hit Savali-villages, but had to give it up. In 1992, I thought I would start travelling through the adivasi villages, collecting their songs and stories; but I did not. At last, in 1996, my body, mind, family and financial condition together gave a go ahead. I was never alone in the work from the very beginning. Everybody helped me. Former students from the Baroda University came as unpaid volunteers. Others started bringing in monetary contributions. Yet others came forward to own the ideas and execute them. Many brought new ideas. Above all, my Adivasi Academy students! (The indigenous peoples in India call themselves "adivasi.") I have never ceased to learn from them. I have not been good at inventing names and so I always chose simple words: "Bhasha" for the Charity Trust, "Adivasi Academy" for the institute of experimental learning, *Dhol* (drums) for the magazine of tribal concerns, *Vacha* (voice) for the museum of voice, *Samveg* for the learning cottage, *Vikas* (development) for the development-projects complex, *Samas* (compound-epithets) for the forum of like-minded literary persons, and simply "Tribals First" for the first adivasi-managed indigenous craft and cultural centre. I thought the fewer the words, the better.

In 1996, I went to Saputara looking for tribal stories. Then some adivasis came forward to share their songs and stories based on their profound memory. They then wanted to try their hand at the print medium. By then, they had started thinking of writing books and publishing them through the Bhasha Research Centre and editing magazines, writing plays and performing them, and organizing adivasi literary meets. They decided to speak. Bhasha facilitated this adivasi voice. I began by asking them to compile anthologies of their oral literature.

Within months of commencing the work on the 20-volume series of folklore anthologies, many adivasi writers and scholars approached me with the idea of starting a magazine in their own language aimed at the adivasi communities and to be read out loud rather than used for individual reading. The magazine was called *Dhol* (drums), a term that has a totemic cultural significance for the adivasis. We started using the state scripts combined with a moderate use of diacritic marks to represent these languages. The response to the magazine was tremendous. More adivasis approached Bhasha and asked for versions of *Dhol* in their own languages. In two years' time, *Dhol* started appearing in ten of the adivasi languages of western India. When the first issue of Chaudhary language *Dhol* was released, it sold 700 copies on the first day. This was a record of sorts for a little magazine. Inspired by the success of the oral magazine, our adivasi collaborators started bringing manuscripts of their autobiographies, poems, essays and even anthropological studies of their communities to Bhasha, which they wanted us to publish. Subsequently, in order to highlight the oral nature of adivasi culture, we launched a weekly radio magazine which was relayed throughout the adivasi areas of Gujarat and Maharashtra. Together, all these initiatives gave birth to a small but focused publishing and book distribution house, the Poorva-prakash (the light of the East), which was not so much a commercial venture as a cultural and literary platform for intellectual concerns and a forum for expression in peoples' own languages.

In its 20 years of existence, Bhasha anchored two movements. One was the movement for the rights of the Denotified and Nomadic Tribes (wrongly branded as "criminal" communities), and the other was the movement for the language rights of the linguistically marginalized communities. In both these movements, the conceptual and the tangible went hand in hand. In relation to the "Bhasha" movement, the main theoretical challenge involved re-stating the precise relationship between language and dialect and understanding how the simplistic co-relation between script and language had adversely impacted history of the minor non-lexical languages.

The immediate reason

When preparations for the 11th Five Year Plan began in India, the Ministry of Human Resource Development (MHRD) established a group to suggest ways of strengthening Indian languages. A sub-group was carved out of the larger group to think about non-scheduled languages. I was asked to chair it. Our recommendations to the MHRD were accepted by the National Planning Commission and funds were allocated as suggested. The MHRD turned the recommendations into a *yojana* (a scheme) – the Bharat Bhasha Vikas Yojana (scheme for developing Indian languages) – and the government-run, directorate-level language institution was assigned the responsibility for implementing the scheme. Two years later, I learnt that it had failed to take off. During the same period, the MHRD had suggested the idea of New Linguistic Survey of India (NLSI). Funds for it, too, had been made available. The same government institution was charged with the responsibility to take the NLSI forward. Two years later, I learnt that the initiative had been cold-stored. This was enough to make one angry, particularly as I had been witnessing the severe gap between the economic development of speakers of some of the scheduled languages and that of the speakers of the indigenous languages. Therefore, I sent out a call to individuals and groups interested in the language issue from all parts of India to assemble in Baroda. I had also written to several hundred linguists. I was not sure how many would turn up. When we met in March 2010, this gathering, convened under the title "Bhasha Sangam" (language confluence), had representatives of 320 languages registered and in attendance. The delegates included 17 vice-chancellors, over a hundred linguists, publishers, writers, language lovers and villagers. They were nearly 800 in number. During the "Bhasha Sangam," speaker after speaker called for a comprehensive survey. As a result, on the morning of the 10 March 2010, I announced to the media that a People's Linguistic Survey of India (PLSI) would be initiated. The news was carried very widely in media in and outside of India.

Obviously, since there was no funding available for the initiative, I could not have thought of setting a grand office for this purpose. Instead, I chose to go from state to state and set up groups of like-minded persons. From May till November of 2010, I had managed to set up state-level committees of the PLSI in Himachal Pradesh, Uttara Khand, Punjab, Rajasthan, Orissa, West Bengal, Jharkhand, Andhra Pradesh (now split into two states), Karnataka, Tamil Nadu, Kerala, Maharashtra and Goa. Yet, many states still remained out of my reach. The entire North-East kept eluding me. Throughout the next year, 2011, I decided to focus on the North-East, Uttar Pradesh and Bihar. During that year, I also managed to constitute a National Editorial Collective of about 60 distinguished scholars, and prepare one or two persons in every state to function as the state coordinator(s) of the PLSI. The movement was capable of moving forward because many capable persons willingly joined it, including several eminent scholars. Just as there were scholars involved in the making of the PLSI, there were lay persons as well. They came from background as varied as agriculture, primary school teaching, casual labour, street entertainment and para-medical professions. In a way, it would not be far from the truth to say that the entire rainbow of social diversity was involved in the PLSI movement (Devy, 2014). In each of the states, a series of training workshops were organized. All this had to be done without any specific funding support. Yet, the urgency of the language issue brought people together and encouraged their spirit of voluntary work. Towards the end of 2011, Tata Trust offered partial support for the PLSI work. The volume of the funds I asked them to offer was significantly lower than what the government had visualized for its aborted NLSI two years prior. These funds helped me organize a series of meetings of the National Editorial Collective and state-level workshops.

In January 2012, I requested the coordinator in every state to come up with their list of languages and a very rough draft of the publication they intended to work on. To my utter surprise, they all complied. And, once again, I could hold a very large conference under the caption "Bhasha Vasudha" (The Language Universe). Scholars from several countries outside of India also participated. And, at the end of the conference, I had 30 rather nicely bound manuscripts in progresses with me, one for each state or union territory in the country. I knew in my heart that the PLSI dream was not impossible to realize. For the next 18 months, I kept frequently travelling to every state, meeting the PLSI teams, helping them improve their work, keeping their teams together, bringing them information resources and working with them through difficulties big and small. During those months, I also kept discussing the arrangements for the eventual publication of the volumes resulting out of the PLSI with various publishers. I drew up, revised and refined the scheme of the volumes, arranged for translators where they were needed and editors for materials that were commissioned. So, the PLSI was, for me, during those crowded years, a people's language movement as well as a serious academic project. Reconciling the diverse demands of these two faces of the PLSI was a stressful work; but I knew that I had to do it.

By early 2013, it was clear that the PLSI volumes would eventually get published. On 5 September 2013, all of the volume editors from every state in India came together in Delhi. By then, nearly 3,000 individuals were involved in the PLSI movement and 780 languages – not dialects – had been identified for inclusion in the volumes. We all went to the "30th January Street" memorial – the Birla House compound, where Mahatma Gandhi was assassinated on 30 January in 1948 – and placed bound manuscripts of the volumes on the ground as a symbolic gesture of dedicating the work to the nation. The date chosen was in memory of a former president of India known for his scholarship. Thus, the symbolism combined the figures of a highly respected president and Gandhi, the Father of the Nation. The volumes had yet to be published, but the PLSI had come into existence. I received a call from the office of the president of India on the eve of this dedication ceremony. On the invitation of the president, my wife and I went to the Rashtrapati Bhavan and offered a copy of the manuscript of the first volume, the *Introduction*, to him. In a purely symbolic way, India had put the seal of acceptance on the PLSI. The news was reported widely in all regional languages, in the national dailies and in newspapers in more than 40 countries outside of India. A unique language movement, whose seeds lay in a four-decades-old and somewhat obscure publication and in a relatively modest community initiative, had come to be a part of the people's history in India.

Though I was at the centre of the entire movement, I am aware that the PLSI has been a collective effort by the people of India to register their "voices." It is not a repeat, a replacement or a substitute for the Grierson-like survey. The parameters for the accomplishments of these two surveys are different. The PLSI is more of an informal attempt to bring to the world's notice the phenomenal language diversity in India, and by extension in the rest of the world, in the interest of keeping the biosphere alive and preserving the democracy that India has acquired through a long and pitched struggle. In order to commemorate the struggle, it was decided to place the following description of the process in the opening pages of every volume of the PLSI series:

> The People's Linguistic Survey of India is a right-based movement for carrying out a nation-wide survey of Indian languages as people perceive them, to identify, document and understand them; especially languages of fragile communities such as nomadic, coastal, island, hill and forest communities. The PLSI is a quick, non-hierarchical, public consultation and appraisal, intended as an aid to cultural impact assessment of development, and as an acknowledgement of the self-respect and sense of identity of all, especially, endangered speech communities of India. The PLSI is carried out by scholars, writers and activists in partnership with members of different speech communities. . . . It is an attempt at reinventing and re-rooting cognitive categories available in languages across political borders, in consonance with ecological regions, for building defences for a *sui generis* Community Intellectual Preservation Regime (C-IPR) as against Individual Intellectual Property Right (I-IPR) protection.

In 1996, when I started work with adivasis in Western India and after the *Dhol* magazine started appearing in 1997, I was nearly convinced that each of the adivasi languages, and the languages like these, deserved to have at least a 60-page quarterly magazine devoted to them. By 2002, I was ready to spread it to about 80 such languages in the country; and to this end, I recall having convened a major conference of representatives of various adivasi languages from Central and Western Indian states like Orissa, Jharkhand, Chhattisgarh, Madhya Pradesh, Maharashtra and Rajasthan. I had to drop the plans, as the printing press in Baroda engaged for printing the ten editions of the *Dhol* magazine was unable to cope with the pressure. Besides the disturbed situation, the post-riot Gujarat created certain other difficulties in pursuing my agenda of promoting language diversity (Devy, 2006).

In 2003, as my way of coping with the post-riots social situation in Gujarat, my adivasi colleagues and I conceptualized the *Bol* magazine, framed in Gujarati, but carrying stories and songs from several adivasi languages within its covers. This was put out as a children's magazine and it achieved a phenomenal success. In a short time, it had over 7,000 schools as subscribers, in addition to an equally impressive number of individual subscribers. I decided, therefore, to cease the publication of the ten versions of *Dhol* and decided to concentrate on the relatively younger age group of readers that the *Bol* magazine had established. If I had commenced the linguistic survey in 2003, I would have probably solely concentrated on the folklore aspect of the languages. My ideas, however, had changed by the time I announced in 2010 that the *People's Linguistic Survey of India* was being proposed. In March 2010, I drew up the first plan for the distribution of the survey material in different volumes. The list of the PLSI volumes I circulated in August 2010 among the colleagues invited to join the National Editorial Collective (NEC) was much different from what it is now that the majority of the volumes are published. The discussion during the National Editorial Collective meeting in August 2010 was not entirely based on the abstract idea of "having to do a linguistic survey of India." The discussion brought several ground realities and considerations with a bearing on the plan of volumes to the NEC forum. I had maintained from the beginning of my work with the adivasi communities that the no credit for intellectual work should be given to individuals, but it should be given instead to the entire collective that makes the product of such work possible. Accordingly, I had suggested to the Editorial Collective that the "authorship" of the *People's Linguistic Survey of India* be stated in the name of all the individuals involved in its making. At the time of the first NEC meeting in Baroda, about 700 individuals had volunteered to contribute or help collect data for the survey. I had estimated this number to go up substantially, as we had still not made a beginning in Bihar, Uttar Pradesh and the North-Eastern States. I had suggested that we print all those 1,000 or more names on the cover pages of the proposed volumes as "authors." My idea did not find favour with the National Editorial Collective. Some of the major scholars from the Southern States clearly stated their desire to be recognized "individually" as the PLSI state coordinators or as "volume editors." Some others expressed concern relating to the publication process. They argued that no good publisher would ever agree to sign a combined contract for the volumes with 1,000 or more "authors." In the past, I had carried out all my work in strict adherence to the principle of "collective intellectual work." While I could have claimed the credit for *Dhol*, *Bol* and all the other publications of the Adivasi Academy and the Bhasha Research Centre, I had always insisted on mentioning the names of the persons from the communities whose language or culture was represented as "editor" or "author." However, in this case, we came to the conclusion that my idea of collective intellectual pursuit was either too late or too early in the intellectual history of India. Besides, there was a strange kind of contradiction between the argument defending language movements and the argument favouring individual authorship. The first pointed to the hunger for a "collective identity," the second to the thirst for an individual identity. However, there were certain practical implications of this work for the participants in the PLSI. Some of them were engaged in universities and colleges as faculty. They were required to justify the use of their professional time that had been used for the PLSI work to their own institutions. Hence, a clear certification or recognition in some conventional form was necessary for them to be able to participate in the work. In the light of the discussion during the National

Editorial Collective, we decided to respect the desire of the state coordinators and the state volume editors to be recognized individually for their specific role. During the months following the meeting, I spent time travelling to various states and union territories to decide in mutual consultation with the teams formed in those states and Union Territories as to who was given the responsibility of coordinating the work for the respective state and who was involved in editing the state volume. Through a long series of meetings, workshops, discussions and the exchange of views, we decided that a volume per state would be a desirable structure for the PLSI series when we come to publishing it. We also decided that for some of the states the volumes would be published first in the main language of the respective state, and then independently in an English translation for further dissemination. From the very beginning of the PLSI, the primary readership for the published volumes was that of the language communities that have kept the languages alive. The growth or survival of a language, particularly a marginalized language, depends more on the "will to survive" that the community has rather than on any other external aid created in support of the language. Hence, we decided that the *People's Linguistic Survey of India* volumes should be primarily published in the languages that are more accessible to the village people and the non-schooled citizens of India. English is clearly not that language. But, at the same time, it was felt that if a vast language survey of this scale was carried out, the world outside India, too, would be interested in knowing the contents of the report. Therefore, we decided that an additional national PLSI series should be published in English. A little later, we decided that all of the volumes would be made available in Hindi as well. As I write this essay, more than 55 titles of the PLSI have already been published and are being used by communities and scholars alike.

It is too early to say what impact that the language movement will have on the destinies of each of the Indian languages. What is clear, however, is that the world and the government establishment in India have conceded that the language diversity of India is very large, though diminishing rapidly. The figure of the Indian languages that the PLSI proposed is now more or less accepted in India in all quarters. So often, in newspapers, radio and TV, one hears clear echoes of the PLSI's description of language diversity. Diversity, as an idea central to democracy and its linguistic demonstration, has been one of the most significant contributions of the PLSI movement.

There will indeed be scholars and linguists in the future who will point out inadequacies in the PLSI volumes. One hopes that they do, which will help in improving the PLSI volumes. However, once the PLSI has come into existence, in no future time will it be easy for any government or political party to favour the imposition of a single language or nationally in any particular state. This movement, unlike any other language movement, was not espousing the cause of a given single language. Rather, it has placed on firm footings the idea that India is, and shall remain, a multi-lingual and therefore a multi-cultural nation. In the times of rapidly shrinking cultural diversity all over the world, and the times when democracies are becoming increasingly "majority-biased," the PLSI foregrounded linguistic diversity and expansion of democracy as significant. This movement may be able to make claim to that achievement.

References

Anthony, David W., 2007, *The Horse, the Wheel and Language*, Princeton and Oxford: Princeton University Press.

Asp, Elissa D. and De Villiers, Jessica, 2010, *When Language Breaks Down*, New York: Cambridge University Press.

Austin, Granville, 2009, 'Language and the Constitution: The Half-hearted Compromise', in *Language & Politics in India*, Asha Sarangi (ed.), New Delhi: Oxford University Press, pp. 41–92.

Austin, Peter, 2008, *One Thousand Languages: Living, Endangered and Lost*, Berkley: University of California Press.

Barber, Charles, Joan C. Beal, and Philip Shaw, 1993, *The English Language: A Historical Introduction*, Cambridge: Cambridge University Press.

Bianco, Joseph Lo, 2012, 'National Language Revival Movements: Reflections from India, Israel, Indonesia and Ireland', in *The Cambridge Handbook of Language Policy*, Bernard Spolsky (ed.), Cambridge: Cambridge University Press, pp. 501–522.

Blench, Roger and Mathew Spriggs (eds.), 1999–2012, *Archaeology and Language: Theoretical and Methodological Orientations*. 4 vols, London and New York: Routledge.

Bragg, Melvyn, 2003, *The Adventure of English: The Biography of a Language*, London: Hodder & Stoughton.

Braggs, I. and H. I. Freedman, September 1993, 'Can the Speakers of a Dominated Language Survive as Unilinguals? A Mathematical Model of Bilingualism', in *Mathematical and Computer Modelling*, Vol. 18 (6), Oxford: Pergamon Press, pp. 9–18.

Corballis, Michael, 2011, *The Recursive Mind: The Origins of Human Language, Thought and Civilization*, Princeton, NJ: Princeton University Press.

Cru, Josep (ed.), 2010, *The Management of Linguistic Diversity and Peace Processes*, Barcelona: UNESCOCAT.

Crystal, David, 2000, *Language Death*, Cambridge: Cambridge University Press.

Dalby, Andrew, 2003, *Language in Danger*, New York: Columbia University Press.

Deshpande, Madhav, 1979, 'History, Change and Permanence: A Classical Indian Perspective,' in *Contributions to South Asian Studies*, Vol. I, Gopal Krishna (ed.), Delhi: Oxford University Press.

Devy, G. N., 2006, *A Nomad Called Thief, The Voice and the Silence of Adivasis*, New Delhi: Orient Blackswan.

Devy, G. N., 2014, *The Being of Bhasha: General Introduction to the People's Linguistic Survey of India*, New Delhi: Orient Blackswan.

Fishman, Joshua A. (ed.), 2001, *Can Threatened Languages be Saved?* Clevedon and Sydney: Multilingual Matters.

Florey, Margaret (ed.), 2010, *Endangered Languages of Australia*, New York: Oxford University Press.

Gillespie, Tarleton, 2007, *Wired Shut: Copyright and the Shape of Digital Culture*, Cambridge, MA: The MIT Press.

Grierson, George Abraham, Serially published in 11 Volumes. 1905–1928. Linguistic survey of India, Calcutta: Government Press.

Harrison, K. David, 2007, *When Languages Die*, New York: Oxford University Press.

Janse, Mark and Sijmen Tol (eds.), 2003, *Language Death and Language Maintenance: Theoretical Practice and Descriptive Approaches*, Amsterdam/Philadelphia: John Benjamin Publishing Company.

Jiarajbhoy, N. A., 1975, 'Music', in *A Cultural History of India*, A. L. Basham (ed.), Oxford: Oxford University Press.

Lukanovic, Sonja Noval (ed.), 2010, *A Shared Vision: International Dialogue – a Global Paradigm to Promote Linguistic and Cultural Diversity*, Ljubljana: Institute for Ethnic Studies.

McMahon, April and Robert McMahon, 2013, *Evolutionary Linguistics*, Cambridge: Cambridge University Press.

Meierkord, Chritiane, 2012, *Interactions across Englishes: Linguistic Choices in Local and International Contact Situations*, New York: Cambridge University Press.

Mosley, Christopher, 2010, *The Atlas of the World Languages in Danger*, Paris: UNESCO.

Nettle, Daniel and Suzanne Romaine, 2000, *Vanishing Voices,* Oxford: Oxford University Press.

Nigam, R. C., 1972, 'Language Handbook on Mother Tongues in Census', *Census of India 1971*, No. 10, New Delhi: Census Centenary Monographs.

Rossi, Paolo, 2006, *Logic and the Art of Memory: The Quest for a Universal Language*, London: Athlone Press.

Sarangi, Asha (ed.), 2009, *Language and Politics in India*, New Delhi: Oxford University Press.

Schreier, Daniel, Peter Trudgill, Edgar W. Schneider, and Jeffrey P. Williams (eds.), 2010, *The Lesser Known Varieties of English*, New York: Cambridge University Press.

Schwartzberg, Joseph E., 2009, 'Factors in the Linguistic Reorganization of Indian States', in *Language and Politics in India*, Asha Sarangi (ed.), New Delhi: Oxford University Press.

Sengupta, Kamalini (ed.), 2005, *Endangered Languages in India*, New Delhi: INTACH.

Wurn, Stephen, 2005, *Atlas of the World's Languages in Danger*, Paris: UNESCO.

3

INDIGENOUS LANGUAGES OF ARNHEM LAND

Dany Adone, Bentley James and Elaine L. Maypilama

In recent years, we have seen an increasing number of studies on the languages of Australia ranging from traditional indigenous languages (TILs), contact languages (e.g., Northern Territory Kriol, or mixed languages such as Gurindji Kriol or light Tiwi), varieties of English and sign languages (both indigenous alternate sign languages and the official sign language of Australia, also known as Australian Sign Language [AUSLAN]).[1] It has long been established that the indigenous people of Australia have shared the southern continent for more than 50,000 years and inherit one of the oldest continuous, sustainable, socio-cultural endowments on the planet. With respect to indigenous languages, it is no exaggeration to say that Australian languages exhibit the complex and fascinating variation and exceptional characteristics of language born of eons of evolution. In many ways they represent some interesting challenges to several linguistic theories. Indeed, the study of these languages provides deep insights into the multifaceted relationship between ephemeral human language and culture.

When Captain Cook landed on the afternoon of Sunday, 29 April 1770, Australia had between 700–800 language varieties including those of Tasmania and the Torres Strait Islands (Koch and Nordlinger 2014). According to Butlin (1983), these language varieties were spoken by a population of about one million people, illustrating a characteristic linguistic diversity extant across the wide brown continent. Although Australia still shows linguistic diversity, it has lost most of its traditional indigenous languages. Worldwide concern for language endangerment has singled out Australia as the continent where languages are disappearing the fastest, with the possibility that all indigenous Australian languages may disappear within the next few decades. Schmidt (1985); Nettle and Romaine (2000); the National Indigenous Languages Survey (NILS) (McConvell et al. 2005); Marmion, Obata and Troy (2014); and Zuckermann (p.c. 2016) all argue that only a handful of the traditional Australian indigenous languages that still survive can be regarded as being in a "healthy state."

In this chapter, we focus on traditional indigenous languages of Australia, more specifically those in Arnhem Land. In the next section, we discuss three central but broader socio-linguistic factors which play an important role in understanding Australia's indigenous languages. The second section provides an overview of indigenous languages across the continent, taking into account current discussions on three principal issues in the field: historical linkages among Australian indigenous languages, their genetic classification and the part played by language contact. In the third section, we take a close look at Arnhem Land, the home of several traditional indigenous languages, with a focus on the Yolngu language family of North-East Arnhem Land as a subgroup of the Pama languages. We examine its status as one of Australia's surviving indigenous languages, focusing on the complex triangulation between Language-Land-People. In the fourth section, we provide an overview into new studies on the signed languages of Arnhem Land. In the final section, we offer a brief conclusion with some prospects for future research.

Background to the study of the traditional indigenous languages of Australia

There are several important factors that need to be taken into account when studying Australia's traditional indigenous languages. These factors offer strong explanatory potential for a fuller understanding of their contexts and use. Recognizing the potentially problematic use of the term traditional, we use it here to simply differentiate those indigenous languages spoken before colonization from those arising after the fact.

The literature reveals a propensity for multilingualism in Australian indigenous societies in which it is not uncommon for large numbers of individuals to speak several languages and to have a passive understanding of a number of others (e.g., Dixon 2002; Evans 2007; Koch and Nordlinger 2014). Earlier studies, such as Voegelin et al. (1963: 25), noted that the "culture of multilingualism" is widespread in Australia. In some places a harsh environment, uncertain ecological holding capacity and subsistence economies promoted long-distance networks of ritual, marital (connubial) and economic relations. Such connections provide a strong impetus for multiple language skills and good relations with geographically distant groups speaking a number of different languages. Studies of multilingualism have only concentrated on spoken languages to a large degree. Kendon (1988), Adone and Maypilama (2014a, 2015), Green (2014) and Adone et al. (2018) have shown that the hearing population of indigenous people in many parts of Australia are also fluent in their local sign languages. Adone and Maypilama (2014a) have argued that indigenous societies are "bimodal bilingual" societies, meaning that the hearing population uses several spoken languages (auditory modality) and may well be experienced in an indigenous sign language (visual modality). Communities using two of the three existing modalities in which human language is expressed are described as bimodal bilingual. Bimodal bilingual is an expression taken from sign linguistics to refer to the ability of people to use both spoken and signed languages to communicate. This type of bimodal bilingualism, while being a common practice in indigenous communities in Australia, is rarely attested elsewhere in the world, with the exception of Native American communities and several indigenous communities of Mesoamerica (see Farnell 1995, 2003 and Fox Tree 2009).

Another key factor to be considered when studying TILs in the Australian context is the very close and complex relationship between Land-Language-People. Indigenous Australian language ideology postulates that a group's ancestrally endowed language is directly related to their inherited land (Stanner 1933; Berndt 1951; Bagshaw 1998; Keen 2004; Rumsey 1993; Baymarrwangga and James 2014). Stanner (1960: 4) characterizes the relationship to land as inherently spiritual and, he argues,

> place was the source of a person's life-force, and he or she was inseparably connected with it. This indissoluble connection of person and place by means of a spiritual link externally manifest in land as an outward and visible sign.

Morphy (2010) describes how a clan's language is closely bound to a pre-existing ancestral geography. The method of the investment of language in people and land is recorded in a complex and profound body of creation myths, i.e., foundational myths in which the ancestors are believed to create the topography and endow it with language as an integral part of the cosmogonic act of creating the land and sea scape (Warner 1937; Williams 1999; Evans 2007). Those inheriting possession of the ancestral geography also inherit the language. The owner group and their "ritual managers" retain the authority to speak about and share details of the particular language with outsiders, e.g., researchers. This elemental connection between Land-Language-People is not just associative, but an ontological reality. Consequently, a high level of informed consent is a precondition to any linguistic research in the field.

A third factor fundamental to a better understanding of TILs is the notion of circumspection. Circumspection is one of the core principles underlying interaction in indigenous societies. Garde (2013: 12) observes that circumspection as a universal operates "in a way so as to not overtly restrict a set of potential referents." This cultural trait, expressed through oblique reference, intentional ambiguity, vagueness and an inhibition to engage has been identified in the literature on TILs. Keen (1994) offers an in-depth discussion on ambiguity in language and ritual practices around rights to know and to speak in an economy of secret knowledge in religious contexts. Oblique reference, indirectness and circumspection about the use of names accounts for a preference in some communities to use nicknames or kin names rather than personal names. Children learn to not pronounce the names of the deceased, a grave offence known as *dudakthun*, meaning "to invoke the name of the dead" (James 2009). Circumspection, for example, may be expressed in the form of general statements that function as open questions, leaving plenty of subjective wiggle room. Walsh and Yallop (1993) and Garde (2013: 11) note that Aboriginal children learn the pragmatics of personal reference at a very early age and are encouraged "to refer to people, places and totemic symbols primarily in terms of kinship relations."

Overview of traditional indigenous languages

In this section, we offer a brief overview on TILs in Australia. Australian indigenous societies, renowned for their linguistic diversity, furnish fertile ground for an emerging collocation of post-settler influenced languages labelled "contact languages" in many areas (e.g., the Torres Straits, Queensland and Western Australia). In the Northern Territory, more precisely in Arnhem Land, we find, for instance, Roper River Kriol or Barunga Kriol, both of which are the outcome of language contact between the indigenous population and the English-speaking population (e.g., missionaries, police and pastoralists). Besides these Creole languages, we also find varieties of English, which we call here "Indigenized Englishes." These varieties of English have emerged under the influence of English and carry in them the durable hallmarks of indigeneity in their structural makeup. Termed Aboriginal Englishes in the literature, it is still not clear how many forms of Aboriginal English exist. Other languages, such as Gurindji Kriol or light Tiwi, are classified as mixed languages. These mixed varieties typically emerged in the context of community bilingualism and display a split ancestry (Matras and Bakker 2003, among others). Gurindji Kriol presents a challenge for some theories of language formation and some interesting potential themes for further investigations in that code-switching has been identified as the key source of its genesis (McConvell and Meakins 2005).

As research on indigenous sign languages in Australia is in its infancy, we do not yet have a complete picture of their distribution and density before colonization. However, findings from recent studies (Walsh 1979; Adone et al. 2018) seem to point strongly towards the existence of these languages long before the arrival of Europeans. We would argue that some indigenous sign languages documented up until now should be regarded as TILs in the signed modality. A strong case exists for Yolngu Sign Language (YSL). Most of the early attempts to describe the languages of Australia were undertaken by missionaries (Teichelmann and Schürmann 1840; Meyer 1843). Grammar descriptions of this era have been found wanting because they typically followed a European traditional grammar framework. This may also be why multimodality was overlooked.

A historical look at the distribution of TILs mapped at the continental level reveals a large proportion of Pama-Nyungan languages. McConvell and Evans (1997: 14–15) state the following, as illustrated on Map 3.1:

> Pama-Nyungan languages are spread in relatively homogenous fashion over seven-eighths of the continent, in contrast with the diverse mosaic of their

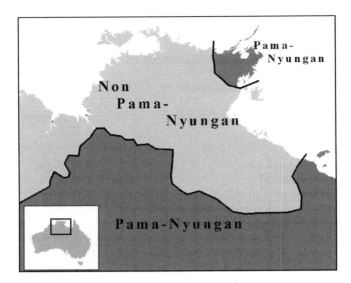

MAP 3.1 The distribution of Pama and non-Pama Nyungan languages in Australia (James and Watkinson 2017a)

non–Pama-Nyungan relatives, which are confined to the Kimberley, Top End and Barkly regions.

Within the group of Pama-Nyungan languages, we find a number of subgroups of languages. The Pama-Nyungan family, according to Koch (2014: 57), encompasses around 200 languages. The label Pama-Nyungan family was first proposed by Hale in 1961 and used in subsequent studies (O'Grady, Wurm and Hale 1966; O'Grady and Hale 2004). Dixon (1980) rejected this label, and Blake (1990), among others, was uneasy about this classification. In spite of this controversy, this label appears to be widely accepted in recent surveys on language classification and textbooks, such as Walsh and Yallop (1993), Campbell and Poser (2008) and Simons and Fennig (2017).

From a morphosyntactic perspective, both the Pama-Nyungan and non–Pama-Nyungan languages have a free word order and have been classified as non-configurational languages (Hale 1992). The Pama-Nyungan languages are homogenous in that they use suffixes; the languages of the non–Pama-Nyungan language group, found in the north of Australia, have both suffixes and prefixes. They are thus sometimes regarded as a morphosyntactic "mixed bag."

An interesting condition that occurs in most traditional indigenous languages is the existence of three core clausal functions (agent, subject and object) and five peripheral clausal functions (including purposive, dative, instrumental, causal and aversive). Further peripheral clausal functions are expressed by genitive, comitative and privative (Dixon 2002). In contrast to European languages, the TILs of Australia have an ergative-absolutive case system. However, we find a split ergative system in many languages in which free and bound pronouns are marked with the accusative case, while nouns are marked with the ergative case.

From a phonological perspective, we find some recurring phonological patterns all over the continent. One of the phonological hallmarks is the complex consonant inventories, multiple places of articulation, absence of contrastive fricatives and a small vowel inventory (see also Capell 1967; Fletcher and Butcher 2014). According to Fletcher and Butcher (2014), the indigenous languages of Australia belong to the small percentage of the world's languages with small vowel inventories, with just between three to five contrastive vowels. Butcher (2006) describes the consonant system found in indigenous languages as "long and thin" due to an absence of voiced and voiceless contrast in the stop series and absence of contrastive fricatives.

From a lexical point of view, we find open word classes (nouns, adjectives and verbs) in most indigenous languages of Australia. Walsh (1996) has argued convincingly that word classes are not always clearly distinguishable from each other, thus resulting in nominal elements with "verby" characteristics and verbal elements with "nouny" characteristics.

A central issue in Australian linguistics is the relationship between these two groups of languages. We refer the reader to Evans (2003, 2005), who discusses the four current models of classification in great detail. As mentioned in the introduction, one of the fundamental issues exercising the minds of those in the field is the genetic classification of TILs. Evans (2005) argues cautiously that there appears to be some evidence pointing towards the unity of all languages that belong to the Australian phylum. The second issue is the role played by language contact. Important studies worth mentioning here are the ones by Heath (1978, 1981), Dixon (1980, 1997, 2001) and McConvell (2010). Heath investigated diffusion, both on the structural and lexical level, in Arnhem Land. He argues that bound morphology can be borrowed. These morphemes include suffixes marking case (ergative and instrumental markers), kin dyads and prefixes marking comitative case, among others. This would count as direct diffusion. Heath uses the term "indirect diffusion" to describe copying patterns which do not show up with the actual form (morphemes or words). This is how the development of bound pronouns in some Yolngu languages, e.g., Ritharrngu, is explained (Heath 1978; Dixon 2002 among others).

The discussion of these issues relates to the question of "exceptionality" of TILs (for a detailed discussion, see Koch 2014). Hale (1983), among others, has discussed the case of non-configurational syntax of Australian TILs. Many of the North-Western languages split event structure into two parts: a set of generic verbs that describe the semantic space of event representations and another set of coverbs that are combined with the generic verbs to describe the event (see, e.g., McGregor 2002). Evans (2007) reports the use of multiple case marking, also known as case stacking, in Kayardild, which is spoken in the South Wellesley islands in North-West Queensland. TILs demonstrate a respect register, also known as the "brother-in-law" or "mother-in-law register," or "avoidance registers." Avoidance registers demonstrate the aforementioned circumspection as polite forms of languages used among certain relatives. In Uw-Oykangand, a language of Cape York, a man talking to his potential mother-in-law uses the mother-in-law register, in which affixes and function words are used but the remaining vocabulary is replaced. A further characteristic of TILs is the elaborate kinship system of "tri-relational" kin terms which allow a number of different ways of referring to kin, based on the relationship of the referent, to the speaker, to the hearer and to the other kin present (see, e.g., Garde 2013). Other registers, such as initiation registers, are common in indigenous communities across Australia in which a uniform adherence to a kin-based universal view appears to have been extant in all corners of the country. This type of register is taught to male ceremonial initiates as part of their age grade tribulations and education (Evans 2007). An interesting example is provided in the case of Warlpiri initiates. Initiates in the liminal stage, at the beginning of their first initiation between childhood and manhood, will for a short time learn the special register *Jiliwirri*. This term usually means "silly, ridiculous or foolish," and is used in this context as a register in which some lexical items are replaced with their opposites. During the liminal state, the world is said to be "upside down" for the boys and returns to normal on their return to society as full men. The sentence "I am sitting on the ground" could be replaced in Jiliwirri by a sentence literally meaning "someone else is standing in the sky" (Evans 2007: 356).

Indigenous spoken languages of Arnhem Land

The greater Arnhem Land covers an area of approximately 50,000 km² and is the home to some 80 different languages (Cole 1979: 26). This is illustrated in Map 3.2. It is also described as Australia's most linguistically complex region (Evans 2003). Predominantly non-Pama-Nyungan languages are punctuated by an enclave of Pama-Nyungan languages (the Yolngu languages).

In this section, we will focus on the Yolngu Matha languages of North-East Arnhem Land. The geographical area of Yolngu-speaking North-East Arnhem Land is about 26,590 km², including coastal islands. Yolngu sea country has 1,597 km of mainland shoreline and the greater 1,778 km of island coastline from the Crocodile Islands in the west to Blue Mud Bay in the east (James 2015: 256). As mentioned, these languages belong to the Pama-Nyungan language group. These Pama-Nyungan Yolngu languages are surrounded to the west and south by several different languages, all members of the non-Pama-Nyungan group.

According to Evans (2003), the Yolngu languages show some important cultural traits that have been diffused. The system of patrimoieties known in Bininj Gun-wok as *Duwa/Yirridja* is known in Yolngu languages as *Dhuwa/Yirritja*. Yolngu people are organized into patrilineal clans that are exogamous. These clans

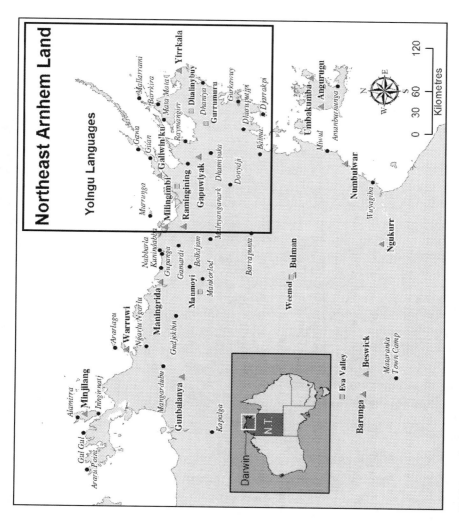

MAP 3.2   Arnhem Land and North-East Arnhem Land communities (James and Watkinson 2017a)

are divided into moieties named Dhuwa and Yirritja.[2] A close look at studies on Yolngu Matha languages reveals the following picture: there are three major subgroupings referred to in the literature as Western/inland, Northern and Southern (Wilkinson 1991). Waters (1989) speculates that surrounding non-Pama-Nyungan languages, such as Burarra and Rembarrnga, may have developed pronounced linguistic differences to Yolngu types in order to protect geographic and resource access boundaries (Waters 1989: 286–7; cf. Schebeck 1968: 51–2). Waters describes the geographical separation of the Yolngu enclave from surrounding non-Pama-Nyungan languages thus:

> A major linguistic boundary occurs at the western border of Djinang territory, the languages to the west (Burarra), southwest (Rembarrnga) and south (Ngandi) being of the prefixing type, and genetically far-removed from the Yolngu languages. To the south east there is Djinba (actually one of a number of clans, each of which speaks closely related dialects – the most numerous one at present being Ganalbingu); To the east there are Dhuwala (Gupapuyngu) and Dhuwal (Liyagalawumirr) and to the north and north east Yannhangu. Djinang, Djinba, Dhuwal/Dhuwala and Yan-nhangu are all Yolngu languages, and are not mutually intelligible.
>
> *(Waters 1989: 286)*

Today, Yolngu people number approximately 7,000, with the majority living in communities of between 500 and 2,000 people which were originally established as Methodist Overseas Missions (MOM). The Rev. James Watson established the first mission at Milingimbi (Yurruwi) Island in 1921. Revs. Chaseling and Wells established a mission in Yirrkala in 1935. The Galiwin'ku mission was started in 1942, and the later Yolngu communities of Gapuwiyak (1969) and Ramingining (1975) started as outstations to Galiwin'ku and Milingimbi, respectively. During the 1970s, many Yolngu people moved back to their traditional lands in what has been called the homelands movement.

Some 60 homelands exist in the Yolngu language domain. These homelands' populations are usually made up of one or two related family groups and their kin living together on their land. The links between patri-language, sacred sites, ceremonies and kin are very strong on the homelands.[3] Homelands are different from the ex-mission communities where many clans coexist, living and working in one place. Life on homelands is more immediately organized around landownership and care, family and ancestral connections (see Slotte 1997; Morphy 2005; Altman 2006; Blakeman 2013). Languages used on the homelands map onto the traditional geographic associations of clans and broader regional connubial connections to place. Morphy (2010) has described a pre-existing ancestral geography depicting the prior network of ancestral sites that link discrete Yolngu clans to others over the entire region. Widespread regional intermarriage through kin-based connubial relations between clans speaking separate languages creates the conditions for prevalent multilingualism among Yolngu speakers. Further, this pre-existing ancestral geography accounts for the pattern of homeland locations in close proximity to a clan's traditional estate. Map 3.3 gives some indication of the geographical spread of homelands inhabited by the Yolngu people across North-East Arnhem Land.

Today, settlements are governed by the Australian federal government from the capital in Canberra and the Northern Territory government in Darwin. Yolngu languages persist in a vigorously monolingual national context. Australia is the continent where all TILs may disappear within the next few decades (Nettle and Romaine 2000: 4–5; National Indigenous Languages Survey [NILS 2005]).[4] The fate of fragile indigenous alternate sign languages is even more grim (Adone and Maypilama 2015). Yolngu languages are one of the top ten strongest indigenous languages (NILS 2005). Australian languages continue to disappear at an alarming rate.[5] However, active local language revitalization in recent Yolngu-driven, place-based, Learning on Country activities are supporting language use. Key examples are community-driven indigenous land and sea management projects, Ranger and Junior Ranger Programs, and homeland-based learning, all of which are substantially strengthening bilingual outcomes. Ecological services collaborations, promoting intergenerational transmission of local knowledge and Caring for Country values, are having outstanding success improving school attendance, literacy, numeracy, and appear to be the best hope for institutional support for local languages learning into the future (Fogarty and Schwab 2015).

Children now grow up in communities speaking the community Yolngu lingua franca almost exclusively, in addition to being taught English in schools. For example, children growing up at Milingimbi use a Milingimbi-style Yolngu Matha at home, a form easily recognizable to Yolngu from elsewhere. A similar situation is extant in all five major Yolngu communities. Shift to a community lingua franca started in the wake of missionization.[6] When people moved to the Milingimbi MOM mission from their traditional homelands in the early 1920s, they spoke eight or nine different Yolngu languages. The routines of mission life made it necessary for them to find a language that they could all communicate in. Speaking traditional patri-linguistic varieties – varieties associated with their clan homelands – could be seen as a sign of discord in the new community polity and, as such, the change to mission residence necessitated a politically neutral "inter-language" lingua franca. Before going on to discuss the nature of this contemporary Yolngu Matha "inter-language" lingua franca in detail, it is very instructive to first outline the somewhat complex socio-linguistic fundamentals of a Yolngu kin-based worldview linking language to land.

It is no exaggeration to say Yolngu people attach enormous significance to the ancestral inheritance of sites and the bestowal of songs, paintings, stories, names and language identified as their ancestral property. They believe that the languages of their respective clans or *bäpurru*[7] and countries were endowed to them by ancestral

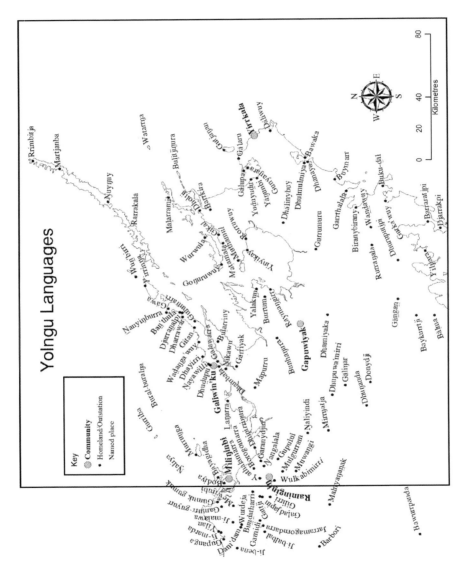

MAP 3.3 Major communities and homelands of North–East Arnhem Land (James and Watkinson 2017b)

wangarr (creator/spirits). The mechanism of this linguistic endowment is described by Williams (1999: 57):

> The spirit beings/ancestral beings/creator beings vested land in particular groups of people in a time long past. Both the beings and the time are locally distinctive, as are the acts of vesting. They all, however, include descriptions of flora and fauna as well as topographical features of the particular land and sea, and most importantly they gave names to them. Usually the language in which these acts are done is also distinctive and pertains to the specific locality.

Williams shows the significance of specific locality, language and the endowment of ancestral names. Names, the sites they refer to and the language they are spoken in are all joined by the crucial notion of shared ancestral essences. Each Yolngu individual and clan "has a primary affiliation to particular territory with which is also allied a particular linguistic variety" (Wilkinson 1991: 1). That is, languages – along with all other aspects of the Yolngu clan or bäpurru (songs, names, estates) – are joined by consubstantial connections.[8]

Schebeck (1968, 2001) provides an analysis of Yolngu language types and Yolngu language theories in his discussion on dialect and social groupings in North-East Arnhem Land. He endeavours to clarify the notional parallelism between social groups and linguistic varieties by addressing the division of speech varieties to regional "this" (proximal demonstrative) types in the Yolngu area. He deploys "native terms" in an attempt to come to an ethnographically accurate separator of Yolngu social structures to show the distinction between the said "native theories" and linguistic categories, and to correlate these to linguistic categories (Schebeck 1968: 27–38). Schebeck demonstrates that there is no one-to-one relationship between *matha* (speech variety) and *mala* (and/or patri-group, clan) or *bäpurru* (language) from a linguistic perspective. At the broadest level, Yolngu language groups sharing the same "this" word, that is, groups with the same proximal demonstrative, are called a dialect group. These dialect groups are divided into different bäpurru group names. Schebeck employs the emic (Yolngu) taxonomy of ways of speaking to distinguish each of eight language groups identified by Yolngu speakers, defined by the proximal demonstrative or word for "this" or "here." As will be seen later, this Yolngu style of language grouping is further dissected along regional, subsidiary linguistic, geographic and ritual lines. For example, Table 3.1 shows eight dialect groups and some examples of bäpurru groups speaking that dialect:

The table shows there is more than one bäpurru speaking any one "this" language as defined by the proximal demonstrative.[9] Keen (1994) calls these "this groups" and reminds us that these "this groups" are not sociological groups, but include patri-filial groups of both moieties, with the exception of Dhuwala and Dhuwal-speaking patri-groups (Keen 1994: 76). However, it must be said that the relationship between a dialect group as defined by its "this" word is a little bit

TABLE 3.1 Yolngu proximal demonstratives and Bäpurru groups

Dhuwal	Djambarrpuyŋu, Liyagawumirr, Marraŋu, Marrakulu, Djapu, Dhäpuyŋu
Dhuwala	Gupapuyŋu, Wubukarra, Munyuku, Madarrpa, Gumatj, Maŋgalili
Dha'yi	Wunuŋumurra, Gumana, Ḏalwaŋu, Djarrwark
Dhaŋu	Wangurri, Rirratjiŋu, Golumala, Gälpu
Djaŋu	Warramiri, Maṉḏatja, Lamamirri, Girrikirri
Djinaŋ	Wulaki, Man-nharrŋu, Murruŋun, Ḏadiwitji
Djinba	Ganalbiŋu, Ḏäbi, Walmapuy, Mandjalpuyŋu
Nhaŋu	Golpa, Walamaŋu, Biṉḏarra, Ŋurruwula, Mälarra, Gamalaŋga, Gurryindi

Source: Based on James (2009)

more complicated than the previous table might reveal at first glance. Attention to emic categories and cultural context improves the sensitivity of research and better renders the ideational categories as conceived by members of the society itself, in so doing, it provides a more nuanced depiction of language.

This logic of shared relationships between matha (speech variety) and mala (and/or patri-group, clan) or bäpurru (language) demonstrates the way Yolngu people from distinct bäpurru draw connection and mark similarities and differences between each other. Keen (1994) shows how Yolngu people invoke connection and difference with distinctive and conventional signifiers from different domains of social life. These linguistic, group and social signs are deployed to locate one's social identity. The Yolngu convention engages the triangulation of these important and recognizable Yolngu signifiers, juxtaposing names denoting contrasting attributes of bäpurru, language and groups in this way:

x matha, y mala (x tongue, y group)
x mala, y bäpurru (x group, y bäpurru)

(Keen 1994: 75)

Triangulation of two or three attributes signifies different kinds of identities. Signalling a bäpurru (estate-holding group) name, a mala (collective group) name and a matha (language) name is the fundamental way of locating individuals and groups in social space. Both the bäpurru (estate-holding group) and the matha (language) are linked by the notion of ancestral essence to the sites of the estate. Yolngu ideology says that each clan has its own land and named variety of language. From a Yolngu perspective, the ancestors that created the different sites, site names, ancestral identities, totems, songs and ceremonies of a clan also invested the clan and its people with their own distinctive languages.

Arising from the Yolngu notion that each of the separate bäpurru is endowed a particular language originating from discrete estates is a critical distinction in language identity, cast by members of Nhangu speaking groups. The Nhangu-speaking Yan-nhangu and Nhangu-mi (Nhangu-mirr) (Zorc 1986) see their languages as being distinct, even though they use the same proximal demonstrative *nhangu*. Members of the Nhangu-speaking bäpurru Golpa (Gutjiway) Barrangu and the now extinct Yalukal see themselves as inheriting distinctive ancestral identities, totems, songs and their own distinctive language they call Nhangu. This emblematic relationship of the bäpurru, country and language has an enormous significance for the Yan-nhangu-speaking people (James 2015: 243–4). Following the same Yolngu logic, the Yan-nhangu-speaking Walamangu, Bindarra, Ngurruwula, Malarra, Gamalangga and Gurryindi see themselves as inheriting distinctive ancestral identities and their own distinctive language they call Yan-nhangu. For the Yan-nhangu, *yan* means "language" and *nhangu* means "this." Yan-nhangu is the language of the people of the Crocodile Islands, its songs, stories and colours (Baymarrwangga and James 2014: 13; see also James 1999, 2003, 2009, 2015). From the Yolngu perspective a particular patri-language is the foundation for locating individuals and groups in cosmic, linguistic and social space. The relationship between a person's linguistic identity and the language they generally speak is changing slowly but surely in light of the legacy of mission residence and the contemporary socio/political context of North-East Arnhem Land.

Today, the Yolngu Matha language variety, also known as the Dhuwal/Dhuwala transitional linguistic form described as Gupapuyngu by Lowe (1957) and Djambarrpuyngu by Schebeck (1968: 61), became an "inter-language" or "comulect," combining parts and modes from each of these two Dhuwal/Dhuwala clan languages. The evolution of this lingua franca is linked with an associated decline in the use of patri-linguistic varieties deployed at Milingimbi concomitant with the evolution of the new mission community. Lowe, as a teacher at Milingimbi, conducted the first substantial linguistic analysis on Milingimbi Island. She started the compilation of a Gupapuyngu dictionary with over 4,000 forms in 1951 (Lowe 1957). Significantly, Lowe had been adopted into the Gupapuyngu family during her stay at Milingimbi, and it was this Yolngu Matha language variety that she worked on. This was a significant factor in the choice of Gupapuyngu as the language to be used in the bilingual program at the school starting in 1974, and gave substantial impetus to continued interest in this variety, leading to a number of contemporary Gupapuyngu language courses. Despite the assertions of senior people of the numerically dominant Gupapuyngu clan, the comulectal style of Yolngu Matha spoken at Milingimbi continues to have more in common with the Dhuwa Djambarrpuyngu language.

The widely practiced Yolngu convention of children learning their patri-linguistic variety, previously the norm for Yolngu groups, has diminished in importance due to new residence patterns. Devlin (1986) demonstrates the decline of children going on to learn their father's clan language and the rise of peer group languages in enclave speech communities.[10] Contemporary linguistic conventions at Milingimbi tend towards a widely understood, yet not homogenized, comulect that is a linguistic variety derived from Dhuwal/Dhuwala sociolects, including locally evolved modes arising from the context of the Milingimbi mission community. In the end it appears that, at Milingimbi at least, the large number of Dhuwa wives – in the order of nine per senior Yirritja men (husbands) – speaking Djambarrpuyngu-related languages, and their considerable numbers of children – again, on average, around eight and nine – continue to speak in their mothers' Dhuwal-style languages. Similarly, conditions derived from contemporary community life in the other major communities of Yirrkala (1935), Galiwin'ku (1942), Gapuwiyak (1969) and Ramingining (1975) have led to the development of their own "comulectal styles."

Despite this language shift to the comulect, in the ceremonial sphere strict adherence to clan patri-languages in accordance with an ontology of immutable language endowment by the ancestors continues to be the rule. It is in this sense that linguistic shift may be of small socio-cultural significance in the short term. Sutton (1999) contends that language filiations are not cancelled by failure to learn the language. The label *Yolngu Matha*, "people's tongue," has become the catch-all signifier for this more complex linguistic situation as it changes in the face of contemporary contexts, an area that could use more detailed linguistic attention.

Indigenous sign languages of Arnhem Land

An area even less well attended to is that of the sign languages of Australia. In this section, we will present some findings on a sign language within the Yolngu Matha language area, also known as Yolngu Sign Language (YSL). We previously noted the paucity of studies on indigenous sign languages in Australia. The use of sign languages in Arnhem Land caught the attention of several anthropologists travelling throughout Arnhem Land between the 1880s and the 1940s (Foelsche in Curr 1886; Webb 1933; Warner 1937; Thomson 1949 among others). A key observation made by several of these scholars is the use of sign languages among groups of people with mutually unintelligible languages.

More recently, Adone and Maypilama (2014b) have discussed a variety of Yolngu Sign Language used on Elcho Island, Milingimbi and in the Yirrkala community. This sign language, similar to the other existing sign languages in Arnhem Land, is an alternate sign language used by both hearing and Deaf signers. It is an alternate sign language because the hearing community uses it as an alternative mode of communication in many contexts in which speech is prohibited (Cooke and Adone 1994, Adone and Maypilama 2013, 2014a, 2014b, 2015). Two major points to be taken into account here are: first, hearing children start signing from an early age. Second, the system used by the hearing signers among each other is somehow different from the one used by the Deaf people when communicating among each other. Adone et al. (2018) have established that signing is used in 17 communities across Arnhem Land.

YSL is used in both the public and private domains in a wide range of contexts such as in hunting and fishing, the preparation of fish traps, for secrecy, long-distance communication, ceremonies, in the proximity of sacred and dangerous sites and spiritual entities in the landscape, etc. (for more details, see Adone et al. 2018). These contexts have also been identified for other alternate sign languages such as the one used in Gunbalanya, Minjilang and Maningrida (Adone and Maypilama 2014a). From a structural perspective, YSL behaves very much like other sign languages in the world. It uses space for both topological and grammatical purposes, and deploys both manual and non-manual components. As it is an alternate sign language used by the hearing population, it displays great variability in many areas of grammar.

Interestingly, we recently discovered a signing system coexisting with the local sign languages and spoken languages. We refer to this signing system as Arnhem Land Signed Lingua Franca (ALSLF) elsewhere (Adone et al. 2018). This signing system is used across Arnhem Land by many different language groups. Its main purpose has been and is still to allow communication among unintelligible language groups. Although this signed lingua franca is used in various contexts such as hunting, fishing and ceremonies, which is a similarity this signed lingua franca shares with the local sign languages, it is restricted to activities among language groups speaking different or unintelligible languages. In Adone et al. (2018) we discuss the contexts of use of this signed lingua franca in detail. We also note the use of either a variety of Aboriginal English or Kriol is sometimes favoured over this signed system. This point is part of our future research agenda.

Conclusion

To recapitulate, in this chapter we set out to give the reader a broad overview on traditional indigenous languages in Australia. A short introduction on the distribution of these languages across the continent reveals that there are two main language families – Pama-Nyungan and non-Pama-Nyungan languages – that have different linguistic profiles. While these languages might share similar cultural practices, we find differences in their grammatical structures. We have also mentioned some of the key factors that need to be understood when working with indigenous Australia. Multilingualism or, more precisely, bimodal bilingualism is common in indigenous Australia. Circumspection expressed in various linguistic forms is another important factor that plays a central role in interaction. Furthermore, the complex connection between Land-Language-People, especially the view of ownership with respect to language, is central to the discussion of indigeneity. Our focus was on Arnhem Land in the Northern Territory of Australia. In this area we find several traditional indigenous languages, with the majority of those languages belonging to the non-Pama-Nyungan language family. A small group of languages known as the Yolngu language family belongs to the Pama-Nyungan language family. Arnhem Land presents a challenge to linguistic theories for many reasons. In an area with such linguistic diversity, language contact is expected to play a role in shaping the development of languages as Heath (1978) has already described. The question, however, is the extent of language contact and which changes can be regarded as contact-induced changes.

The Yolngu language family has been presented against the ethno-linguistic background of the discussion on the triangulation between Land-Language-People. The issue of language endangerment and the degree of endangerment of these languages has also been touched upon. Besides the spoken languages in Arnhem Land, we have also introduced the reader to the signed languages (e.g., YSL among others and a signed lingua franca). While YSL is used among the Yolngu language groups, we notice the widespread use of a signed lingua franca across Arnhem Land. As the study of indigenous sign languages in Australia is relatively recent, more studies have to be conducted in order to provide us with some insights into the complex relationship between spoken and signed languages in indigenous Australia.

Notes

1   We wholeheartedly thank Astrid Gabel, Kathrin Brandt and Melanie Brück for reviewing, editing and proofreading this chapter. Thank you to the editors Devy and Davis for their support and patience. All shortcomings in this chapter are ours.
2   Dhuwa and Yirritja are two halves, or moieties, of the Yolngu system of thought that divide the world into two categories, classifying every aspect of the physical and spiritual world. These moieties are characterized by complementary reciprocal relations understood to create the fundamental conditions for life.
3   Previously, the estimated 560 outstations/homelands/communities of fewer than 100 people in the Northern Territory, comprising approximately 10,000 people (the number having dropped substantially), have been denied their human rights as a people to live on their land by the Northern Territory government. The "Stronger Futures" policy has further disadvantaged another 40,000 people residing primarily in larger "townships" in the region (Altman 2006; Altman, Biddle and Hunter 2008: 2).
4   A view supported in the report of the Second National Indigenous Languages Survey (Marmion, Obata and Troy 2014).
5   Truscott and Malcom (2010) show how a weakly funded but vibrant Northern Territory bilingual education program running during the 1970s and 1980s was closed down without consultation by the Northern Territory government in 1998 along with punitive welfare reform. The Northern Territory government decreed English-only teaching as part of a schizophrenic and invisible assimilationist political agenda contradicting Australia's international posture on indigenous and human rights covenants (Truscott and Malcom 2010: 15).
6   The earlier norm of transmission of the father's bäpurru patrilect after learning the mother's tongue declined because the majority of people at Milingimbi mission were women speaking closely related Dhuwal languages, so most children grew up speaking these Dhuwal languages without learning their father's language.
7   The term "clan" is now usually replaced by the term "bäpurru," as it denotes a more complex meaning closer to Yolngu conceptions. Bäpurru have been described as complex, multilayered, focal social categories sharing common ancestral identity, existing in shared ancestral essences (see Keen 1978, 1994, 1995; Toner 2005; Baymarrwangga and James 2014).
8   To be consubstantial with something is to be identified with it at the elemental level, to be of identical substance. Consubstantial identification constitutes the principal ontological basis of ownership of the elements of the bäpurru, sites, madayin and the ancestral essences of their living descendants (see also Bagshaw 1998: 162).
9   A number of other possible schemes for organization into linguist groups appear in the literature: Schebeck (1968); Zorc (1986); Heath (1980); and Morphy (1983).

10 The decline in the significance of linguistic identification with one's father's clan (bäpurru) language has affected a younger generation living in ex-mission communities and more unfamiliar with their land and sea country which may be very distant more directly. Homeland life provides strong links of language to country and close proximity to sacred sites, whereas more recently, homelands are being dismantled by settler policies to mainstream and assimilate Yolngu life projects.

References

Adone, D. and E. Maypilama. 2013. 'Yolngu Sign Language: An Undocumented Endangered Language of Arnhem Land', *Learning Communities: International Journal of Learning in Social Contexts*, 13: 37–44.

Adone, D. and E. Maypilama. 2014a. 'Research Report: Bimodal Bilingualism in Arnhem Land', *Australian Aboriginal Studies* (AIATSIS), 2: 101–106.

Adone, D. and E. Maypilama. 2014b. *A Grammar Sketch of Yolngu Sign Language*. München: Lincom.

Adone, D. and E. Maypilama. 2015. 'The Sociolinguistics of Alternate Sign Languages of Arnhem Land', *Learning Communities: International Journal of Learning in Social Contexts*, 16: 13–23.

Adone, D., E. Maypilama, and M.A. Brück. 2018. 'A Signed Lingua Franca in Arnhem Land', in B. Neumeier, B. Braun and V. Herche (eds), *Nature and Environment in Australia. KOALAS*, Vol. 13. Tier: Wissenschaftlicher Verlag Trier.

Altman, J.C. 2006. *In Search of an Outstations Policy for Indigenous Australians*. Centre for Aboriginal Economic Policy Research Working Papers 34/2006. Centre for Aboriginal Economic Policy Research, ANU.

Altman, J.C., N. Biddle and B.H. Hunter. 2008. *How Realistic are the Prospects for 'closing the gaps' in Socioeconomic Outcomes for Indigenous Australians?* Centre for Aboriginal Economic Policy Research, College of Arts and Social Sciences, The Australian National University. No. 287 CAEPR Canberra ACT.

Bagshaw, G. 1998. 'Gapu Dhulway, Gapu Maramba: Conceptualization and Ownership of Saltwater among Burarra and Yan-nhangu Peoples of North-East Arnhemland,' in N. Peterson and B. Rigsby (eds), *Customary Marine Tenure in Australia, Oceania Monograph 48*, pp. 154–178. Sydney, NSW: University of Sydney.

Baymarrwangga, L. and B. James. 2014. *Yan-nhangu Atlas and Illustrated Dictionary of the Crocodile Islands*. Sidney/Singapore: Tien wah Press.

Berndt, R.M. 1951. *Gunapipi*. Melbourne, VIC: Cheshire.

Blake, B.J. 1990. 'The Significance of Pronouns in the History of Australian Languages', in P. Baldi (ed.), *Linguistic Change and Reconstruction Methodology*, pp. 435–450. Berlin/Boston: De Gruyter Mouton.

Blakeman, B. 2013. 'An Ethnography of Emotion and Morality: Toward a local Indigenous Theory of Value and Social Exchange on the Yolngu Homelands, NE Arnhem Land, Australia'. PhD dissertation, The Australian National University, Canberra, Australia.

Butcher, A. 2006. 'Australian Aboriginal Languages: Consonant-salient Phonologies and the "place-of-articulation imperative"', in J.M. Harrington and M. Tabain (eds) *Speech Production: Models, Phonetics Processes and Techniques*, pp. 187–210. New York/Hove: Psychology Press.

Butlin, N.G. 1983. *Our Original Aggression: Aboriginal Populations of Southeastern Australia, 1788–1850*. Sydney/Boston: G. Allen & Unwin.

Campbell, L. and W.J. Poser. 2008. *Language Classification. History and Method*. Cambridge: Cambridge University Press.

Capell, A. 1967. 'Sound Systems in Australia', *Phonetica*, 16(2): 85–110.

Cole, K. 1979. *The Aborigines of Arnhem Land*. Adelaide: Rigby.

Cooke, M. and D. Adone. 1994. 'Yolngu Signing – Gestures or Language?', *Centre for Australian Language and Linguistics (C.A.L.L) Working Papers*. 1–15.

Curr, E.M. 1886. *The Australian Race*, 4 vols. Melbourne: Govt. Printer.

Devlin, B.C. 1986. *Language Maintenance in a North East Arnhem Land Settlement*. Columbia University Teachers College: University Microfilms.

Dixon, R.M.W. 1980. *The Languages of Australia*. Cambridge: Cambridge University Press.

Dixon, R.M.W. 1997. *The Rise and Fall of Languages*. Cambridge: Cambridge University Press.

Dixon, R.M.W. 2001. 'The Australian Linguistic Area', in A.Y. Aikhenvald and R.M.W. Dixon (eds), *Areal Diffusion and Genetic Inheritance: Problems in Comparative Linguistics*, pp. 64–104. Oxford: Oxford University Press.

Dixon, R.M.W. 2002. *Australian Languages: Their Nature and Development*. Vol. 1. Cambridge: Cambridge University Press.

Evans, N. (ed.). 2003. *The Non-Pama-Nyungan Languages of Northern Australia: Comparative Studies of the Continent's Most Linguistically Complex Region*. Vol. 552. Canberra: Pacific Linguistics.

Evans, N. 2005. 'Australian Languages Reconsidered: A Review of Dixon (2002)', *Oceanic Linguistics*, 44(1): 242–286.

Evans, N. 2007. 'Warramurrungunji Undone: Australian Languages in the 51st Millennium', in M. Brenzinger (ed.), *Language Diversity Endangered*, pp. 342–373. Berlin: Mouton de Gruyter.

Farnell, B. 1995. *Do You See What I Mean? Plain Indian Sign Talk and the Embodiment of Action*. Austin: University of Texas Press.

Farnell, B. 2003. 'Plains Indian Sign Language', in S.I. Kutler (ed.), *The Dictionary of American History. 3rd Edition*, pp. 357–358. New York: Scribner.

Fletcher, J. and A. Butcher. 2014. 'Sound Patterns of Australian Languages', in H. Koch and R. Nordlinger (eds), *The Languages and Linguistics of Australia: A Comprehensive Guide*, Vol. 3, pp. 91–138. Berlin: Mouton de Gruyter.

Fogarty, W. and R.G.J. Schwab. 2015. 'Land, Learning and Identity: Toward a Deeper Understanding of Indigenous Learning on Country', *UNESCO Observatory Multi-Disciplinary Journal in the Arts*, 4(2): 1–16.

Fox Tree, E. 2009. 'Meemul Tziij: An Indigenous Sign Language Complex in Mesoamerica', *Sign Language Studies*, 9(3): 324–366.

Garde, M. 2013. *Culture, Interaction and Person Reference in an Australian Language: An Ethnography of Bininj Gunwok Communication*. Amsterdam/Philadelphia: John Benjamins Publishing.

Green, J. 2014. *Drawn from the Ground: Sound, Sign and Inscription in Central Australian Sand Stories (Language Culture and Cognition)*. Cambridge: Cambridge University Press.

Hale, K. 1983. 'Warlpiri and the Grammar of Non-configurational Languages', *Natural Language & Linguistic Theory*, 1(1): 5–47.

Hale, K. 1992. 'Basic Word Order in two "free word order" Languages', in D. Payne (ed.), *Pragmatics of Word Order Flexibility*, pp. 63–82. Amsterdam/Philadelphia: John Benjamins.

Heath, J. 1978. *Linguistic Diffusion in Arnhem Land* (Australian Aboriginal Studies Research and Regional Studies, 13). Canberra, ACT: Australian Institute of Aboriginal Studies.

Heath, J. 1980. *Dhuwal (Arnhem Land) Texts on Kinship and Other Subjects with Grammatical Sketch and Dictionary* (Oceania Linguistics Monographs, 23). Sydney: University of Sydney.

Heath, J. 1981. 'A Case of Intensive Lexical Diffusion: Arnhem Land, Australia', *Language*, 57(2): 335–367.

James, B. 1999. 'The Yan-nhangu and the Implications of Djambarrypuyngu at Murrungga'. Unpublished MA dissertation, Northern Territory University.

James, B. 2003. *Yan-nhangu Dictionary*. Darwin, NT: Northern Territory University Press.

James, B. 2009. 'Time and Tide in the Crocodile Islands: Change and Continuity in Yan-nhangu Marine Identity'. PhD Dissertation, Canberra, ACT: A.N.U.

James, B. 2015. 'The Language of Spiritual Power: From Mana to Märr on the Crocodile Islands', in P.G. Toner (ed.), *Strings of Connectedness: Essays in Honour of Ian Keen*, pp. 235–262. Canberra, ACT: ANU Press.

James, B. and S. Watkinson. 2017a. 'Map 4.1: Arnhem Land and North-East Arnhem Land Communities'.

James, B. and S. Watkinson. 2017b. 'Map 4.2: Major Communities and Homelands of North-East Arnhem Land'.

Keen, I. 1978. 'One Ceremony, One Song: An Economy of Religious Knowledge among the Yolngu of North-East Arnhem Land'. PhD dissertation, Australian National University, Canberra, ACT.

Keen, I. 1994. *Knowledge and Secrecy in an Aboriginal Religion*. London: Oxford University Press.

Keen, I. 1995. 'Metaphor and the Metalanguage: "Groups" in North-East Arnhem Land', *American Ethnologist*, 22(3): 502–527.

Keen, I. 2004. *Aboriginal Economy and Society: Australia at the Threshold of Colonization*. South Melbourne/Oxford: Oxford University Press

Kendon, A. 1988. *Sign Languages of Aboriginal Australia*. Cambridge: Cambridge University Press.

Koch, H. 2014. 'Historical Relations among the Australian Languages: Genetic Classification and Contact-based Diffusion', in H. Koch and R. Nordlinger (eds), *The Languages and Linguistics of Australia: A Comprehensive Guide,* Vol. 3, pp. 23–90. Berlin: Walter de Gruyter.

Koch, H. and R. Nordlinger. 2014. 'The Languages of Australia in Linguistic Research: Context and Issues', in H. Koch and R. Nordlinger (eds), *The Languages and Linguistics of Australia: A Comprehensive Guide,* Vol. 3, pp. 3–22. Berlin: Walter de Gruyter.

Lowe, B.M. 1957. *Grammar Lessons in Gupapuyngu. A North East Arnhem Land Dialect.* Mimeograph.

Marmion, D., K. Obata and J. Troy. 2014. *Community, Identity, Wellbeing: The Report of the Second National Indigenous Languages Survey*. Canberra. ACT: AIATSIS Australian Institute of Aboriginal and Torres Strait Islands Studies.

Matras, Y. and P. Bakker. 2003. 'The Study of Mixed Languages', in Y. Matras and P. Bakker (eds), *The Mixed Language Debate*, pp. 1–20. Berlin/Boston: Mouton de Gruyter.

McConvell, P. 2010. 'Contact and Indigenous Languages in Australia', in R. Hickey (ed.), *Handbook of Language Contact*, pp. 770–779. Chichester/Singapore: Wiley-Blackwell.

McConvell, P. and N. Evans. 1997. 'Clues to Australia's Human Past: Pulling Together the Strands', in P. McConvell and N. Evans (eds), *Archaeology and Linguistics: Aboriginal Australia in Global Perspective*, pp. 1–16. Melbourne: Oxford University Press Australia.

McConvell, P., D. Marmion, and S. McNicol. 2005. *National Indigenous Languages Survey Report*. NILS AIATSIS Australian Institute of Aboriginal and Torres Strait Islands Studies and the Federation of Aboriginal and Torres Strait Islander Languages. Canberra, ACT: FATSIL.

McConvell, P. and F. Meakins. 2005. 'Gurindji Kriol: A Mixed Language Emerges from Code-Switching', *Australian Journal of Linguistics*, 25(1): 9–30.

McGregor, W.B. 2002. *Verb Classification in Australian Languages* (Empirical Approaches to Language Typology Vol. 25). Berlin/New York: Mouton de Gruyter.

Meyer, H.A.E. 1843. *Vocabulary of the Language Spoken by the Aborigines of the Southern and Eastern Portions of the Settled Districts of South Australia, . . . Preceded by a Grammar, Showing the Construction of the Language as Far as at Present Known.* Adelaide: James Allen.

Morphy, F. 1983. 'Djapu: A Yolngu Dialect', in R.M.W. Dixon and B. Blake (eds), *Handbook of Australian Languages*. Canberra, ACT: Canberra University Press.

Morphy, F. 2005. 'The Future of the Homelands in North-east Arnhem Land'. Paper presented at the Centre for Aboriginal Economic Policy Research, Australian National University. Canberra: ACT, 05. December.

Morphy, F. 2010. '(Im) mobility: Regional Population Structures in Aboriginal Australia', *Australian Journal of Social Issues*, 45(3): 363–382.

Nettle, D. and S. Romaine. 2000. *Vanishing Voices, The Extinction of the World's Languages*. New York: Oxford University Press.

O'Grady, G. N. and K.L. Hale. 2004. 'The Coherence and Distinctiveness of the Pama-Nyungan Language Family within the Australian Linguistic Phylum', in C. Bowern and H. Koch (eds), *Australian Languages: Classification and the Comparative Method* (Amsterdam Studies on the Theory and History of Linguistic Sciences Series 4), pp. 69–92. Amsterdam/Philadelphia: John Benjamins.

O'Grady, G. N., S.A. Wurm and K.L. Hale. 1966. *Aboriginal Languages of Australia: (a Preliminary Classification)*. Victoria, BC: Department of Linguistics, University of Victoria.

Rumsey, A. 1993. 'Language and Territoriality in Aboriginal Australia', in M. Walsh and C. Yallop (eds), *Language and Culture in Aboriginal Australia*, pp. 191–206. Canberra, ACT: Aboriginal Studies Press.

Schebeck, B. 1968. 'Dialect and Social Groupings in North East Arnhem Land', MS held at the Australian Institute of Aboriginal Studies, MS 351, 352.

Schebeck, B. 2001. *Dialect and Social Groupings in North East Arnhem Land*. München: Lincom Europa.

Schmidt, A. 1985. *Young People's Dyirbal. An Example of Language Death from Australia*. Cambridge: Cambridge University Press.

Simons, G.F. and C.D. Fennig (eds). 2017. *Ethnologue: Languages of the World, Twentieth Edition*. Dallas, TX: SIL International. www.ethnologue.com/ (accessed on 23 March 2017).

Slotte, I. 1997. 'We Are Family, We Are One: An Aboriginal Christian Movement in Arnhem Land'. PhD dissertation, Australian National University, Canberra, ACT.

Stanner, W.E.H. 1933. 'The Daly River Tribes: A Report of Field Work in North Australia', *Oceania*, 3(4): 377–405.

Stanner, W.E.H. 1960. *On Aboriginal Religion II* (Oceania monographs 30(4)). Sydney: Oceania Publications.

Sutton, P. 1999. 'The System as it was Straining to Become: Fluidity, Stability, and Aboriginal Country Groups', in J.D. Finlayson, B. Rigsby and H.J. Bek (eds), *Connections in Native Title: Genealogies, Kinship and Groups*, pp. 13–57. Canberra: Centre for Aboriginal Economic Policy Research.

Teichelmann, C.G. and C.W. Schürmann. 1840. *Outlines of a Grammar, Vocabulary, and Phraseology of the Aboriginal Language of South Australia*. Adelaide: Published by the authors.

Thomson, D.F. 1949. 'Arnhem Land: Explorations among an Unknown People Part III. On Foot across Arnhem Land', *The Geographical Journal*, 114(1): 53–67.

Toner, P. 2005. 'Tropes of Longing and Belonging: Nostalgia and Musical Instruments in North-East Arnhem Land', *Yearbook for Traditional Music*, 37: 1–24.

Truscott, A. and I. Malcom. 2010. 'Closing the Policy-Practice Gap: Making Indigenous Language Policy More than Empty Rhetoric', in J. Hobson, K. Lowe, S. Potesh, and M. Walsh (eds), *Re-Awakening Languages*. Australia: Sydney University Press.

Voegelin, F.M., S. Wurm, G. N. O'Grady, T. Matsud, and C.F. Voegelin. 1963. 'Obtaining an Index of Phonological Differentiation from the Construction of Non-existent Mini-max Systems', *International Journal of American Linguistics*, 29(1): 4–28.

Walsh, G.L. 1979. 'Mutilated Hands or Signal Stencils? A Consideration of Irregular Hand Stencils from Central Queensland', *Australian Archaeology*, 9: 33–41.

Walsh, M. 1996. 'Vouns and Nerbs: A Category Squish in Murrinh-Patha (Northern Australia)', in W. McGregor (ed.), *Studies in Kimberley Languages in Honour of Howard Coate*, pp. 227–252. München: Lincom Europa.

Walsh, M. and C. Yallop (eds). 1993. *Language and Culture in Aboriginal Australia*. Canberra: Aboriginal Studies Press.

Warner, L.W. 1937. *A Black Civilization: A Social Study of an Australian Tribe*. London: Harper and Brothers Publishers.

Waters, B.E. 1989. *Djinang and Djinba: A Grammatical Historical Perspective*. London: Pacific Linguistics.

Webb, T.T. 1933. 'Tribal Organization in Eastern Arnhem Land', *Oceania*, 3(4): 406–411.

Wilkinson, M.P. 1991. 'Djambarrpuyngu a Yolngu Variety of Northern Australia'. Unpublished PhD thesis, Department of Linguistics, Sydney University.

Williams, N. 1999. 'The Nature of "Permission"', in J.C. Altman, F. Morphy and T. Rowse (eds), *Land Rights at Risk? Evaluations of the Reeves Report*, pp. 53–64. Canberra, ACT: Centre for Aboriginal Economic Policy Research.

Zorc, R.D. 1986. *Yolngu Matha Dictionary*. Darwin, NT: School of Australian Linguistics, Darwin Institute of Technology.

4

ORALITY AND WRITING IN SPANISH AMERICA

A translation perspective

Roberto Viereck Salinas[1]
Translated by Jonathan Alderman

Orality, writing and translation

Perhaps one of the most important theoretical undertakings in the field of Latin American studies in recent years has been the attempt to identify and understand the social, cultural and historical tensions that have formed in the structure of Latin American writing as a result of the contact between European man and indigenous societies in the New World. Renowned critics, such as Antonio Cornejo Polar, Walter D. Mignolo, Martin Lienhard, Enrique Dussel, Nathan Watchel, Mercedes López Baralt, Rolena Adorno and Juan Ossio, among many others, have emphasized from a variety of theoretical perspectives the importance of not only recognizing the coexistence of an indigenous oral code within the literary production of the new continent, but also the need to understand the subversive function that orality fulfils in order to fully understand the textuality of indigenous – and by extension, Latin American – authorship (the latter can be observed particularly in the case of the *First New Chronicle and Good Government* of the indigenous chronicler Felipe Guaman Poma de Ayala [Guaman Poma de Ayala 1987 (1615)]).

The recognition that processes of colonization and decolonization are deeply intertwined in Latin America through the violent incursion of alphabetic writing has opened up numerous analytical perspectives which have provided us with the tools to understand, for example, the work of Antonio de Nebrija, the complexity of Andean Quipus, the Aztec and Mayan codes, and indigenous and mestizo chronicles, with greater nuance, as well as enabling us to critically analyze the contemporary contribution of the oral code in the work of authors such as José María Arguedas or contemporary indigenous poetry. Beyond positions that relativize or deny the existence of the oral–writing conflict, the high intellectual yield of this theoretical perspective appears to be irrefutable proof that it is currently unsustainable to propose an analysis that does not contemplate orality from a critical perspective as an inescapable topic in research and academic discussion on Latin America. Moreover, the widespread references to orality in specialist studies invite us to question the ultimate meaning of the relationship (be it conflictive, tense or complementary) between orality and the written alphabet. The problem appears to have historical roots in the colonial complexity of the continent and the so-called *discovery* and conquest of America. We therefore have to incorporate other problems deriving specifically from the interaction between codes that was performed in the asymmetrical context of the political–military invasion that was the conquest. We must assume the concept of the *border* as an inescapable reality in the framework of the socio-cultural process characterized by the continuous inter-linguistic and intersemiotic transference between the two cultures in question, just as much as between the two codes principally associated with each. In other words, in referring to a border and transference, we are implicitly referring to translation in the broad sense of *transmutation*, from one sign to another (Jakobson 1959), as evidenced literally through the Latin verb *traducere* ("to lead across") from which it derives. A number of practices (particularly discursive) and forms of knowledge that result from this particular interactive dynamic conform to what has become known as *border thinking* (Mignolo 2003) or the *space in-between* (Silvano 2012) within the field of decolonial studies.

From the very first contact between European and indigenous worlds, this process of transference appears decisive not only in the redefinition of the means of information and expression of native culture, but also in the conformation of the Spanish American self. The latter transcends the instrumental limits of intercultural communication, making it possible to view this dynamic as having played an active role in the formation of an aesthetic: of a distinct and differentiated Spanish American form of writing.

From a general perspective, from the Columbian texts of the discovery it is already possible to perceive a *first moment* in which the problem of the interpretation of the New World was set up, at the heart of which is translation as a semiotic mechanism generating meaning in written form. The first tension to emerge is the one set up between *invention* and *invasion*, a tension that persists until the present day and confronts, from a theoretical perspective, the approaches of recognized scholars like, for example, Edmundo O'Gorman on the one hand, and Enrique Dussel and Miguel León-Portilla on the other. While from the theoretical-methodological perspective of the former, America appears as a self that has been monologically *invented* through the European gaze (O'Gorman 1993); for the latter – although each one rooted in very different ideological assumptions – America emerges as a *dialogic* entity (Dussel 1994) that can only be completed, as such, in the ethnohistorical framework of the *victor-vanquished* relationship (León-Portilla 1966) imposed by the Spanish conquest on the indigenous world. This type of debate undoubtedly accounts for the profound and conflictive epistemological imbalance that uprooted the American self at the end of the 15th century, and also underlines the importance of this transmutation as a generator of meaning. The American self has been defined from the beginning by the concept of the border and the self-other dichotomy that was ideologically imposed in the context of the conquest and the *intersemiotic* and *interlinguistic* translation processes (Jakobson 1959) that followed it (namely, the translation of orality and native languages into the written alphabet and the Spanish language, respectively) to guarantee its successful achievement.

Within this first moment, we also see other equally important tensions and conflicts emerge which have endured until the present day. For example, the debate over the label attached to the Amerindians of the continent, who are not really *Indian* (as the Asian hypothesis of Columbus would have it), nor, according to the present-day cultural perception of American ethnic groups, are they all homogeneously indigenous. Also, the vision of American soil as *plunder* (Ortega 1988) stands in opposition – perhaps now more than ever – to the ancestral vision of the Earth as mother and home of native cultures. Likewise, the sinful or infantilized association of the exhibition of the indigenous body with the savage or child is in marked opposition to a notion of indigenous nudity that does not take as its reference point Euro-Christian moral qualities. These conceptual tensions, among others, are added to a long list of contradictory interpretations that acknowledge the inescapable presence of an epistemological border created early on by cultural contact between natives and Europeans that, as with translation itself, has acted as a mechanism (and weapon) in the transmutation between the European (linguistic and semiotic) system of communication and both orality and indigenous languages.

Since the first half of the 16th century it has been possible to identify a *second moment* characterized by an intense instrumental application of intersemiotic and interlinguistic translation. Through the first translation, undertaken by the interpreters Diego Colón (Guanahaní, San Salvador) and Guatícabanu or Juan Mateo (The "Taino" from La Española), and later in other languages and by other translators such as Julianillo and Melchorejo (Yucatec Mayas), Francisco (Náhuatl from Veracruz), Felipillo, Martinillo and Francisquillo (Quechuas from Tumbes, Perú), María (Cumanagota from Venezuela), Luisa (Cacica from Ocoroni, Sinaloa, Baja California), Catalina (Calamarí from Colombia), La Malinche (a Maya chontal from Veracruz and Náhuatl) or the Catalan Ramón Pané, who together with Guatícabanu (Juan Mateo) undertook the first ethnographic work in the New World, among many others, highlight early on in the so-called *spiritual conquest* of the native peoples a series of names, principally of missionary friars, connected to an enormous corpus of transcription and translation of oral works (songs, prayers, narratives, etc.) and the indigenous languages to Latin and/or Spanish. These were conformed of grammar, vocabulary, catechism books and missals, and all provide incontrovertible evidence that from the moment that the Spanish Crown understood the enormous linguistic diversity in the native American world, it made the practice of translation a priority. Added to this, the difficulty the natives experienced in learning Spanish (an attempted imposition of the Crown from the beginning) was an unavoidable obstacle in the successful administration of the missions.

The importance of these documents is incalculable. Beyond the socio-cultural, historical and political implications, the fixation on native orality highlights the central problem that interests us in this chapter; that is, the early intertwining of two types of translation of Spanish American discourse: interlinguistic translation (between Spanish and native languages) and intersemiotic translation (between the written and oral code), following the well-known classificatory proposal of Roman Jackobson, previously mentioned. Such a distinction becomes highly relevant in the formation of the first Spanish American textuality. This is because the process of translation involved a process of *literaturization* that at the same time triggered the embryonic process of *fictionalization* that would, with time, marginalize orality (as it did with other native non-alphabetic forms of communication, such as pictographs, hieroglyphs and quipus). This was precisely because it involved a translation between codes, rather than just between languages. The native subject was soon displaced from the system of production, distribution and consumption of their own cultural material. The consequence of the *poetic* transcription of native songs and prayers, for example, was not only that these *historical* materials (from the oral mythic and ritual perspective) would enlarge the corpus of the European literary tradition, but also that they would become part of the Western tradition of the *lie*, given the association in popular culture between *fiction*, *falsehood* and *tricks* (Segre 1985).

However, these were not the only consequences, as we shall see in the section dealing with the Inca Garcilaso and Guaman Poma de Ayala. The irruption of the written alphabet in the New World led to *textual resistance* that aimed at repositioning, albeit symbolically, the forms of native expression that had been appropriated, marginalized and disparaged within the new system of colonial communication. This gave way to a *third moment*, which was key in the formation of Spanish American literary discourse. We refer here to the emergence of the first distinct textuality that incorporates not only the dominant language and code, but also the translation itself as a mechanism of generating writing. This writing was characterized until the second half of the 19th century by two complementary currents that stemmed from the same translationary matrix,[2] as well as two foundational aesthetic models that emerged from the author's engagement with the tense relationship between both orality and the written alphabet, and native languages and Spanish.

Translation and the literaturization of prehispanic Quechua poetry

To transcribe – to write across a border – was, as we have already indicated, the first mode of intersemiotic translation that permitted the Spanish to register and set in stone native oral expressions. They would not only be locked up within the "illuminated prison of the alphabet,"[3] as Ángel María Garibay would refer to Latin writing, but would be fictionalized due to the distinction Western rationality introduced through which the mythic and oral cosmovision of native peoples was viewed. Native songs, prayers, narratives, etc., came to be governed by laws of verisimilitude (of the possible/credible) imposed in the written translation onto an oral code that does not itself create distance between the discourse and its originator. Nor does the oral code conceptualize such discourses as self-referential mimetic units that only metaphorically allude to the truth, but rather understands them as the truth in themselves. This is in contrast to the Western literary tradition, with its distinction between fiction and non-fiction, and history and literature (Viereck Salinas 1995). In other words, we refer here to the first step in the creation of what is today understood as *precolombian literature* or *indigenous literature*. This, of course, includes the three genres found in Western literature: lyric, epic and dramatic, as well as other relatively recent and less Western genre classifications that, while being frames in the possibilities and limitations of written discourse, nonetheless attempt to convey the aesthetic specificity of the precolombian poetic corpus. This can be seen, among others, in Quechua, in work by Jesús Lara, most notably *La poesía quechua (Quechua Poetry)*, published in 1947 (and republished in 1969, 1980 and 1985), and in Mesoamerican languages (principally Náhuatl and Maya Ki'che), in which the research of Miguel León-Portilla (*El destino de la palabra* 1996; *Antigua y nueva palabra* 2004) and Carlos Montemayor (*La voz profunda* 2004), focussing on precolombian and contemporary indigenous literary production, respectively, are particularly prominent.

The production-creation of an indigenous literature, since these first writings, not only enabled the conquerors to perfect a written instrument of domination, and paradoxically allow us mediated access in the present day to the voices of the colonized. It also set up the framework through which an indigenous or mestizo counterdiscourse could emerge – for example, that of the Inca Garcilaso or Felipe Guaman Poma de Ayala – that would incorporate and *elevate*, to a literary and aesthetic plane, the conflictive and tense border dynamic of the first instrumental (intersemiotic) translations.

Garcilaso and Guaman Poma faced the same problem: the tension between orality and writing inscribed in target texts (the poems themselves, in this case) that both the author and the reader would have to *resolve*, using their own cultural, linguistic and communicative framework. The border situation within which poetic texts emerged must be recognized not just as a historical reference point that serves to enrich the discussion concerning the problem of access to the original indigenous orality (a problem that even today is the cause of conflict within Latin American nation states). Above all, it is a semiotic double condition of opening and self-referentiality (closing), which is inalienable to the poems themselves as written texts, with respect to the orality that they aspire to integrate.

Two textual mechanisms appear to be key in so-called precolombian *poetry* in order to understand the first Spanish American literary corpus. The two semiotic dynamics of *integration* and *disintegration*[4] created the conditions by which the border would emerge as a semantic matrix of Spanish American discourse. On the one hand, in addition to the regulation of transcriptions within the generic boundaries of Western lyric poetry, the texts contain features of oralization that respond just as much to the oral resonances of European lyric poetry – and by extension, to the whole written alphabet – as to the specificities of native orality. We refer here to *oral traces* that allow us to visualize the presence of this code in the texts through the identification, firstly, of a psychodynamic typical of illiterate thought. This can trigger, in effect, a fissure in the written target text with respect to the oral text (its original starting point). The disintegration of the written text occurs simultaneously alongside the literary procedures characteristic of written expression, which enable it to be *closed* semiotically with respect to indigenous orality and to pass, along the border, into the genre of Western lyrical poetry.

Various poetic anthologies have elaborated on this method of compiling and/ or *salvaging* the precolombian indigenous voice. Well-known names such as Ángel María Garibay, Miguel León-Portilla or Mercedes de la Garza, for Mesoamérica (Náhuatl and Maya); or Jesús Lara, Alcina Franch or Edmundo Bendezú, for the Andean area (Quechua), appear associated, among others, to important works of dissemination and critical recovery of indigenous textuality which are the result of a long and complex process of intersemiotic and interlinguistic reformulation, rooted, as we have previously pointed out, in the first moment of contact between Spanish and natives in 1492.

The texts that Jesús Lara offers in his celebrated book of Quechua poetry, *Literature of the Quechuas* (*La literatura de los quechuas: ensayo y antología*) (1969) (a corrected and expanded reedition of *Poesía quechua*, published in 1947), are presented in a bilingual (Quechua-Spanish) version, divided into *prehispanic, colonial* and *republican* sections, and classified according to different types of genre classification – namely, *jalli, arawi, wawaki, taki, wayñu, qhashwa, aránway* and *wanka*. Besides which, all of the texts also correspond to transcriptions, but to transcriptions made in the 16th and 17th centuries towards a written Quechua standardized by Spaniards and later translated into Spanish (by chroniclers, missionaries or by Lara), the language in which the texts would find a wider readership. This process, as we shall see, has left a recognizable imprint of tension between oral traces and writing in the corpus of indigenous texts. Such a tension not only doubly links the corpus of indigenous texts, but also places it in a border situation that makes its nature heterogeneous by destabilizing the nature of the text itself as literary, autonomous and self-referential, supposedly governed and explained only by Aristotelian laws of verisimilitude.

For Walter Ong, thought and expression in a primarily oral culture can be divided between nine different types. These structures are "additive rather than subordinate," "aggregative rather than analytic," "redundant or copious," "conservative or traditionalist," "conservative and traditionalist," "close to the human lifeworld," "agonistically toned," "empathetic and participatory rather than objectively distanced," "homeostatic" and "situational rather than abstract" (Ong 2002). From the perspective of Ong and other well-known authors of studies concerning orality, such as David Olson and Nancy Torrance (1998), orality and writing appear as two distinct, though complementary, codes. Orality is associated with dialogue, and is circular and unifying (harmony: sound); meanwhile, writing is monological, lineal and differentiating (detail: sight). These associations point to the totalizing qualities that Lévi-Strauss characterized as *savage thought* (Levi-Strauss 1966).

In the poems compiled, classified and analyzed by Lara, not only is the connection between written-lyrical poetry and speech made explicit (the first *originality* of the word, according to Octavio Paz, 1992), but also the categories proposed by Ong as characterizing primary orality. The mere versal arrangement of the texts implies a decision on the part of the translator/transcriber to assimilate the native oral texts to the rhythm of song in order to liberate them from the limits imposed by writing. This would go some way towards conveying the intention of establishing the content in the collective memory of the community through the accumulative uses of speech represented when conveyed in Spanish, particularly by the intensive use of conjunctions, epithets and anaphoric redundancy.

In the sacred jalli, *Manco Qhapaj's Prayer* (*Oración de Manco Qhapaj*), compiled by Lara from *Relación de antigüedades deste Reyno del Pirú [Narrative of the Ancient History of the Kingdom of Peru]* by Joan de Santacruz Pachacuti Yamki Sallqamaywa (1968 [1613]), we find the use of the conjunction *y* (and) in an introductory position, four times throught the text:

Rijsiytan munayki.	Ansío conocerte.	Desperate to know you.
Rikújtiy,	Cuando yo pueda ver,	When I can see,
yachájtiy,	Y conocer,	And know,
Unanchájtiy,	Y señalar,	And show,
Jamut'ájtiy,	Y comprender,	And understand,
Rikuwankin,	Tú me verás	You will see me
Yachawankin.	Y sabrás de mí	And know about me.

(Lara 1969: 186)

In the poem *Runa Kamaj* (*Leader of Men*), taken from the collection of Ismael Vásquez, almost all of the verses present an accumulation through the use of the conjunction, with those whose position remarkably introduces the stanza, creating an enumerative linking:

Wayrari tantan	Y el viento junta	And the wind collects
Sach'a purata,	Las copas de los árboles	The tops of the trees
Rijranta sh'ajrin	Y sacude sus ramas	And shakes its branches
Jánaj pachaman.	Y las yergue hacia el cielo.	And raises them up to the sky.
Sách'aj sunqonpi	Y en el ramaje de los árboles	And in the branches of the trees
takikun phichiu,	Los pajarillos cantan	The little birds sing
anchá upaykun	Y rinden el fervor de su	And pay homage fervently
Pachakamajta.	homenaje	To the governor of the world.
	Al regidor del mundo.	

(Lara 1969: 191–2)

On the other hand, the poem *Súmaj ñust'a*, taken from *Historia de los Incas [History of the Incas]* by Blas Valera (1945), constitutes a good example of use of epithet:

Súmaj ñust'a	Bella princesa,	Beautiful princess
Turallaykin	Tu propio hermano	Your own brother
P'uñuykita	Es quien destroza	Is who destroys
P'akirqayan.	Tu cantarillo.	Your pitcher
. . .	Y tú, princesa,	And you, princess,
Qanri, ñust'a,	Mandas tus aguas	Send your waters
Unuykita	En fresca lluvia	In fresh rain.
Paramunki.		

(Lara 1969: 179)

In the same vein, in *To all of the Wak'as* (*A todas las Wak'as*), Viracocha is never simply the "Creator," but the "Nearby Creator":

QayllaWiraqucha,	Cercano Hacedor,	Nearby Creator
Tijsi Wiraqucha,	Raíz del ser, Viracocha,	Root of being, Viracocha,
Llapa k'ánchaj,	Lumbre universal,	Universal light,
Wallpay wañuypa	Dios de la creación	God of creation
Wiraquchan.	Y de la muerte.	And death.

(Lara 1969: 181)

Equally, in the *Manco Qhapaj's Prayer*, Viracocha is not just the *root of being*, but the *powerful* root of being or the *supreme judge*; and not just the *judge*, as the sources are understood, above all, as sacred:

Yau, Wiraqucha,	Oh, Dios soberano,	Oh, sovereign God,
Tijsi qhápaj,	Poderosa raíz del ser, Tú	Powerful root of being,
"Kay qhari kachun	que ordenas: "Éste sea	You who order: "This
Kay warmi kachun,"	Varón, y ésta mujer"	shall be
Willka ullqa apu,	Señor de la fuente sagrada,	Man, and this woman"
Jinantinmi	Tú que inclusive tienes	Lord of the sacred
Chíjchiy kámaj,	Poder sobre el granizo,	fountain,
Maypin Kanki	¿No me es posible verte?	You that even have
Manachu rikuykiman	¿Dónde te encuentras?	Power over hail
Jananpichu,	¿Dónde está: arriba,	Can I not see you?
Urinpichu,	O abajo,	Where can you be found?
Kinrayninpichu,	O en el intermedio	Where are you?
Qhápaj usnuyki?	Tu asiento de supremo	Where is: above,
	juez?	Or below,
		Or in the middle
		Your supreme judge's seat?

(Lara 1969: 186)

With respect to redundancy, in the previous poem, *To All of the Wak'as* (*A todas las Wak'as*), we can clearly observe the use of this device, both with reference to literal reiteration and to metonymical reiteration, when Viracocha is named in a variety of different ways, with the objective of fixing his name mnemonically through his noble attributes:

QayllaWiraqucha,	Cercano Hacedor,	Nearby Creator,
Tijsi Wiraqucha,	Raíz del ser, Viracocha,	Root of being, Viracocha,
Llapa k'ánchaj,	Lumbre universal,	Universal light,
Wallpay wañuypa	Dios de la creación	God of creation
Wiraquchan.	Y de la muerte.	And of death.
Sh'anka wiraqucha,	Dios de las roquedas,	God of the rocks,
Ajna Wiraqucha,	Dios de los rituales,	God of the rituals,
Jatun wiraqucha,	Dios inconmensurable	Incommensurable God
Qaylla Wiraqucha	Cercano Hacedor	Nearby Creator.

(Lara 1969: 181)

Similar examples can be found in the poem *Manco Qhapaj's Prayer* or in the *Song of Bravery* (*Canción de gallardía* [*Warijsa Arawi*]), taken from the *First New Chronicle and Good Government* (*Nueva Corónica y buen gobierno*) of Felipe Guaman Poma de Ayala (1987 [1615]), in which the expression of jubilation "hurrah" is repeated five times in the last five lines:

¡Ajailli, chaymi palla!	¡Hurra, sí esa es la dama!	Hurrah, this is the lady!
¡Ajailli, patallanpi!	¡Hurra, ahí está, en el borde!	Hurrah, there she is, on the bank!
¡Ajailli, chaymi ñust'a!	¡Hurra, sí, esa es la infanta!	Hurrah, yes, that's the infant!
¡Ajailli, chaymi sijlla!	¡Hurra, sí, esa es la hermosa!	Hurrah, yes, this is the beautiful one!
¡Ajailli!	¡Hurra!	Hurrah!

(Lara 1969: 201)

For Ong, other formulaic expressions can be added to these marks of orality. These are *parallelisms* (a stylistic characteristic common in precolombian poetry) and *pseudoquestions* that are also abundant in the precolombian lyrical corpus. The former is notable for its relation to the dual vision of precolombian culture in general, and Andean culture in particular. The sacred *jailli*, *Manco Qhapaj's Prayer*, contains various examples of antithetical expressions that contain this oral Andean form:

Kay qhari kachun	Tú que ordenas: "Éste sea	You that order: "This shall
Kay warmi kachun,	Varón, y ésta mujer"	be man, and this woman"
. . .		

Jananpichu,	¿Dónde está: arriba,	Where is: up
Urinpichu,	O abajo,	Or down,
Kinrayninpichu,	En el intermedio	In the middle
Qhápaj usnuyki?	Tu asiento de supremo juez?	Your supreme judge's seat?

Jay nimulláway,	Escúchame,	Listen to me,
Janan qhochapi	Tú que extiendes	You that extend
Mant'aráyaj,	En el océano del cielo	In the ocean of the sky
Urin qhochapi	Y que también vives	And that also live
Tiyákuj,	En los mares de la tierra.	In the sea of the earth.
. . .		

| Killaqa, | El Sol y la Luna | The sun and moon |
| P'unchauqa, tutaqa, | El día y la noche, | The day and night, |

| Puquyqa, chirauqa, | El otoño y la primavera | The autumn and spring |

Manan yanqhachu,	No son en vano	Are not in vain
Kamachisqan purin,	Obedecen a un mandato,	They obey your mandate
Unanchasqaman,	De modo previsto	In a manner predicted
Tupusqamanmin	Y medido	And measured
Chayamun.	Llegan	They arrive.

(Lara 1969: 186–7)

Finally, in the poems *First Prayer for the Creator* (*Oración primera al Hacedor*), compiled in *Fábulas y ritos de los Incas* [*Tales and Rituals of the Incas*] by the cuzqueño Cristóbal de Molina (1989 [1575]) and *Manco Qhapaj's Prayer*, we also find the use of pseudo-questions to corroborate and establish beliefs and/or ideological affirmations associated with cultural tradition:

First Prayer for the Creator:

¿Maypin kanki?	¿Dónde te encuentras?	Where can you be found?
¿Jawapichu,	¿Fuera del mundo,	Outside the world,
Ukhupichu,	Dentro del mundo,	Inside the world,
phuyupichu,	En medio de las nubes	In the middle of the clouds
Llanthupichu?	O en medio de las sombras?	Or in the middle of the shadows?

(Lara 1969: 180)

In *Manco Qhapaj's Prayer*:

Maypin Kanki	¿No me es posible verte?	Isn't it posible for me to see you?
Manachu rikuykiman	¿Dónde te encuentras?	Where can you be found?
Jananpichu,	¿Dónde está: arriba,	Where is: up
Urinpichu,	O abajo,	Or down,
Kinrayninpichu,	En el intermedio	In the middle
Qhápaj usnuyki?	Tu asiento de supremo juez?	Your supreme judge's seat?

(Lara 1969:186)

In addition to the marks described here, Ong highlights the conservative tradition of oral cultures, a characteristic that other writers, such as Diego Catalán, have underlined in the context of studies of the Spanish Romance (Catalán 1997). The objective of the use of the various mnemonic devices is therefore the conservation of memory and to preserve community traditions from change over time, endangering cultural identity. In other words, oral cultures do not look kindly on innovation, nor on individual deviations that could appropriate and distort the communitarian ethic of traditional narratives. At the same time, we can find evidence for a paradox that Ong shows, with nuance, through three of the remaining four categories: "close to the human lifeworld," "empathetic and participatory rather than objectively distanced," "homeostatic and situational rather than abstract." Here, we refer to the fact that traditional memory cannot be conserved without transforming the original text, or without a connection with the context in which it will be received. As such, the narrative needs to be connected to the lives of its audience in order to update its content and – above all – its ancestral meaning:

> Of course oral cultures do not lack originality of their kind. Narrative originality lodges not in making up new stories but in managing a particular interaction with this audience at this time – at every telling the story has to be introduced uniquely into a unique situation, for in oral cultures, an audience must be brought to respond, often vigorously. But narrators also introduce new elements into old stories. In oral tradition, there will be as many minor variants of a myth as there are repetitions of it, and the number of repetitions can be increased indefinitely.
>
> *(Ong 2002: 40–1)*

A good example of the fundamental/essential content of the Quechua poetry compiled by Jesus Lara is the Jailli cited by the Inca Garcilaso in his *Royal Commentaries* (Garcilaso de la Vega 1989 [1609]) and attributed to the Jesuit priest Blas Valera. The text uses myth to explain the climatic phenomenon of rain, thunder and lightning concretely:

Súmaj ñust'a	Bella princesa,	Beautiful princess
Turallaykin	Tu propio hermano	It is your own brother
P'uñuykita	Es quien destroza	Who destroys
P'akirqayan.	Tu cantarillo.	Your jug.
Jinamantari	Y de este modo	And in this manner
Kunuñunun	Retumban truenos	Thunder resounds
Illapántaj.	Y caen rayos.	And the lightning falls.
Qanri, ñust'a,	Y tú, princesa,	And you, princess,
Unuykita	Mandas tus aguas.	Send your waters.
Paramunki.	En fresca lluvia.	In fresh rain.
Mayninpiri	Y algunas veces	And sometimes
Chijchimunki,	Granizo envías	You send hail
Rit'imunki.	Y a veces nieve.	And sometimes rain.
Pacharúraj,	El que nos crea	He who created us
Pachakámaj	Y nos gobierna,	And who governs us
Wiraqucha	Dios soberano,	Sovereign God.
Kay jinápaj	Este destino	This destiny
Churasunki,	Te ha concedido	Has been appointed to you
Kamasunki.	Y así te ordena	And thus directs you.

(Lara 1969: 179)

Ong highlights the predominance of context-specific content over the abstract construction of oral thought, which, like homeostasis, also connects the need to establish such content in the present through the selection (or oblivion) of all the information that is not relevant in the context of discursive production.

In *First Prayer for the Creator*, we observe, for example, the specific details used in defining Viracocha, the supreme god:

Tijsi Wiraqucha,	Raíz del ser, Viracocha,	Root of being, Viracocha,
Qaylla qaylla	Dios siempre cercano,	Always present God
Wiraqucha,	Dios siempre cercano,	Always present God
T'ukapu	Señor de vestidura	Lord of dazzling vestments
Ajnupujuy	Wiraqucha.	Deslumbradora
Kámaj, chúraj,	Dios que gobierna y preserva,	God that governs and preserves,
Qhari hachun,	Que crea con sólo decir:	That creates with only words.

(Lara 1969: 180)

Something similar can be observed in the poem *To all the Wak'as*:

Qaylla Wiraqucha,	Cercano Hacedor,	Always present God
Tijsi Wiraqucha,	Raíz del ser, Viracoch	Root of beng, Viracocha
Llapa k'ánchaj,	Lumbre universal,	Universal light,
Wallpay wañuypa	Dios de la creación	God of creation
Wiraquchan.	Y de la muerte.	And of death
Sh'anka wiraqucha,	Dios de las roquedas,	God of the rocks
Ajna Wiraqucha,	Dios de los rituales,	God of the rituals,
Jatun wiraqucha,	Dios inconmensurable	Incomensurable God
Qaylla Wiraqucha	Cercano Hacedor,	Always present God
Túkuy runata	Que otorga el don del habla	That gives the gift of speech
Jay níchij, juñúchij,	Y junta a todos los hombres	And joins all men together
Lliulli jina	A fin de que aprendan	That they may learn
Yachakunánpaj,	Con la fuerza de la luz,	Through the force of light
Jawapi, ukhupi	Dondequiera que	Where they must go
vayan, Purispapas.	Por fuera o por dentro	Outside or inside.

(Lara 1969: 181)

Furthermore, in these examples and others, only those qualities that need to be remembered are referred to – a mechanism that evokes oral Incaic history, in which the amautas and quipucamayus erased those names or events that it was not in their interests to be remembered in the present for various reasons from the chronology, above all because they concerned events or people that discredited the dynastic past and could therefore put the present stability of the political system at risk.

With respect to the marks of orality, just as with their eminently empathetic and participatory character, some good examples of Quechua poetry illustrate the characteristics that emphasize, in the last instance, the importance of the dialogic dimension of discourse. Felipe Guaman Poma de Ayala shows us in his *Song of Bravery* how dialogue structures the text:

Qoyas y ñust'as	**Reinas e infantas**	**Queens and girls**
¡Arawi!	¡La canción!	The song!
Hombres	**Hombres**	**Men**
¡Warijsa, ayay warijsa,	¡La gallardía, ah, la gallardía!	The bravery! Ah, the bravery!
Chamay warijsa,	¡Cómo me gusta la gallardía!	How I love the bravery!
Ayay warijsa!	¡Ah, la gallardía!	Ah, the bravery!
Qoyas y ñust'as	**Reinas e infantas**	**Queens and girls**
¡Ayay warijsa!	¡Ah, la gallardía!	Ah, the bravery!

Hombres	**Hombres**	**Men**
¡Ayau jailli, yau jailli!	¡Oh, el cantar, el cantar!	Oh, the song, the song!
¿Uchuyujchu chajrayki?	¿Tienes ají en tu sementera?	Do you have chilli in your field?

(Lara 1969: 201)

As with *payas* (a challenge between two poets to improvise sung verse), the dialogue structures the text. Within the text we can appreciate not just the redundancy, but also the duality and confrontational character of struggle or competence that we tend to observe in orality:

> Many, if not all, oral or residually oral cultures strike literates as extraordinarily agonistic in their verbal performance and indeed in their lifestyle. Writing fosters abstractions that disengage knowledge from the arena where human beings struggle with one another. It separates the knower from the known. By keeping knowledge embedded in the human lifeworld, orality situates knowledge within a context of struggle. Proverbs and riddles are not used simply to store knowledge but to engage others in verbal and intellectual combat: utterance of one proverb or riddle challenges hearers to top it with a more apposite or a contradictory one.
>
> *(Ong 2002: 43)*

Finally, we can complete the review of the traces of orality that appear in the Quechua poetry compiled by Lara with the poem *Manco Qhapaj's Prayer*. In the thematic context of uncertainties over the origin of the world and human existence on Earth, the poem also incorporates the tendency towards communitarian identification in its verses, as well as an identification with the already known, not permitting the separation of subject and object imposed by literate ways of thought:

Pachakámaj,	Gobierno del mundo,	Government of the world,
Runa wállpaj, apu	Creador del hombre.	Creator of man.
Inkaykuna jina	Como los señores Inkas	Like the Lord Inkas
Allqa ñawiywan	Con mis áridos ojos	With my arid eyes
Rijsiytan munayki.	Ansío conocerte.	I long to know you
Rikújtiy,	Cuando yo pueda ver,	When I can see
yachájtiy,	Y conocer,	And know,
Unanchájtiy,	Y señalar	And show
Jamut'ájtiy,	Y comprender,	And understand,
Rikuwankin,	Tú me verás	You will see me
Yachawankin.	Y sabrás de mí	And you will know of me.

(Lara 1969: 186)

Understood as double and heterogeneous discursive frameworks in a tension between two cultural universes, the marks of orality that we have seen constitute undeniable proof not only of the presence of a border, and consequently of a *translative* process of transcription-translation, but also of the communicative and literal decision on the part of the transcriber-translator to *uproot* the reader, as F. Schleiermacher and later José Ortega y Gasset put it, from their own cultural setting and throw them into the *strangeness* of the (oral) culture of origin (Schleiermacher 1992 [1813]; Ortega y Gasset 1983). However, we cannot ignore the fact that the mechanism for the oralization of the text is only possible in the framework of a simultaneous coexistence with a series of other literary hallmarks that, for obvious reasons, do not tend to stand out. In the context of the border texts generated through the process of translation, reformulation became unavoidable in guaranteeing the literary effect of literaturization and fictionalization that is required to incorporate the oral into the written text, and to domesticate the indigenous voice and permit the Western reader to absorb the content without great effort or cultural confusion.

As is well-known, many of the transcriptions of indigenous songs and prayers were not originally structured into lines, a concept that, as Ong explains, in itself belongs to literary rather than oral culture:

> "Line" is obviously a text-based concept, and even the concept of a "word" as a discrete entity apart from a flow of speech seems somewhat text-based. Goody . . . has pointed out that an entirely oral language which has a term for speech in general, or for a rhythmic unit of a song, or for an utterance, or for a theme, may have no ready term for a "word" as an isolated item, a "bit" of speech, as in, "The last sentence here consists of twenty-six words." . . . The sense of individual words as significantly discrete items is fostered by writing, which, here as elsewhere, is diaeretic, separative.
>
> *(Ong 2002: 59–60)*

Cristóbal de Molina, for example, transcribed the poem that would be presented by Jesús Lara under the title *First Prayer for the Creator:*

> A ticsi uiracochan caylla uiracochan tocapo acnupo uiracochan camachurac caricachon huarmicachon nispallutac rurac camascayque churascaiqui casilla quespilla cauca musac maipimcanqui ahuapichu ucupichu puyupichu llantupichu hoyarihmay hayniguai ynihuai may pachacama cauca chihuay marcarihuay hatallihuay cay cullcaitari chasqui huaimay piscapapis viracochaya.
>
> *(de Molina 1989 [1575]: 81)*

And translated this into Spanish (here rendered into English):

> O creator, you who are without equal in the whole world, that gave life and worth to men and said: you will be man, and to the women: you will be woman; saying this you made them and formed them. You made them, you

take care of them so that they live safe and sound without danger, in peace. Where are you? Are you high in the heaven or below in the thunder of the clouds and the storms. Listen to me, respond to me and give in to me and give us eternal life, so that we may always be at your side, and receive this offering wherever you are, O creator.[5]

As we have previously indicated, over the years this text has been structured into verse, and is presented in the following manner in the anthology of Jesús Lara:

First Prayer for the Creator

Tijsi Wiraqucha,	Raíz del ser, Viracocha,	Root of being, Viracocha, Always present God,
Qaylla qaylla Wiraqucha,	Dios siempre cercano,	Lord of dazzling vestments,
T'ukapu Ajnupujuy Wiraqucha.	Señor de vestidura, Deslumbradora	
kámaj, chúraj,	Dios que gobierna	
y preserva, "Qhari hachun,	Que crea con sólo decir:	God that governs and preserves,
warmi kachun"	"Sea hombre,	That creates only by saying:
Ñispa rúraj	Sea mujer,"	"Be are a man,
Kamasqayki,	El ser que pusiste	Be a woman,"
Churasqayki	Y criaste	The being you put
Qasilla, qhespilla	Que viva libre	And created
Kausamuchun.	Y sin peligro.	That lives free
¿Maypin kanki?	¿Dónde te encuentras?	And without danger
¿Jawapichu,	¿Fuera del mundo,	Where can you be found?
Ukhupichu,	Dentro del mundo,	Outside the world,
phuyupichu,	En medio de las nubes	Inside the world,
Llanthupichu?	O en medio de las sombras?	In the middle of the the clouds
Uyaríway,	Escúchame,	Or in the middle of the shadows?
Jay nímúway.	Respóndeme.	Listen to me,
Yurajyánay	Haz que viva	Answer me.
Pacha kama,	Por muchos días,	Make me live
Ashka p'unchau kama	Hasta la edad en que deba	For many days,
Kausachíway,	Encanecer,	Until the age at which
Marq'aríway,	Levántame,	I go grey,
Jatarichíway,	Tómame en tus brazos	Lift me up, Take me in your arms,

Saykújtiyri	Y en mi cansancio	And in my tiredness,
Sh'askichíway,	Auxíliame,	Help me
Maypi kaspapas,	Doquiera estés,	Wherever you are,
Wiraqocha Yaya.	Padre Viracocha	Father, Viracocha.

(Lara 1969: 180)

Beyond the evident transformations the text has undergone over time, which we can observe through the differences between the two versions, it is important to point out the process of literary *genre creation* which was the result of successive retranslations. Specifically, the conversion of ritual song into indigenous writing, and later into Spanish writing, appears to be the first step in a process of textual solidification which makes it feasible to create versions that depart further and further from the original orality. The process of retranslation progressively incorporates a series of generic rules that make it possible (and credible) that such oral indigenous rituals can be, at present, received primarily as lyrical *poetry*.

The literaturization of indigenous orality is not limited to a literary genre through versification in the case of Quechua songs and prayers. The meter, as we shall see, also fulfils an important role in this process in that through it we realize the significant impact that suprasegmental characteristics of Spanish have in the construction of the musicality of prehispanic Quechua poetry.

As such, it is worth noting that Quechua poetry tends to be written in short verses, predominantly pentasyllables. According to Lara, this coincides with the phonic tendency of spoken Spanish, and consequently, also with its literary composition. Through an analysis of a corpus of 190 verses translated from Quechua to Spanish compiled by Lara, we can observe that the majority (63.5%) contain verses of between five and seven metric syllables, with pentasyllables presenting the highest percentage of occurrence (27.4%). This tendency coincides, as we have indicated, with the explanation that the Bolivian poet and researcher offered in 1947, but which he (curiously) omits in the 1969 edition:

> In the testimonies that we have access to, what jumps out is the predilection of the *arawicus* for short verse, what the Spanish versifiers would call a minor art. There are few poems composed in verses of more than eight syllables. Rather, there are a large amount with four or six, with five being the most common; there are also quite a few with eight [syllables]. This is explained by the orientation of the song, which taking into account the technical possibilities of the music, always sought short verse.[6]

What stands out, however, is the fact that in Spanish we can also observe this tendency towards short phonic periods, a characteristic presented by Lara among other authors, as specific to Quechua poetry. With respect to this, Gili Gaya explains:

> In ordinary conversation, phonic groups are generally shorter and distinct in themselves than in speeches or in written compositions. Classical rhetoritians

and our own sixteenth century writers considered colloquial language as not being *numbered*, and they contrasted this with *numbered prose*, created with a conscious artistic purpose. In narrative and descriptive prose, the preference for short or long units depends on the style of each author and of the prosodic qualities of the language in which they write. According to studies recently conducted by Navarro Tomás, the Spanish language shows a marked preference towards phonic groups of between 5 and 10 syllables, of which the most frequent are those of 7 and 8. The proportion of octosyllabic lines is 25 per cent of the total.[7]

While it is known that in Spanish, metric lines are produced in groups of around eight syllables, and in Quechua poems (the translations) they are around five, there is a general tendency in both cases towards phonic groups of eight or less syllables. As such, according to our calculations, the percentage of heptasyllables is 21.6%, a figure not too far away from 27.4% of pentasyllables – just eleven verses more in a total of 190.

Taking these observations concerning the Quechua poetry complied by Lara as a starting point, it is possible to infer that the precolombian Spanish American poetry appears, by extension, to be equally inseparable from the process of transcription and translation that indigenous orality was subject to as a consequence of the Spanish conquest. Due to the natural limitations of an essay such as this, we cannot expand the present analysis to the Mesoamerican precolombian literary corpus or offer a detailed reflexion on this textual corpus. Nevertheless, it is worth pointing out, at least, that besides the tensions between orality and written Quechua poetry reviewed according to translation theory, there are several other problems with using this same perspective to analyze Nahuatl poetry or Maya literature. Many pages have been written concerning the disagreement between Amos Segala and Miguel León-Portilla concerning the supposed authenticity and correct interpretation of the translations of Nahuatl poetry published by the latter. Similarly, the problem with the authenticity of texts such as the *Popol Wu'j* continues to stimulate research supporting the translation of the text and its paratexts. Regardless, in every case we come up against the same inevitable (though theoretically and aesthetically stimulating) problem: the existence of a prehispanic/oral–colonial/literate border that simultaneously makes heterogeneous and creates tension within precolombian texts. In the 16th century this made the emergence of a protoaesthetic translationary form possible, which is perhaps one of the most defining characteristics of Spanish American writing.

Writing and orality: translation as aesthetics

As we have previously outlined, the process of reformulation (transcription-translation) that made the emergence of a first precolombian textuality possible, and its insertion into the Western literate and literary universe, would constitute the necessary base for the foundation of a distinct protoaesthetic that incorporates not only the dominant language and code (the written alphabet), but also the tensions which emerge in the process of translation and the border problems that this implies. As we will see further on, this *moment* can be visualized through two authors who were fundamental to understanding the 16th century Andean world: Inca Garcilaso de la Vega and Felipe Guaman Poma de Ayala. Through the *Comentarios reales de los Incas* (Garcilaso de la Vega 1989 [1609]) and the *Primer nueva corónica y buen gobierno* (Guaman Poma de Ayala 1987 [1615]) we see two distinct forms of symbolic resolution of the tensions imposed by the conquest: firstly, between orality and the written alphabet; and secondly, between indigenous languages and Spanish.

1 The (free) road of the Inca

On the one hand, we see a model of *trust* in translation, which finds in the *Royal Commentaries of the Incas* by Inca Garcilaso de la Vega its best exemplar. The project of transposing the indigenous orality (of the Inca period) to the written alphabet is performed by the mestizo chronicler by adjusting the universe through the language and code into which they are being translated (that is, Spanish and the written Spanish alphabet), and, as such, enabling the process of translation itself to *disappear*.[8] In other words, this work, inspired by the translation that Inca Garcilaso had already conducted with León Hebreo's *Diálogos de amor [Dialogues of Love]*, inaugurated a style of writing that aesthetically incorporated *free* translation (a mode of translation followed by humanists in the era of Garcilaso) which was defined by Friederich Schleiermacher in 1813 in conjunction with literal translation: "Either the translator leaves the writer alone as much as possible and moves the reader toward the writer, or he leaves the reader alone as much as possible and moves the writer toward the reader" (Schleiermacher 1992: 41–2). In order to *leave the reader in peace as much as possible and move the writer towards the reader* (free translation), as we know thanks to translation theory, it is necessary for the translator (author) to remove all traces of their presence, becoming *invisible*, as Lawrence Venuti (Venuti 2008) puts it, in order to leave the reader with the impression that the target text (the chronicle written in Spanish by Garcilaso) produces the same effect that the original oral and Quechua text produced before the Spanish conquest.

In the *Royal Commentaries*, starting from the *Preface to the Reader* the writing of Garcilaso de la Vega is presented as a retranslation – an undertaking that proposes to translate the history of the Inca Empire again, but with restructured criteria for linguistic competence that enables one to understand the true history of the Incas through the accuracy of translation, with its roots deep in Andean orality:

> I have fuller and more accurate information than that provided by previous writers. It is true that these have dealt with many of the very remarkable achievements of that empire, but they have set them down so briefly that, owing to the manner in which they are told, I am scarcely able to understand even such matters as are well known to me. For this reason, impelled by the

natural love for my native country, I have undertaken the task of writing these *Commentaries*, in which everything in the Peruvian empire before the arrival of the Spaniards is clearly and distinctly set down, from the rites of their vain religion to the government of their kings in time of peace and war, and all else that can be told of these Indians, from the highest afairs of the royal crown to the humblest duties of its vassels. I write only of the empire of the Incas, and do not deal with other monarchies, about which I can claim no similar knowledge. In the course of my history I shall affirm its truthfulness and shall set down no important circumstances without quoting the authority of Spanish historians who may have touched upon it in part or as a whole. For my purpose is not to gainsay them, but to furnish a commentary and gloss, and to interpret many Indian expressions which they, as strangers to that tongue, have rendered inappropriately. This will be fully seen in the course of my history, which I commend to the piety of those who may peruse it, with no other interest than to be of service to Christendom.

(Garcilaso de la Vega 1989 [1609]: 4)

Trusting in the translation as a useful instrument for resolving the contradictions imposed by cultural difference and its border, Garcilaso proposes himself as the "interpreter" of "indian terms" that were interpreted out of context because they were "foreign" in the language of the Spanish chroniclers. This established an unprecedented relationship between translation and writing that would become crucial in the transformation of Spanish American literary discourse, especially when dealing with prehispanic oral tradition. Critics such as Alberto Escobar (1995), Susana Jakfalvi Leiva (1984), Mercedes Serna (2000) and Max Hernández (1991), among others, have highlighted the significance of language and translation in the work of the Inca:

> As Francisco Rico points out, the point of departure for humanistic education (undertaken by Lorenzo Valla and followed by Antonio de Nebrija) is the rejection of corrupt medieval Latin in favour of primitive Latin, the Latin of the classics, the true one. Fidelity becomes an essential concept. The Inca Garcilaso applies this same procedure when he accuses the Spanish chroniclers of ignoring the original language, in this case Quechua. Thus, he claims for himself the role of maximum authority on Inca history; in addition to presenting himself as a descendant of the indigenous nobility, he offers himself as a source of direct first hand knowledge.[9]

As we can see, for the Inca, *to write is to translate*, and to translate is to interpret the oral history of the Inca period *faithfully*, which also implies assuming the epistemological consequences of a criteria of historiographic truth put forward by the figure of the interpreter (the translator) as an ideal model of a historian. In the border context of the conquest of America, this equates to proposing, unequivocally, the

importance of the historian/writer having first-hand knowledge not only Quechua, the language of the Inca empire, but also indigenous orality in itself in order
to achieve the level of veracity required by History as a discipline:

> I declare that I shall simply tell the tales I imbibed in my mother's milk and
> those I have since obtained by request from my own relatives, and I promise
> that my affection for them shall not cause me to stray from the true facts
> either by underestimating the ill or exaggerating the good they did. . . . I
> shall merely as a commentator to reveal and amplify much of what they have
> begun to say, but have left unfinished for lack of full account. Much will be
> added that is missing in their histories but really happened, and some things
> will be omitted as superfluous because the Spaniards were misinformed,
> either because they did not know how to ask for information with a clear
> idea of the different periods and ages and divisions of provinces and tribes, or
> because they misunderstood the Indians who gave them it, or because they
> misunderstood one another on account of the difficulty of the language. The
> Spaniard who thinks he knows the language best is ignorant of nine-tenths
> of it, because of the many meanings of each word.
>
> *(Garcilaso de la Vega 1989 [1609]: 51)*

But perhaps there is no better example in the whole chronicle of the close relationship that Garcilaso establishes between orality, writing and translation than the
dialogue evoked by the mestizo chronicler in the *Commentaries* between him and
his uncle the Inca in his childhood:

> Inca, my uncle, though you have no writings to preserve the memory of
> past events, what information have you of the origins and beginnings of our
> kings? For the Spaniards and the other peoples who live on their borders have
> divine and human histories from which they know when their own kings
> and their neighbours' kings began to reign and when one emire gave way to
> another. They even know how many thousand years it is since God created
> heaven and earth. All this and much more they know through their books.
> But you, who have no books, what memory have you preserved of your
> antiquity? Who was the first of our Incas? What was he called? What was the
> origin of his line? How did he begin to reign? With what men and arms did
> he conquer this great empire? How did our heroic deeds begin?
>
> *(Garcilaso de la Vega 1989 [1609]: 41)*

And his uncle responds:

> Nephew, I will tell you these things with pleasure. Indeed it is right that you
> should hear them and keep them in your heart (this is their phrase for "in
> the memory").
>
> (ibid.)

The vision of oral memory as a source of historical truth is clear. It is the trigger for a translation in a wider sense; that is, a passage from the forgotten towards the remembered, bringing up to date not only the importance of memory for the oral psychodynamic, but also for the classical world, where the metaphorical (and oral) meaning of the Latin word *recordis* (return to the heart) is laid bare. The answer that the Inca puts in the mouth of his uncle, in this sense, appears obvious.

2 The literal *writing of Felipe Guaman Poma de Ayala*

On the other hand, we follow a current that *distrusts* the translation that emerges from the need to express (or, up to a certain point is not able to hide) the conflict between the codes and languages implicated in the violent process of domination that was the Spanish conquest. Here, we refer to texts such as the *First New Chronicle and Good Government* by Felipe Guaman Poma de Ayala that make explicit the border imposed by the Spanish invasion of the indigenous world; texts that reveal their *needlework*, making them an expressive spectacle. In the particular case of the indigenous chronicler, his work constitutes a protomodel for a *literal* translation that does not disturb the (anonymous) author's work, but rather brings the reader to it, obliging them to plunge themselves into the *strangeness* and *otherness* of the oral, principally Quechua world, extremely far from the comfort of their own (literary and Spanish) world. As research by Mercedes López-Baralt (López–Baralt 1988), Rolena Adorno (Adòrno 2000, 2003), Nathan Wachtel (Wachtel 1973), Juan Ossio (Ossio 1973) and others have shown, the presence of the border and its conflict comes to be aesthetically evident, even inevitable, for Guaman Poma, to the point that we could say paradoxically that it forces the reader to develop an intercultural competence that enables them to read, through *other* eyes, the chronicle's profound, complex and subversive content.

With reference to the 399 drawings in the chronicle, Rolena Adorno has indicated:

> In the present case, a specifically Andean pattern of spacial significance is pertinent. I propose reading the pictorial text by superimposing on it a grid of Andean spatial symbolism; I would argue that the arrangement of icons in space allows for an additional visual interpretation and is responsible for an additional level of pictorial meaning. Thus, although pictorially expressing himself in ways that are comprehensible to the European reader, Guaman Poma employs and remains true to his own authochtonous values of symbolic representation.
>
> *(Adorno 2000: 89)*

Both Rolena Adorno and Mercedes López-Baralt have highlighted the tremendous multicultural challenge that Guaman Poma faced. In this context, the presence of a rhetorical *other* that fulfils the function of subverting the Western rhetorical cannon just as much in the written as in the visual code is remarkable. Nathan Wachtel and Juan Ossio, amongst others, have done in-depth studies of the system of internal categorization within Andean culture from an anthropological and historical-anthropological point of view. For these researchers, it is possible to demonstrate the existence of a system of categories of Andean thought, organizing the narrative structure of the chronicles of Guaman Poma. For Wachtel, for example, what other researchers, such as Raúl Porras Barrenechea, have associated with *barbarity* and *chaos* (Porras Barrenechea 1971 [1948]) constitutes precisely the proof that the discourse of the Yarovilca chronicler is of another type altogether:

> If such barbarity exists, it is without a doubt necessary to regard it, following Claude Lévi-Strauss as savage thought. Guaman Poma perceives the colonial world through authentically indigenous categories, that nonetheless continue to be ruled by rigorous logic. However, the system of thought is still different to our own. The chronicle of Guaman Poma is only confusing if we measure it against our own Western criteria; if we want to escape the vertigo of Raúl Porras Barrenechea we should return to the mechanism of indigenous thought. It is under this apparent chaos that the coherence and meaning of the work of Guaman Poma will be revealed to us. . . . Guaman Poma offers precisely the example of an acculturation where the Western elements are absorbed by the system of indigenous thought that, at the cost of a series of adaptations and transformations, manages to conserve its original structure.[10]

Juan Ossio, on the other hand, has said with respect to the mythical conception of time in Guaman Poma's work:

> Guaman expresses himself using concepts belonging to contemporary European historiography and to the language in which he was writing (Spanish). This is signalled in the very title of the work (New Chronicle), in his objectives, and (according to him, preserving the memory of acts of certain persons), in his claimed search for authenticity, in his conception of time, etc. However, after a detailed examination of the manuscript, I realised that these concepts had been badly assimilated by Guaman Poma, noting a haphazard tone similar to that of modern scholars. Under the foreign apparel emerged a way of thinking marked by categories foreign to the European world contemporary to him, and which we can classify as mythical in the sense that they carry a static conception of time, an interest in the past to justify the present, and a unitary vision of the cosmos and social relations. Thus, through Guaman Poma, I have been able to confirm that oral traditions were effectively dispossessed by Europeans of their original meaning.[11]

The subtextual and subversive dimension of Guaman Poma's text not only illustrates the implicit intention of the chronicle to hurl the non-indigenous reader into the cultural otherness of Andean orality. The reader, according to Schleiermacher and Ortega y Gasset, is uprooted from the comfort of their language and culture, but also permitted to understand, with anthropological precision, the importance for the Andean writer of *visibilizing* the border that other chroniclers, from a *free* translation and ideologically *appropriative* perspective, try to make invisible. In effect, one of the recurring motifs in the work of Guaman Poma is the *upside-down world*, which aims to both directly denounce the catastrophic state of post-conquest colonial Peru and, as an ideological plan, to use the latent concept in the Andean myth of *pachacuti* to *invert* and *separate* two worlds that, for the Andean chronicler, should never come into contact with one another, never mind mix.

> for Guaman Poma the conquest was not an historical event, but rather a cosmic cataclysm, a "pachakuti", to use the Andean term, in which the world had been turned upside down and left in in the reverse order.[12]

In effect, the Peruvian researcher is right when he highlights, as others such as Tom Zuidema (1964) and Wachtel (1973) himself have, that the indigenous vision of Guaman rejects all types of mixing that disturb the order based on the traditional hierarchies of space, time and lineage, *hanan* and *hurin* being the best representation of Andean dualism that Guaman Poma used to write his chronicle. From Ossio's perspective, Guaman Poma's rejection of any kind of mestizaje leads him to propose a systematic separation of components as a measure of re-establishing lost equilibrium:

> Until now, we have seen that the image that Guaman Poma has of the disorder of this world comes principally from the fusion of two principles "Hanan" and "Hurin". Order is only restored by keeping both principles apart. That is, keeping the Spanish separate from the Indians would permit the latter to return to their previous positions, which has been altered by the conquest. These positions were the property of Andean territories and their respective status within the hierarchical order was immutable.[13]

Regarding the separation as ideal, Guaman Poma vehemently denounced the mixing between Indians and Spaniards:

> In the service of God and of the royal crown of his majesty, said author, having entered the city of the kings of Lima, saw it crowded with absent Indians and runaways slaves who had become yanaconas [servants], officials who became mitayos [those who do the work], low-lying Indians who pay tribute, who had put on a collar and dressed as Spaniards, carrying swords, while while others shaved their heads to avoid paying tribute or serving in the the mines. Here we see the world upside-down.
>
> And so, as these absent Indians are seen, other Indians leave their villages and there is no one to pay the tribute, nor to work in the mines. And said

author also saw very many Indian prostitutes loaded with mestizos and mulatos, all with underskirts, ankle boots and head-dresses. Even though they are
married, they walk about with Spaniards and Blacks. And so, others do not
want to marry Indians, nor want to leave said city for not leaving the whor-
ing. The rancherias of said city are full of Indians, and there is no remedy.
They make offence in the service of God, our Lord, and his Majesty. And so,
said Indians of this kingdom do not multiply.[14]

As we can see, for the Andean chronicler, the event was a catastrophic event –
a real *pachacuti* (cataclysm) caused by the contact and mixing between Spaniards
and indigenous people. In the Andean cosmovision that subtextually governs the
chronicle, neither world should come into contact with the other, and therefore
constitute a border that permits the aberrations that produce the mestizaje that
Guaman Poma refers to. In this sense, from the ideological perspective latent in
the *New Chronicle*, the border symbolizes, paradoxically, the possible solution to
the conflict that this mixing represents and that propels the aesthetics of counter-
writing and cultural recognition. The need to separate the worlds that the Spanish
conquest had mixed is combined with the urgency to forge a discourse that not
only highlights the urgency to recognize and reinforce the border that others do
not see or try to blur, but also to symbolically resolve the tensions that imply the
imposition of the need to negotiate a border through the violent imposition of the
written alphabet and translation, both indisputable arms of the so-called spiritual
domination of American Indians. The writing of Guaman Poma, then, follows
the separation of the European and indigenous worlds ideologically, Spanish and
indigenous languages, and alphabetic writing and orality, identifying them with the
Andean cultural principles of *hanan* y *hurin*, respectively, but paradoxically does not
have any other method of doing so than through the written word. Lettered discourse creates the *literary* effect that such a separation is both *possible* and *credible* in
the framework of the written alphabet and the visual rhetoric of the drawings that,
as Rolena Adorno notes, predated the redaction of written script (Adorno 2003).

Guaman Poma was therefore forced to write from a border that he himself
attempted to negotiate. This implied a series of decisions in relation to the translation (forced equally by the complex political and multicultural circumstances) that
determined if the reader could relax without having to make any attempt to understand the original text, or whether they had to be torn from their own surround-
ings and propelled into the strangeness of the text. The answer to this dilemma
can be found in the strange quality of the chronicle – the same quality that led
Porras Barrenechea to describe the writing of Guaman Poma as "pure mental disorder,"[15] an epithet that, fortunately, has not held back subsequent research. In fact,
perhaps there are no better words than those of Ortega y Gasset to assess the ultimate sense of literalism that drives the writing in the *New Coronica*. Although the
Spanish philosopher reflects particularly on translation (or "pseudo-translations,"
as he describes them) (Ortega y Gasset 1983: 26), his conclusions can be perfectly

applied to the work of Guaman Poma since in the chronicle, the border and silence existing between languages and the cultural systems associated with them appear visible, obliging the reader to move towards the (oral) source text, resulting in a strange or *ugly* text (as Ortega y Gasset would call it). This happens, firstly, because it is written; and secondly, because it is written primarily in Spanish, but thought (and drawn) from an oral perspective drawing on an indigenous language, which also forces, in a gesture of counterdiscourse and counterculture, the recipient of the lettered discourse (the King, Felipe III) to expand the border of his own language and code in order to really understand the difference that all source texts have to offer the curiosity of those approaching them from a foreign perspective. As Ortega y Gasset explains, as if he were defending the difference that others rejected in Guaman Poma's writing:

> Only when we force the reader from his linguistic habits and oblige him to move within those of the author is there actual translation. Until now there has been hardly anything except pseudo-translation. . . . I imagine, then, a form of translation that is ugly, as science always is, one that does not insist on literary grace, one that is not easy to read. . . . It is necessary for the reader to know beforehand that when he reads a translation he is not going to read a text that is beautiful.
>
> *(Ortega y Gasset 1983: 28–30)*

The lettered voice: current indigenous poetry in perspective

As we have seen up to now, the path that the indigenous voice has had to walk has rested on columns of either cultural or pragmatic translation (interpretation, transcription and interlinguistic translation). Missionaries, as well as Spanish, indigenous and mestizo chroniclers, have faced the complex task of translating indigenous orality into the written alphabet, Spanish and (usually standardized)[16] indigenous languages across a tense and conflictive border that has been ignored and made invisible by some and highlighted by others. From the time of Columbus and the first interpreters until mestizo and indigenous authors such as Inca Garcilaso de la Vega; Felipe Guaman Poma de Ayala or Joan de Santa Cruz Pachacuti Yamqui Salcamaygua; Titu Cusi Yupanqui, in the Andean area; or Fernando Alvarado Tezozomac, Fernando Alva Ixtlilxóchitl and Domingo Francisco de San Antón Muñón Chimalpáhin Cuatlehuanitzin, in Mesoamerica; among others, be they collective, individual or anonymous, this path has principally used the written alphabet and/ or the Spanish language as the principal code for transmission, solidifying, reformulation and resistance of indigenous oral memory. However, as we have seen in terms of the differences in translation in the writing of Inca Garcilaso and Guaman Poma, the ideological purpose of this reformulation is not always to visibilize the border that separates orality and writing (or indigenous people from Spaniards).

Moreover, in the Andean context, we can see that privileging the universe created by the Spanish conquest can lead to a literary silencing of the indigenous voice, as occurred for approximately a century after the consolidation of the colony, as Martin Lienhard explains:

> The definitive consolidation of the Colony, relatively late in Peru, ends with a literature that draws strength from the cultural dialogue between the "vanquished" and the "winners". Over the course of more than a century, no significant text in Spanish opens to a hispanic-Quechua interaction. In the context of "Andean" conscious-raising from which the chain of insurrectional events of the eighteenth-century spring, finally arise a literature (composed fundamentally of letters and memorials of "principal caciques") that critically examine again the relationship between the "Republic of Indians" and that of the Spanish. The authors of this literature, members of the neo-Inca aristocracy, opt in their discursive-linguistic practice, for unreserved submission to the requirements of the dominant culture.[17]

The *indigenism* of the 19th and 20th centuries, on the other hand, does not demonstrate any substantial changes to this situation. The *free* aesthetic used by authors to write about the indigenous world produces texts that show the exoticism of the indigenous language, but do not manage to propose a border discourse that makes the tensions on the process of translation imposed evident since the colonial period, as we have examined in the preceding pages. In effect, in the works of authors such as Clorinda Matto de Turner, Enrique López Albújar, Mariano Melgar or Ciro Alegría (in Peru), Alcides Arguedas (in Bolivia), Jorge Icaza (in Ecuador), Miguel Ángel Asturias (in Guatemala), Gregorio López y Fuentes, Ricardo Pozas or Muricio Magdaleno (in Mexico), among many others, there is no aesthetic that speaks of the Indian from the border, as Guaman Poma does.

However, the most notable exception in the context of the first half of the 20th century, and specifically in the Andean context, was the work of José María Arguedas, whose own aesthetic is marked by an *indigenism* that neither assimilates nor idealizes indigeneity. Rather, he visibilizes indigeneity thanks to anchoring it in the Andean present, interpreting the interference between indigenous languages and Spanish as a verbal performance of cultural resistance and persistence, similar to that which we can find in the writing of the Andean chronicler:

> In very broad terms, the linguistic paradigm of the Arguedian narrative, as with that of Guaman Poma or of Pachakuti (although there are significant differences from one work – or version – to another), is the "translinguistic" . . . tendency of openness to the copresence or the imbrication of Spanish and Quechua elements. The Quechua lexis and syntax, or discursive fragments in Quechua (above all, novels, the transcription of songs), do not appear, in any way, "as strange bodies", artificially arranged in the texts, but as symbols

in a (precisely) translinguistic code. Rather than simply in Spanish or in Quechua, Arguedas writes in "Andean", if by this term we wish to understand a conflictive, open and dynamic system of multiple expression, that bit by bit has come to constitute Andean history.[18]

The aesthetic challenge that Arguedas faced, and the enormous tensions that the Quechua-Spanish imposed on him, can be seen as a fundamental milestone in the complex trajectory the indigenous voice has taken towards the present. In fact, this *alternative*[19] and lettered journey through indigenous orality – of which we cannot offer more than a condensed version – does not manage to open its own space of expression until the 1970s, when capitalist and neoliberal politics were adopted by Latin American governments, triggering a new series of migratory displacements and indigenous claims that would lead the way to a new indigenous Spanish American writing, led principally by "bilingual teachers, cultural promotors and indigenous intellectuals of the communities where indigenous languages are spoken" (Waldman 2003: 68).

One example of this is the flourishing of a new indigenous poetry across the whole American continent. In countries such as Mexico and Guatemala, this new "indigenous word or *Yancuic Tlahtolli*" (León-Portilla 2004: 19) reveals a clear insertion of this phenomenon in the wider context of the long indigenous trajectory of counter-appropriation of the written alphabet, just as much as Spanish, as the dominant language of communication. In this sense, the poetic work of authors such as Humberto Ak'abal (Maya *k'iche'* from Guatemala), Calixta Gabriel Xiquín (Maya Kaqchikel from Guatemala), Briceida Cuevas Cob (Maya from Yucatán, México), Natalio Hernández (*Nahuatl* from México), Natalia Toledo (Zapoteca from Oaxaca, México), Waldemar Noh Tzec (Maya from Campeche), Víctor de la Cruz (Zapoteco from Oaxaca, México), María Sabina (Mazateca from Oaxaca, México) and Juan Gregorio Regino (Mazateco from Oaxaca, México), among others, constitute voices representative of the indigenous struggle to recuperate their *voice* through the appropriation of the written alphabet, the written word, and, specifically, a fictional literary discourse that in this new context functions as a literary convention and creates the conditions for the repositioning of orality and myth at the centre of a system of production from which they had been marginalized following the conquest.

Examples of this literature have proliferated throughout America. An understanding of these texts requires an engagement with the persistence and resistance that has characterized indigenous orality until the present day. In the majority of cases we are referring to a literature written "at the bottom of the source," as defined by the Mapuche poet Elicura Chihuailaf (Viereck Salinas 2012: 207–8): an *oraliture*[20] that reminds us of the literal and translinguistic quality of the writing of indigenous authors who, like Guaman Poma de Ayala during the colony, pulled the readers out of the comfort of their Hispanic and literate environment to plunge them into the difference of the oral indigenous world. Such aesthetics drive the symbolic reconfiguration of the colonial border on the basis of a new mode of communication that highlights precisely – as in the *New Chronicle* of Guaman Poma – the importance of the border in conveying an indigenous voice, written by indigenous authors, that is effectively adjusted to the parameters of the ancestral cosmovision of indigenous peoples.

In the case of the most widely adopted genre – poetry – in the context of Spanish American countries, Ecuador, Peru and Chile stand out, as well as Mexico and Guatemala, as previously mentioned. Ariruma Kowii, a Quechua-speaker from Otavalo in Ecuador, is perhaps the most noteworthy figure in the indigenous poetic scene from that country. His book *Mutsuctsurini* (Kowii 1988), published entirely in Quechua, stands out in the period of Andean production as a radical example of expression and the affirmation of cultural difference. In his collection of poems, the border appears aesthetically invisible due to the monolingualism of the publication. This is exacerbated by being a written text aimed at a literate indigenous readership that barely existed in Spanish American countries. For this reason, in contrast to Ariruma Kowii's challenging collection of poems, the majority of indigenous poetry currently being published has been written in what Iván Carrasco referred to as a *double register* (Carrasco 1991). That is, a bilingual, indigenous and Spanish version, which means that the text achieves not only the objective of a wider potential readership, but also makes the importance of the border, difference, and translation as inherent dimensions of contemporary indigeneity visible.

Thus, in the Andean context, we can add the names of Eduardo Ninamango Mallqui, Dida Aguirre, Susy Delgado or Odi González, some of the most well-known Quechua poets in Peru, to a long list of Mapuche poets in Chile and Argentina that, with a varying fluency in Mapudungun[21] (the indigenous language of the Mapuche people), successfully burst onto the contemporary publishing scene in their respective countries. Among the latter, the most notable is Elicura Chihuailaf Nahuelpan, whose work is perhaps only comparable in terms of international recognition to the Maya Ki'che' work of Humberto Ak'abal from Guatemala. Along with the stand-out figure of the Araucanian Chilean poet, we can find the award-winning poetic works of Leonel Lienlaf and Lorenzo Aillapan Cayuleo, Mapuche-Lafkenche poets from Chile, and the work of Mapuche-Huilliche poets from the regions of Osorno, Valdivia and Puerto Montt (also in Chile), such as Jaime Huenún, Roxana Miranda Rupailaf, Adriana Paredes Pinda, Juan Paulo Huirimilla, Bernardo Colipán, David Aniñir Guilitraro, Graciela Huinao, María Teresa Panchillo, María Inés Huenuñir Antihuala or Eliana Pulquillanca Nahuelpan, as well as the Mapuche poet from Argentina, Liliana Ancalao, among various others. However, despite finding themselves relatively late in the process of learning (or *recuperation*, as many have declared)[22] their indigenous languages, we can observe the bilingualism and double codification as a constant cultural and ideological gesture. As we have underlined, the concepts of the border and translation position this production in the historical perspective of the appropriative tradition of persistence and cultural resistance that has marked the transformation of the indigenous voice within a literary circuit since the end of the 15th century.

On the other hand, it is important to point out that such a cross-sectional characteristic of the production of Mapuche poetry, and Spanish American poetic production in general, should not be interpreted as synonymous with an absolute lack of aesthetic heterogeneity between texts belonging to the same author or two different authors, whether or not they belong to the same cultural community or speak the same language. Any study that attempts to evaluate the discursive strategies that each author and/or text specifically brings into play to resolve the tensions between orality and the written word would, without a doubt, shed relevant light on the problems of continuity and rupture that have followed translations at the hands of the indigenous subject, as well as the manner in which writings/translations have attempted to symbolically and culturally resolve and negotiate the border that was imposed by the violent imposition of the written alphabet.

In the particular case of current Mapuche poetry, however, the apparent homogeneity of the textual corpus appears to be relativized by the possibility of identifying at least three distinct aesthetics: the *literal*, the *free* and the *irreverent*. In the case of the first two, the author is left alone and the reader is made to meet him or vice versa, respectively; while in the third, the poem and original text relationship appears incorporated into the discourse from a perspective that conceives the written version as an insubordinate text with respect to the original one.

Amongst this production, above all we can find an example of the literal aesthetic in many of the poems of Aillapán Cayuleo. His works expose the reader to a writing adjusted to the parameters of the lifeworld of the original indigenous orality, confronting it with all the cultural competencies necessary to understand it. This aesthetic reminds us of the Arguedian option for non-professional writing, as we can observe in the following poem, titled *Manke* (Cóndor):

Kuyfi müleken tachi doy fütra üpünfe   An ancient bird that flies at a great height
rumel küntraymiyaukey ko meu reke   always majestic in the air, like a boat in
   kürüf meu   the water
– doy kim üñum – kimche reke   Incredible bird just like a wise man
– doy nor üñum – norche reke   Incredible bird just like a rightous man
– doy küme üñum – kümche reke   Incredible bird just like a kind man
– doy newen üñum – newenche reke.   Incredible bird just like a powerful man
Maaaannkkeeee – maaaannkkeeee – affkape
maaaannkkeeee – maaaannkkeeee – affkape
Fey meu inarumeley newen ka ngülam   Living people following this exemplary
   pu mülenche   truth and reason
rumel mülekelu kam tañi mapu meu   just like a bird always around its dear
   ayiwün duam   terrain
fey Lakukonkey allanagechi mañke   becoming the legitimate namesake of
   üñum meu   the Condor
Miyaukelu fill ad ad mapu püle witran   symbol of the traveller in their original
   reke   prohibited territory

wefrumekey dulliñ üy mañkelef pingelu	from there was born the name
che	"Mañkelef – quick Condor"
Mañkengean üytukuwi doy	The most inspired put
poyeayiumalu.	"Mañkengean = I will be Condor"
Maaaannkkeeee – maaaannkkeeee – affkape	
Maaaannkkeeee – maaaannkkeeee – affkape	

Es un pájaro milenario que vuela a gran altura
siempre majestuoso en el aire como nave en el agua
Pájaro sobresaliente igual a un sabio
Pájaro sobresaliente igual a un justiciero
Pájaro sobresaliente igual a un bondadoso
Pájaro sobresaliente igual a un poderoso.

Esta verdad y razón ejemplar personas vivientes lo sigue
igual que el ave siempre alrededor de su amado terruño
llegando a ser legítimo tocayo del ave Cóndor
símbolo del viajero en territorio original prohibido
de ahí nace nombre propio "Mañkelef – cóndor veloz"
el más inspirado se puso "Mañkengean = cóndor seré"
(Aillapan 2003: 116)

On the other hand, we can find a good example of the *free* aesthetic in the poems *Se notó tu ausencia en el Domingo de Ramos [I felt your absence on Palm Sunday]* by Bernardo Colipán, or *Salmo 1492 [Psalm 1492]* by Graciela Huinao. In these texts, the procedure is to privilege the code and language into which the poem was translated (Spanish), despite the ideological context of the text. While Colipán's text belongs to a monolingual edition in Spanish (an exception in the context of lyrical poetry), in both cases the nature of the texts is adjusted to meet the parameters of the literary discourse of the dominant language. This gives the effect of a text that was written in Spanish, in which the marks of orality, and therefore translation, have been made aesthetically invisible. One would have to consider this to be a minor factor behind the aesthetic, since the author cannot translate themselves, as in the case of the poem of Graciela Huinao and other authors whose texts have been translated, for example, by the teacher and translator Clara Antinao or the poet and translator Víctor Cifuentes:

I felt your absence on Palm Sunday

You tell us in your letter, Carmen, that Santiago
is a great city, cheap and with many lights
That you have a personal stereo and listen to Michael Jackson.

That you wear a miniskirt that you never showed here.
That your happiness is a CD that you play loudly at night
We – your Friends in the neighbourhood – with a plaster cover your emptiness.
On Palm Sunday we felt your absence.
Johnny found work and no longer remembers you.
Carmencita – your daughter – is already four years old.
It will do Carmen good to return to Rahue

Se notó tu ausencia en el Domingo de Ramos

Nos dices en tu carta, Carmen, que Santiago
es una gran ciudad, barata y de muchas luces.
Que tienes un personal estéreo y escuchas a Michael Jackson.
Que usas la minifalda que acá nunca mostraste.
Que tu felicidad es un CD que tocas por las noches
a todo volumen.
Nosotros – tus amigos del barrio- con un parchecurita
sellamos tu vacío.
El domingo de Ramos se notó tu ausencia.
El Johnny consiguió trabajo y aún se acuerda de ti.
Carmencita – tu hija – ya tiene cuatro años.
Bien te haría Carmen volver a Rahue

(Colipán 2005: 47)

Salmo Waranka, Meli Pataka, Ailla Mari Epu	Salmo 1492	Psalm 1492
Turpu ngünel	Nunca fuimos	We never were
Trokiñchenoefl iñchiñ	el pueblo señalado	The chosen people
Welu langümngekeiñ	pero nos matan	But they kill us
Küruz ñi duam meu	en señal de la cruz	At the sign of the cross
		(Huinao 2009: 20)

Lastly, the *irreverent* aesthetic articulates a series of compositional decisions which are clearly aligned with the discursive procedures of the literary avant-guard and produce a textuality that plays – in a manner reminiscent of Borges[23] – with the process of translation and the concept of the border. As we will see with the poem *Rituals for the blue serpent* (*Rituales de la serpiente azul*) by Roxana Miranda Rupailaf, these poems exemplify the relationship between the written text and indigenous orality that appears to be interchangeable in the framework of an *appropriative* conception of translation. This could even lead us to see this type of writing as an extreme variant of the free aesthetic, if it were not for the fact that these texts not only adjust the poem to the parameters of the code and language into which the poem is translated, but also produce a modern effect of *adaptation* to the present that incorporates the desacralization of primary orality. Aligned with a conception of a living contemporary indigenous culture, these texts appropriate and subvert alongside the literary stamp of the author's Western individualism, the mythology just as much as the oral content of the tradition, among other similar topics associated with conservative indigenous tradition. Miranda Rupilaf's poem is divided into two parts and preceded by an epigraph (verses by Adriana Paredes Pinda) that allude to the main cultural text appropriated by the poem, the Mapuche myth of *kai-kai filu*:

> *What are we going to do Kai-kai filu*
> *So that we do not drown in your ritual*
> *of fear and thickness*

I

Water makes you and cracks
your skin

Devour me with your heartbeats and mountains.
Pursuing the screams of death
That resist the choking of fish
of the blood.
I carry out my body in waves
of salt and madness

I bite earth in the corners of the blue.

The cries and anger
fragment in the eyes of life.

II

Blood enters mouths
And its drum spins in skin.
Breath flutters
until the water with which I support the Spring
and go running
screams at me
the bird
that does not show its feathers while it dreams:
their dream is deeper in the night.
Blood runs, cutting my tongue.

In hardstep
I dance
towards the outside.

Blood runs through my teeth
That I couldn't grit enough
when blue castaways
passed
in the salt

Qué haremos Kai-kai filu
para no ahogarnos en tu rito
de miedo y espesura

I

Agua hacerte y agrietarte
por las pieles.

Devorarme tus latidos y montañas.
Persiguiendo los gritos de la muerte
que se resiste al atorarse de los peces
de la sangre.
Cuerpo arrastro en oleajes
de sal y de locura.

Muerdo tierra en los rincones de lo azul.
Los llantos y las rabias
fragmento en los ojos de la vida.

II

Entra sangre adentro de las bocas
y gira en piel su tambor.
Convulsiona el aliento
hasta gritarme el agua
en que sostengo la primavera
en que seguir corriendo
al ave
que no muestra las plumas mientras sueña:
que el sueño es más profundo en lo nocturno.

Anda sangre cortándome la lengua.

En danza de golpear
me baila el acento
hacia el afuera.

Sangre corre por los dientes
que no pudieron apretar lo suficiente
cuando pasaron
náufragos azules
en la sal
      (Miranda Rupailaf 2008: 69–70)

As we have shown, through this introductory and panoramic tour through written translations of the indigenous voice from soon after the so-called discovery of America until the present day, it is not possible to understand the true significance of Spanish American writing outside the frame of meaning imposed by translation due to the violent imposition of the written alphabet on the oral indigenous world. As we have seen, the application of some concepts used in translation, especially those related to methods of translating, permit us to visualize discourses that become relevant in the discussion over the literary configuration of the indigenous voice in Spanish America from an intellectual perspective. These discourses contribute to the stimulation of cultural, historical and social debate around the conflict between orality and writing. Other explanatory models have tried to tackle these conflicts through concepts such as *transculturation* (Fernando Ortíz 2002), *heterogeneity* (Antonio Cornejo Polar 2003), *hibridity* (Néstor García Canclini 1995) or *diglossia* (Martin Lienhard 1990), among others, which have enabled the opening up of a path of critical alternatives to the traditional biological focus of miscegenation that for a long time confined the problem of Latin American specificity to the interests of an oligarchic minority that attempted to leave behind the conquest and colonial contradictions in favour of a supposed homogeneity that would have contributed to the construction of nation state in Latin America.

Viewing the problem through the lens of *translation*, as we have, through a panorama of three foundational moments (oral interpretation, transcription to literaturization and the aestheticization of translation), plus a fourth moment of contemporary continuity and rupture (current indigenous poetry) that appears to be a necessary interpretative framework through which to expand the analytic possibilities of other explanatory models, aligns them implicitly with the concept of the "translation turn" proposed by Susan Basnett and André Lefevre (1998: 123) two decades ago, with the postcolonial theories of Gayatri Spivak (1993) or Hommi Bhabha (2005), and the concept of the "translation zone," proposed by Emily Apter (2006). In the latter, the use of the word "zone," as explained by Edwin Gentzler in his book *Translation in the Americas: New Directions in Translation Theory*, makes reference to a "theoretical space, one that is not defined by language, politics or nation, but is broad enough to include the aftershocks of translation" (Gentzler 2008: 3).

A focus such as this on the (conflictive and tense) interactions between orality and writing locates translation in the centre of discussions regarding the impact of the border and the relevance of the orality-writing relationship in the configuration of the Latin American lettered corpus. However, this has been done so far without understanding, from our perspective, that translation is much more than an accident or a medium through which content is conveyed that was previously expressed in another language. Genztler himself, in relation to the postcolonial approach of Homi Bhabha, explains this as follows:

> America is a mistranslation. . . . As postcolonial theorists such as Homi Bhabha talk about culture as "transnational and translational" to refer to a new hibridized condition that is indicative of contemporary culture (1994:172), so too might translation studies scholars begin to recognize the fundamental role translation plays in the construction of individual identity.
>
> *(Gentzler 2008: 5, 7)*

While explanations such as this appear regularly in the context of theoretical and cultural discussions regarding translation, we cannot say the same about Latin American approaches.

Despite this, it is pertinent to conclude this essay with two quotes from two notable exceptions. The first one relates to the *space in-between* concept developed by Santiago Silvano. For the Brazilian researcher:

> America is transformed into a copy, a simulacrum that wants to become more and more like the original, even when its originality cannot be found in the copy of the original model, but in an origin that was completely erased by the conquerors. Through the constant extermination of original strokes and the oblivion of origin, the phenomenon of duplication is established as the only valid rule of civilization.[24]

The second one – directly linked to the thesis of this chapter – is a citation of the final paragraph of the article *La interrelación creativa del quechua y del español en la literatura peruana de lengua española* [*The creative interrelationship between Quechua and Spanish in Peruvian literatura and the Spanish language*] by Martin Lienhard (1992). It shows not only how translation stands up – repeatedly – as an explanatory tool to understand Latin American culture, but also underlines the coherence with which we can use it as a theoretical perspective in itself, beyond the inevitable differences that authorship stamps onto the work of each individual author. In this sense, the traductological perspective with which he systematizes the thesis in his article is noteworthy, as is the prominence given to the writing of the Inca Garcilaso and Felipe Guaman Poma de Ayala in explaining the *literary effects* of translation in the Andean area and, by extension, from the point of view of this essay, in Latin America:

> As can be seen from our trip through the manifestations of the interaction between Quechua and Spanish in Spanish-language Peruvian literature, the authors of "Andean" texts in Spanish show, throughout Andean history, three basic literary-linguistic attitudes: total submission to the norms of Spanish writing (that can hide – Tupac Amaru – the protection of the autonomy of Quechua orality), the "linguistic mimicry" which advocates a radical pluriculturism [sic] and, finally, the "semantic-poetic translation" of Quechua (which fosters the incorporation of a "filtered" Andean culture into the "universal" Western framework). In the last few decades, the validity of the former appears to have suffered (in strictly "Andean" literature), a collapse that could be interpreted as the recognition on the part of the authors of the definitive interpenetration of two primitive "worlds", respectively the "Quechua" and the "Western". Currently, the principal "debate" is between the second ("linguistic mimicry") and the third ("the semantic-poetic translation of the Quechua"), sometimes within the work itself – Arguedas – of a single author. This "debate" translates, in some form, the dilemma between the desire to powerfully anchor the texts in a concrete cultural context, and that of offering them a "universal" way out: neither more nor less than the the the dilemma whose poles represent, almost at the beginning of the Colony, Guaman Poma de Ayala and Garcilaso de la Vega. While a colonial "framework" persists in Peruvian culture, this dilemma will continue, without a doubt, to produce its literary effects.[25]

Notes

1 Every effort has been made to trace and contact copyright holders of the text and poetry extracts contained in this chapter and the author is thankful for the permissions. Perceived omissions, if brought to notice, will be rectified in future printing.
2 As we will see later on, when we review some examples of current indigenous poetry, since the beginning of the 20th century a third irreverent variant emerges that – in what Sergio Waisman (2005) would describe as the Borgesian manner of understanding translation – does not recognize the need to bow the knee to the original version, nor accept the ontological pre-existence of this original version. This leads to the aesthetic possibility of an interchangeability of parts between the original and the translated version.
3 "La luminosa prisión del alfabeto" (León-Portilla 1996a: 362).
4 For a detailed examination of the application of these concepts, see *La traducción como instrumento y estética en la literatura hispanoamericana del siglo XVI*, Roberto Viereck Salinas's doctoral thesis (Viereck Salinas 2003b).
5 "O Hacedor que estás en los fines del mundo sin igual, que deste ser y balor a los hombres y dijiste: sea éste hombre, y a las mugeres: sea esta muger; diciendo esto, los hiziste y los formaste y diste ser. A éstos que hiciste, guárdalos que vivan sanos y salvos sin peligro, viviendo en paz. ¿Adónde estáis? ¿Estáis en lo alto del cielo o avajo en los truenos en los nublados de las tenpestades? Oyeme, respóndeme y concede conmigo y danos perpetua vida, para siempre tenednos de tu mano y esta ofrenda recíbela adoquiera que estuvieres, O Hacedor" (de Molina 1989 [1575]: 82).

6 "En los testimonios que poseemos salta a la vista la predilección de los *arawicus* por el verso breve, de arte menor como dirían los verificadores españoles. Son raros los poemas compuestos en versos mayores de ocho sílabas. En cambio abundan los de cuatro y seis, siendo los de cinco los más corrientes; pero tampoco son escasos los de ocho. Esto se explica por la orientación del canto, el cual, teniendo en cuenta los recursos técnicos de su música, buscaba siempre el verso corto" (Lara 1947: 69).

7 "En la conversación ordinaria, los grupos fónicos son, por lo general, más cortos y distintos entre sí que en el discurso o en la composición escrita. De aquí que los retóricos antiguos, y con ellos nuestros escritores del siglo XVI, considerasen el lenguaje coloquial como *no numeroso*, y lo opusiesen a la *prosa numerosa* elaborada conscientemente con intención artística. En la prosa narrativa y descriptiva, la preferencia por las unidades breves o largas depende del estilo de cada autor y de las cualidades prosódicas del idioma en que escribe. Según los cuidados recuentos llevados a cabo por Navarro Tomás, tiene la lengua castellana de todos los tiempos una preferencia muy marcada a los grupos fónicos de 5 a 10 sílabas, y entre ellos son más frecuentes los de 7 y 8. La proporción de octosílabos viene a ser el 25 por 100 del total" (Gili y Gaya 1993: 83).

8 The idea that translation can *disappear* through use has been influenced by the phenomenological thought of Martin Heidegger concerning the structure of works of art. Specifically, translation is revealed as useless whenever it is ineffective or a relationship of distrust emerges that makes the translation itself visible, losing its instrumental quality and becoming in itself a *work* capable of taking on a life of its own (Heidegger 1969). Similarly, this idea has also been proposed from a traductological perspective by Lawrence Venuti in *The Translator's Invisibility. A History of Translation* (2008).

9 "Como señala Francisco Rico, el punto de partida de la enseñanza humanista (emprendido por Lorenzo Valla y seguido por Antonio de Nebrija) es el rechazo del corrompido latín medieval para acudir al latín primitivo, el de los clásicos, el verdadero. La fidelidad se convierte en un concepto esencial. El Inca Garcilaso aplica este mismo procedimiento cuando acusa a los cronistas españoles de ignorar la lengua original, el quechua en este caso, y de este modo se atribuye el papel de máxima autoridad en la historia Inca, pues, además de presentarse como descendiente de la nobleza indígena, se ofrece como depositario directo de fuentes de primera mano. . . . Desde el inicio de la obra el Inca Garcilaso se presenta al lector como intérprete ideal y el mejor historiador de la vida de sus antepasados incas, en concreto de los reyes del Perú" (Serna 2000: 43).

10 "Si existe tal barbarie, sin duda es preciso tomarla en el sentido de un pensamiento salvaje, tal como lo rehabilita Claude Lévi-Strauss. Guaman Poma percibe el mundo colonial a través de categorías auténticamente indígenas, que no por eso dejan de estar regidas por una lógica rigurosa. Pero su sistema de pensamiento es diferente al nuestro. La crónica de Guaman Poma no es confusa sino en la medida en que la juzgamos a partir de nuestro criterio occidental; si queremos escapar al vértigo de Raúl Porras Barrenechea debemos restituir el mecanismo particular del pensamiento indígena. Entonces, bajo el caos aparente, se nos revelará la coherencia y el sentido de la obra de Guaman Poma. . . . Guaman Poma ofrece precisamente el ejemplo de una aculturación donde los elementos occidentales están como absorbidos por el sistema de pensamiento indígena que, al precio de una serie de adaptaciones y transformaciones, logra conservar su estructura original" (Wachtel 1973: 166–8).

11 "Al finalizar mi investigación pude concluir que las categorías con que Guaman Poma pensó su pasado eran distintas de aquellas que utilizó al expresarse y por lo tanto distintas a las de sus colegas europeos contemporáneos. Es decir, Guaman al expresarse utiliza conceptos propios de la historiografía europea que le es contemporánea y que le viene a través del lenguaje que escribe, que es el castellano. Esto se advierte en el mismo título de su obra (Nueva Crónica), en los propósitos que dice buscar (conservar en la memoria los hechos de algunos personajes), en su pretendida búsqueda por la autenticidad, en su conceptualización de lo temporal, etc. No obstante, y luego de un examen detenido del manuscrito, advertí que aquellos conceptos habían sido mal digeridos por Guaman Poma, notándose un tono paporretesco propio de nuestros escolares modernos. Por

debajo de aquel ropaje extranjero emergió un pensamiento que se enmarcaba en categorías ajenas al mundo europeo que le era contemporáneo y que bien las podríamos calificar de míticas en el sentido que conllevan una concepción estática del tiempo, un interés en el pasado para justificar el presente y una visión unitaria del cosmos y de las relaciones sociales. Así, a través de Guaman Poma, he podido constatar que las tradiciones orales fueron efectivamente despojadas por los europeos de su sentido original" (Ossio 1973: 156).

12 "para Guaman Poma – apunta Ossio – la conquista no fue un acontecimiento histórico, sino más bien un cataclismo cósmico, un 'pachacuti' según el término andino, por el cual el mundo se había volteado y puesto al revés" (Ossio 1973: 157).

13 "Hasta el momento hemos visto que la imagen que Guaman Poma tiene del desorden de su mundo es dada principalmente por la fusión de los principios 'Hanan' y 'Hurin'. El orden sólo se restauraría manteniendo a ambos principios separados. Es decir, a los españoles separados de los indios para permitir a estos últimos retornar a sus posiciones pasadas alteradas por la conquista. Estas posiciones eran la propiedad de los territorios andinos y sus rangos respectivos dentro del orden jerárquico inmutable" (Ossio 1973: 187).

14 "En seruicio de Dios y de la corona rreal de su Majestad el dicho autor, auiendo entrado a la dicha ciudad de los Reys de Lima, uido atestado de indios ausentes y cimarrones hechos yanaconas [criado], oficiales ciendo mitayos [que presta rabajo], indios uajos y tributarios, se ponía cuello y cí bestía como español y se ponía espada y otros se tresquilaua por no pagar tributo ni seruir en las minas. Ues aquí el mundo al rreués.

Y ací, como uen estos indios ausentes, se salen oros yndios de sus pueblos y no ay quien pague el tibuto ni ay quien cirua en las dichas minas. Y asimismo uido el dicho autor muy muchas yndias putas cargadas de mesticillos y de mulatos, todos con faldelines y butines, escofietas. Aunque son casadas, andan con españoles y negros. Y ancí otros no se quieren casarse con indio ni quiere salir de la dicha ciudad por no dejar la putiría. Y están lleenos [*sic*] de yndios en las dichas rancherías de la dicha ciudad y no ay rremedio. Y hazen ofensa en el seruicio de Dios, nuestro señor, y de su Majestad. Y ancí no multiplican los dichos yndios en este rreyno" (Guaman Poma de Ayala 1987: 1198).

15 "Pura behetría mental" (Porras Barrenechea 1971 [1948]: 6).

16 As is well-known, indigenous languages went through a process of linguistic standardization at the hands of Spanish missionaries. Languages used extensively, such as Nahuatl, Quechua or Tupi-Guaraní, were reduced to dialectical variants as missionaries attempted to construct a simpler and more homogeneous code of communication that would permit them to evangelize more effectively. For indigenous people this was disastrous. As Felipe Guaman Poma de Ayala conveys through one of his drawings of the "Sermon of the priests" in the *New Chronicle*, the discourses of the missionaries were boring because the language that they were using – in this case Quechua – was artificial and bordering on incomprehensible.

17 "La consolidación definitiva de la Colonia, relativamente tardía en el Perú, acaba con una literatura que extrae su fuerza del diálogo cultural entre los 'vencidos' y los 'vencedores'. Durante más de un siglo, ningún texto significativo en español se abre a alguna interacción cultural hispano-quechua. En el contexto de la toma de conciencia 'andina' que supone la cadena de acontecimientos insurreccionales del siglo XVIII surge, finalmente, una 'literatura' (compuesta fundamentalmente por cartas y memoriales de 'caciques principales') que vuelve a plantear críticamente, en términos temáticos, la relación entre 'República de los Indios' y la de los españoles. Los autores de esta literatura, miembros de la aristocracia neoinca, optan, en cuanto a su práctica lingüístico-discursiva, por la sumisión sin reservas a las exigencias de la cultura dominante" (Lienhard 1992: 40).

18 "A muy grandes rasgos, el paradigma lingüístico de la narrativa arguediana, como el de Guaman Poma o de Pachacuti, aunque con grandes diferencias de una obra (o versión) a otra, es tendencialmente 'translingüístico' . . ., abierto a la copresencia o a la imbricación de elementos españoles y quechuas. Los quechismos léxicos y sintácticos, o los

fragmentos discursivos en quechua (sobre todo, en las novelas, la transcripción de can-tos) no aparecen, de ningún modo, en efecto, como 'cuerpos extraños' artificialmente dispuestos en el texto, sino como signos de un código (precisamente) translingüístico. Más que en castellano o en quechua, en efecto, Arguedas escribe en 'andino', si se quiere entender por este término un sistema de expresión múltiple, conflictivo, abierto, dinámico, tal como lo fue constituyendo, poco a poco, la historia andina" (Lienhard 1992: 43).

19 We have taken the notion of an "alternative literature" from the reflections of Martin Lienhard concerning the *traces* of orality in Latin America (Lienhard 1990).

20 The term *oraliture*, used by Chihuailaf, was originally proposed by the African historian Yoro Fall (1992). It is explained by a Chilean Araucanian poet as follows: "I write about this and from things that I have lived through and I am not sitting in judgement over anyone when I say that orality is a device, that the oraliture is a device that gets close to a device, and that literature is a device springing from a device, because in literature one can write about Paris without ever having been to Paris, through research" ("yo escribo sobre cosas y desde cosas que me ha tocado vivir y no estoy haciendo juicio de ningún tipo cuando digo que la oralidad es un artificio, que la oralitura es un artificio que se acerca al artificio y que la literatura es un artificio del artificio, porque uno en la literatura puede escribir sobre París sin haber estado nunca en París, haciendo una investigación") (Viereck Salinas 2012b: 226).

21 Other names for the language are Mapuzungun or Mapuchezungun.

22 This is the description used by many Mapuche-Huilliches poets in interviews I con-ducted between 2009 and 2014 in Chile and Argentina.

23 Sergio Waisman, in his book *Borges and Translation: The Irreverence of the Periphery*, con-ducts a detailed analysis of the translation theory of J.L. Borges. While our proposal identifies – following Ortega y Gasset – the *bad* writing with the literal aesthetic, we have taken the concept of aesthetic *irreverence* associated in the reflections of Waisman with *mistranslations* (from the margins) from his book (Waisman 2005) but within our own framework and perpective.

24 "América se transforma en copia, simulacro que desea asemejarse cada vez más al origi-nal, incluso cuando su originalidad no puede ser encontrada en la copia del modelo original, sino en un origen que fue completamente borrado por los conquistadores. Mediante el exterminio constante de trazos originales y el olvido del origen, el fenó-meno de la duplicación se establece como la única regla válida de civilización" (Silvano 2012: 63).

25 "Como se desprende de nuestro recorrido a través de las manifestaciones de la interac-ción del quechua y del español en la literatura peruana en español, los autores de textos 'andinos' en español manifiestan, a lo largo de la historia andina, tres actitudes lingüístico-literarias básicas: la sumisión total a las normas de la escritura del español (que puede ocul-tar – Tupac Amaru – la protección de la autonomía de la oralidad quechua), el 'mimetismo lingüístico' que aboga a favor de un pluriculturismo radical y, finalmente, la 'traducción semántico-poética' de lo quechua (que auspicia la incorporación una cultura andina 'fil-trada' a la cultura 'universal' de marca occidental). En los últimos decenios, la vigencia de la primera parece haber sufrido (en la literatura propiamente 'andina') un colapso, lo que se podría interpretar como el reconocimiento, por parte de los autores, de la definitiva interpenetración de los dos 'mundos' primitivos, respectivamente 'quechua' y 'occiden-tal'. Actualmente, el 'debate' principal se da, por lo tanto, entre la segunda ('mimetismo lingüístico') y la tercera ('traducción semántico-poética de lo quechua'), a veces en el interior de la obra – Arguedas – de un solo escritor. Este 'debate' traduce, de algún modo, la disyuntiva entre el deseo de anclar poderosamente los textos en el contexto cultural concreto, y el de ofrecerles una salida 'universal': ni más ni menos la disyuntiva cuyos polos representan, casi al comienzo de la Colonia, Guaman Poma de Ayala y Garcilaso de la Vega. Mientras prevalezca, en la cultura peruana, una situación de 'marca' colonial, tal disyuntiva seguirá, sin duda, produciendo sus efectos literarios" (Lienhard 1992: 46–7).

References

Adorno, Rolena. 2000. *Guaman Poma: Writing and Resistance in Colonial Peru*. Austin, TX: University of Texas Press, Austin/Institute of Latin American Studies.

———. 2003. 'A Witness unto Itself: The Integrity of the Autograph Manuscript of Felipe Guaman Poma de Ayala's *El primer nueva corónica y buen gobierno* (1615/1616)', in Rolena Adorno et al. (eds.), *New Studies of the Autograph Manuscript of Felipe Guaman Poma de Ayala's Nueva corónica y buen gobierno*, pp. 7–106. Copenhagen: Museum Tusculanum Press.

Aillapan Cayuleo, Lorenzo. 2003. *Üñumche. Hombre pájaro*. Santiago de Chile: Pehuén.

Apter, Emily. 2006. *The Translation Zone: A New Comparative Literature*. Princeton, NJ: Princeton University Press.

Basnett, Susan, and André Lefevere. 1998. *Constructing Cultures: Essays on Literary Translation*. Clevedon, UK: Multilingual Matters.

Bhabha, Homi, K. 2005. *The Location of Culture*. London and New York: Routledge.

Carrasco, Iván. 1991. 'Textos poéticos de doble registro', *Revista chilena de literatura*, 37: 113–122.

Catalán, Diego. 1997. *Arte poética del romancero oral* (Parte I). Madrid: Siglo XXI.

Colipán, Bernardo. 2005. *Arco de interrogaciones*. Santiago de Chile: LOM.

Cornejo Polar, Antonio. 2003. *Escribir en el aire*. Lima: CELACP, Latinoamericana Editores.

Dussel, Enrique. 1994. *1492: El encubrimiento del Otro*. Bolivia: Plural editores.

Escobar, Alberto. 1995. 'Lenguaje e historia en los Comentarios reales', in *Patio de Letras*, 3: 1–22.

Fall, Yoro. 1992. 'Historiografía, sociedades y conciencia histórica en África', in Celma Agüero (ed.), *África: inventando el futuro*. México: El Colegio de México.

García Canclini, Néstor. 1995. *Hybrid Cultures: Strategies for Entering and Leaving Modernity*. Minneapolis: University of Minnesota Press.

Garcilaso de la Vega, Inca. 1989 [1609]. *Royal Commentaries of the Incas, and General History of Peru (translated with an introduction by Harold V. Livermore)*. Austin: University of Texas Press.

Gentzler, Edwin. 2008. *Translation and Identity in the Americas: New Directions in Translation Theory*. New York: Routledge.

Gili Gaya, Samuel. 1993. *Estudios sobre el ritmo*. Madrid: Istmo.

Heidegger, Martin. 1969. *Sendas perdidas*. Buenos Aires: Losada.

Hernández, Max. 1991. *Memoria del bien perdido: conflicto, identidad y nostalgia en el Inca Garcilaso de la Vega*. Madrid: Siruela.

Huinao, Graciela. 2009. *Walinto*. Santiago de Chile: Cuarto propio.

Jakfalvi Leiva, Susana. 1984. *Traducción, escritura y violencia colonizadora: un estudio de la obra del Inca Garcilaso de la Vega*. Syracuse – Nueva York: Maxwell School of Citizenship and Public Affairs.

Jakobson, Roman. 1959. 'On Linguistics Aspects of Translation', in R. A. Brower (ed.), *On Translation*, pp. 232–239. Cambridge, MA: Harvard University Press.

Kowii, Ariruma. 1988. *Mutsuctsurini*. Quito: Corporación Editora Nacional.

Lara, Jesús. 1947. *La poesía quechua*. México: Fondo de Cultura Económica.

———. 1969. *La literatura de los quechuas: ensayo y antología*. La Paz: Librería y Editorial Juventud.

León-Portilla, Miguel. 1996. *El destino de la palabra: de la oralidad y los códices mesoamericanos a la escritura alfabética*. México: Fondo de Cultura Económica.

———. 2004. *Antigua y nueva palabra: antología de la literatura mesoamericana desde los tiempos antiguos hasta el presente*. México: Aguilar.

Levi-Strauss, Claude. 1966. *The Savage Mind*. London: Weidenfeld & Nicolson.

Lienhard, Martin. 1990. *La voz y su huella: escritura y conflicto étnico-social en América Latina (1492–1988)*. La Habana: Casa de las Américas.

———. 1992. 'La interrelación creativa del quechua y del español en la literatura peruana de lengua española', *Senri Ethnological Studies*, No. 33 (27–49), http://hdl.handle.net/10502/668 (accessed on 12 September 2017).

López-Baralt, Mercedes. 1988. *Icono y conquista: Guaman Poma de Ayala*. Madrid: Hiperión.

Mignolo, Walter D. 2003. *Historias locales/diseños globales: Colonialidad, conocimientos subalternos y pensamiento fronterizo*. Madrid: Akal.

Miranda Rupailaf. 2008. *Pu llimeñ ñi rulpázuamelkaken. Seducción de los venenos*. Santiago de Chile: LOM.

Molina, Cristóbal de (el cuzqueño).1989 [1575]. *Relación de las fábulas y ritos de los incas*. Madrid: Historia 16.

Montemayor, Carlos. 2004. *La voz profunda*. México: Joaquín Mortiz.

O'Gorman, Edmundo. 1993. *La invención de América*. México: Fondo de Cultura Económica.

Olson, David y Torrance, Nancy. 1998. *Cultura escrita y oralidad*. Barcelona: Gedisa.

Ong, Walter. 2002. *Orality and Literacy: The Technologizing of the Word*. London and New York: Routledge.

Ortega, Julio. 1988. 'Para una teoría del discurso latinoamericano: Colón, Garcilaso y el discurso de la abundancia', *Revista de Crítica Literaria Latinoamericana*, 28: 101–115.

Ortega y Gasset. 1983. 'The Misery and Splendour of Translation', *Translation Review*, 13(1).

Ortíz, Fernando. 2002. *Contrapunteo cubano del tabaco y el azúcar*. Madrid: Cátedra.

Ossio, Juan. 1973. 'Guaman Poma: Nueva corónica o carta al Rey. Un intento de aproximación a las categorías del pensamiento del mundo andino', in Juan Ossio (ed.), *Ideología mesiánica del mundo andino*, pp. 155–213. Lima: editorial Ignacio Prado Pastor.

Paz, Octavio. 1992. *El arco y la lira*. México: Fondo de Cultura Económica.

Poma de Ayala, Felipe Guaman. 1987 [1615]. *Nueva corónica y buen gobierno*. Madrid: Historia 16.

Porras Barrenechea, Raúl. 1971 [1948]. *El cronista indio Felipe Huamán Poma de Ayala*. Lima: Mercurio peruano.

Santacruz Pachacuty, Yamqui Sallkamaywa, Juan de. 1968 [1613]. *Relación de antigtüedades deste reyno del Pirú*. Madrid: Biblioteca de Autores Españoles.

Santiago, Silvano. 2012. 'El entre-lugar del discurso latinoamericano', in Mary Luz Estupiñán and Raúl Rodríguez Freire (eds. and trans.), *Una literatura en los trópicos*, pp. 57–76. Escaparate ediciones.

Schleiermacher, Friedrich. 1992 [1813]. 'From *on the Different Methods of Translating*', in Reiner Schulte and John Biguenet (eds.), *Theories of Translation. An Anthology of Essays from Dryden to Derrida*, pp. 36–54. Chicago: The University of Chicago Press.

Segre, Cesare. 1985. *Principios de análisis del texto literario*. Barcelona: Crítica.

Serna, Mercedes. 2000. 'Introducción biográfica y crítica', in Mercedes Serna (ed.), *Comentarios reales*, pp. 9–91. Madrid: Castalia.

Spivak, Gayatri Chakravorty. 1993. 'The Politics of Translation', in M. Barret and A. Phillips (eds.), *Destabilizing Theory: Contemporary Feminist Debates*, pp. 179–200. Cambridge: Polity Press.

Valera, Blas. 1945. *Las costumbres antiguas de Perú y La historia de los Incas*. Lima: Francisco A. Loayza.

Venuti, Lawrence. 2008. *The Translator's Invisibility: A History of Translation*. New York: Routledge.

Viereck Salinas, Roberto. 1995. 'Literatura e Historia: una tensión impuesta por la conquista', *Revista chilena de humanidades*, 16: 13–25.

————. 2003. *La traducción como instrumento y estética de la literatura hispanoamericana del siglo XVI* (Tesis doctoral). Madrid: Universidad Complutense de Madrid.

————. 2012. *La voz letrada: Diálogos con seis poetas amerindios contemporáneos.* Quito: Abya Yala.

Wachtel, Nathan. 1973. *Sociedad e ideología: ensayos de historia y antropología andinas.* Lima: Instituto de estudios peruanos.

Waisman, Sergio. 2005. *Borges and Translation: The Irreverence of the Periphery.* Lewisburg: Bucknell University Press.

Waldman, Gilda. 2003. 'El florecimiento de la literatura indígena actual en México. Contexto social, significado e importancia', in José Emilio Ordóñez Cifuentes (ed.), *El derecho a la lengua de los pueblos indígenas*, pp. 63–72. México: UNAM-Instituto de Investigaciones Jurídicas.

Zuidema, R. Tom. 1964. *The Ceque system of Cuzc: The Social Organization of the Capital of the Inca.* Leiden: International Archives of Ethnography.

5

"HOW TO WRITE AN ORAL CULTURE"

Indigenous tradition in contemporary Canadian native writing

Geoffrey V. Davis[1]

> Did you ever wonder how it is
> we imagine the world in the way we do,
> how it is we imagine ourselves,
> if not through our stories.
>
> *(King,* The Truth about Stories *95)*

The Black British author of the novel *Small Island*, Andrea Levy, when asked in a recent interview about her debt to the oral culture of her Caribbean origins, surprised her listeners by remarking that in her home, the only manifestation of a storytelling tradition had been the long-running soap *Coronation Street* on her family's television set.[2] This witticism might be taken to suggest that in some societies the oral tradition is no longer a source of creative inspiration and has been replaced by more modern modes of communication. Quite the opposite impression will have been gained by anyone who witnessed the inauguration of Nelson Mandela as president of South Africa in 1994, since the ceremony was preceded by a traditional praise poem spoken by the "people's poet," Mzwakhe Mbuli. In South Africa, it would seem oral culture is very much alive and there are numerous examples of its continuing to be practiced. One only has to recall the example of Alfred Qabula, a Durban migrant worker, who with his "Praise poem to FOSATU" revitalized the form of the traditional isiZulu *izibongi* he had heard as a child as a highly effective tool of mobilization during the trade union campaigns of the 1980s.[3]

★★★

My interest in orality was aroused primarily through the recent series of Chotro conferences held here in India. The word "chotro" in the Bhil language means "a place where villagers gather" or a "public platform" (Devy et al. [ed.], *Voice and Memory* xiii). Accordingly, it was our intention to bring together indigenous people – Adivasis from India, Maori from New Zealand, Aboriginals from Australia and First Nations from Canada – as well as scholars interested in their cultures and socio-political situation as "an exercise in reducing our collective ignorance about the communities generally described as 'indigenous'" (Devy et al. [eds.], *Voice and Memory* xiv).

The topics discussed came from the fields of literature, linguistics, language policy, history, sociology, media, film studies, theatre, music and visual culture. Some idea of the astonishing range of presentations which these conferences generated may be gleaned from the two volumes of proceedings already published.[4] These included popular culture in Malawi, endangered languages in Kenya, the situation of indigenous women in New Zealand, ethnic life writing in Canada, language revitalization in Ireland, indigenous cultural festivals in Australia, dramatizations of Mexican indigenous history and Adivasi Museums in India.

Orality played a significant role in the Chotro project. Thus, we heard papers on orature in South India, oral traditions in Kenya, the traditional folksongs of the Bodo, gender and empowerment in the folklore of Garhwal, the oral cultural expression of the Zulus, and so on. While many of the speakers dealt with oral tradition amongst indigenous peoples, others focused on the literary transformation of orality in recent written texts. One presentation which particularly impressed me was by the Métis scholar Jo-Ann Episkenew from the First Nations University in Regina, Saskatchewan (Canada). It was devoted to "Contemporary Indigenous Literatures in Canada: Healing from Historical Trauma"[5] and I shall return to this paper later on, since it significantly informs my own presentation today.

★★★

In the present chapter I wish to examine some of the ways contemporary indigenous literature has used, or in some cases transformed, oral culture. In the main I shall use Canadian examples: *Halfbreed*, the autobiography of Maria Campbell; *In Search of April Raintree*, the autobiographical fiction by Beatrice Culleton; *Three Day Road*, Joseph Boyden's novel on Cree participation in the First World War; and *Kiss of the Fur Queen*, the novel by Tomson Highway. Following the thesis put forward by Episkenew, I shall be focusing – in part – on how indigenous storytelling is being used as a means of healing the historical traumas arising from colonialism.

★★★

In recent decades, much has been done in many countries towards rediscovering oral traditions. In Australia, Canada and New Zealand, anthologies of indigenous writing have been published which consciously include orature. In Australia, a volume like *Paperbark: A Collection of Black Australian Writings*,[6] which spanned the period 1840 to the present day, memorably brought together Aboriginal work from all over the country, including transcriptions of oral literature. In Canada, a volume like *An Anthology of Canadian Native Literature in English* made traditional orature available in print to a wide readership.[7] In New Zealand, Witi Ihimaera's five-volume collection *Te Ao marama* presented written and oral literature by Maori since 1980.[8] The editors of these anthologies have, to borrow a phrase from Terry Goldie (the co-editor of the Canadian anthology), done "a little bit to get the Native voice heard" ("Preface: Two Voices" in *An Anthology of Canadian Native Literature*, xii). The impact such publications can have on native writers themselves has been acknowledged by Daniel David Moses[9] who, in introducing the Canadian volume, speaks of how "the example of traditional Native story-telling, its orality" is for him, as a native writer, "a freeing thing" ("Preface: Two Voices," xiii).

That it has proved necessary to "rediscover" the oral tradition is due in large part to the impact of colonialism, which sought to replace traditional indigenous myths by new settler myths.

The Canadian Jo-Ann Episkenew, for example, wonders

> what happens . . . to peoples of oral cultures if invaders wrest control of the education of their children . . . systematically de-educating the children so that they lose their ability to communicate in their native languages and, therefore, lose access to those foundational narratives of their people?
>
> *(Taking Back Our Spirits 4)*

She speaks for many in deploring the way the Canadian educational system, and particularly the residential school system which many native children experienced, worked to undermine traditional cultures and languages. This has remained a constant theme in Canadian native society.[10] Chief Roger William of the Xeni Gwet'in nation of British Columbia, for example, criticizes the way the process of passing on knowledge to children through story was "broken by the residential school experience" (quoted by Mildon in Hulan and Eigenbrod 91). The native scholar Andrea Bear Nicholas of the Maliseet First Nation believes that "our oral traditions [have] been outlawed, stolen and disfigured" (Hulan and Eigenbrod 33).

★★★

In the introduction to their study *Aboriginal Oral Traditions*, Hulan and Eigenbrod define their subject as follows: "Oral traditions form the foundation of Aboriginal societies, connecting speaker and listener in communal experience and uniting past and present in memory" (7). If we look at statements by Canadian native writers, we will find much to corroborate this view. Oral narratives are "passed down through the generations, [they] explained the history of the peoples, reinforced cultural practices and norms, and articulated the peoples' relationship with the world" (Episkenew, *Taking Back Our Spirits* 4). They constitute "the traditional means of preserving and transmitting traditional knowledge" (Greg Young-Ing in Hulan and Eigenbrod 61) and they serve as "vessels for passing along teachings, medicines, and practices that can assist members of the collective" (Kovach 95).

That the functions of oral narratives, of story, were so fundamental to the fabric of aboriginal societies no doubt contributed to the fact that they survived the impact of cultural imperialism in the colonial period. Orality should thus not be seen as a mere precursor of the written text, as something "we slough off . . . and leave behind" as we "move from the cave to the condo," as King puts it (*The Truth about Stories* 100); it continues to thrive and to inform evolving indigenous cultural practices. Indeed, as King maintains, native oral and written literatures "occupy the same space, the same time" (*The Truth about Stories* 101–2).

What interests me in this paper is the way native writers have set out to integrate traditional orature in their writing in recent decades, so that the texts they produce retain characteristics of oral culture. As such, they are examples of what Susan Gingell has usefully termed "textualized orality" (Gingell, quoted in Hulan and Eigenbrod 7), that is, hybrid productions which mix the oral and the written, the native and the Western, and work with innovative narrative strategies. The genre known in both Canada and Australia as life-writing, for example, lends itself, as we shall see, particularly well to native writers, who "wish to allow modalities of oral and written composition to coexist within the text" (Grossman in Hulan and Eigenbrod 114).[11]

★★★

There are, of course, numerous examples in the written literatures in English the world over of the shaping influence of orality. In some parts of the world, Africa for example, orality "remains predominant." Not for nothing does the critic Abiola Irele suggest that "oral literature . . . represents the basic intertext of the African imagination" (Irele 56). "The oral tradition has," according to him, "come to govern the processes of creation in the work of . . . African writers" (Irele 62). Evidence for this can be found across the continent: in Chinua Achebe's novel *Things Fall Apart*, which integrates African speech patterns, folktales and proverbs; in Chenjerai Hove's fiction *Bones*, which draws on the Shona oral tradition of Zimbabwe; in Bessie Head's stories of rural life in Botswana; or in Sindiwe Magona's Xhosa storytelling techniques in her South African autobiographies.

In New Zealand and Australia, too, indigenous writers have had abundant recourse to the oral traditions of their countries. One thinks of Witi Ihimaera, who asserts in his "Author Notes" to *The Whale Rider*, that "Maori and Polynesian stories come from a different source, a different inventory than western tradition" (173), and thus incorporates Maori mythology and language into the story of Paikea; or of Jack Davis, whose play *The Dreamers* proceeds from the oral tradition embodied in the Aboriginal creation story of the Dreamtime; and of Sally Morgan, who in her famous autobiography *My Place* records how in retrieving the Aboriginal family history of which she had long been unaware she used the oral histories of family members to tell it.

It is, however, to Canada that I wish to turn my attention. In the same manner as the indigenous writers just referred to, contemporary Canadian writers – be they First Nations, Métis or Inuit – draw on traditional oral culture. Their writings abound in instructive examples of the many productive ways this has been done.

★★★

By way of introduction, I want first to turn to the important paper by Jo-Ann Episkenew on "Contemporary Indigenous Literatures in Canada: Healing from Historical Trauma" I mentioned earlier (Episkenew in Devy et al. [eds.], *Indigeneity. Culture and Representation* 77–86), since this will provide a useful framework for my discussion.[12] Episkenew first offers a damning political analysis of the impact of colonialism on indigenous people in Canada, dismissing white superiority as a foundational myth of settler society which has had traumatic effects on the health and well-being of indigenous people (77–8) and has inflicted a "soul wound" on them (78). The pressure to acculturate to settler society exerted over centuries on indigenous people (78) has resulted in what she terms "postcolonial stress disorder" and brought about social abuses such as poverty, alcoholism and violence.

Indigenous literature must, in her view, challenge the "master narrative" of white settlers in Canada through articulating a "counterstory" which will redress the falsities of an imposed history from a native perspective. Indigenous literature for her is a form of counter-discourse (76). Stories and indigenous literature in general have "healing power" (76). "Indigenous people," she says, "have believed in the healing power of language and stories since time immemorial and today's Indigenous writes continue to apply this belief to the creation of works of literature and theatre in English" (80). When indigenous people articulate their own narrative of their own history, the effect is therapeutic and transformative. It brings people out of their isolation, establishes a commonality of experience and provides people with the means to engage with historical trauma.

Episkenew does not criticize the use of English by native writers, since the language has become the *lingua franca* for many indigenous people and since its use has, in her view, enabled them "to create literary works that aspire to accomplish many of the same aims as the oral stories did: to explain the history of the people, to buttress cultural practices and norms, and to articulate their relationship with the world" (80). The language also offers them the opportunity to reach a wider readership and thus to educate contemporary Canadian society.

Episkenew's thesis may be validated by reference to the work of numerous native writers. Jeannette Armstrong (Okanagan), for example, sees her writing "as part of a healing process for my children and my people who have been so damaged, so brutalized" (quoted by Hubbard in Hulan and Eigenbrod 139). Catherine Martin (Mi'kmaw), holds a similar view:

> The telling of the story as a way to begin a healing process is one of the most powerful methods that I know to help begin a dialogue over what many have been silent about. . . . The truths are within our collective memories, the identity that we so desperately need in order to heal our communities

after five hundred years can be found through the process of telling our own stories, in our own way, from our own perspective, our own eyes and from our collective memories as a people.

(Hulan and Eigenbrod 55, 58–9)

Daniel David Moses (Delaware) relates healing to the basic function of the native writer as artists:

> One of the words that always comes up in Native gatherings, and particularly among Native artists, is that it is part of our jobs as native artists to help people heal. Whether we're talking about native people taught by residential schools or whether we're talking about white people who've just been in a car accident, that's what we see as our job; we're looking for the meaning of life to explain the injustices of reality.
>
>

("Preface: Two Voices" in An Anthology of Canadian Native Literature, *xvii)*

Qwo-Li Driskill (Cherokee) sees in the theatre an opportunity to contribute to healing the kind of historical trauma caused, for instance, by the experience of residential schools: "Theatre . . . holds potential for our collective healing by offering a medium to tell our stories" (Driskill in Hulan and Eigenbrod 156, 165). Thomas King (Cherokee) puts the issue in a nutshell: Stories are a survival mechanism: "they help keep me alive" (*The Truth about Stories* 119).

★★★

Canadian native writers integrate and transform oral culture in the written text in different ways. One of them is indigenous autobiography, which has also been one of the prime genres chosen "to help Indigenous readers heal from . . . trauma" (Episkenew, *Taking Back Our Spirits* 73). I want, therefore, to look briefly at two works which fall into that category: Maria Campbell's *Halfbreed* (1973) and Beatrice Culleton's *In Search of April Raintree* (1983).

Maria Campbell is Métis, that is, of mixed race, the daughter of a native mother and a Scottish father. She writes not only for herself and for her own people, but also for non-native readers in the wider society. In a much quoted passage, she has stated:

> I write this for all of you, to tell you what it is like to be a Halfbreed woman in our country. I want to tell you about the joys and sorrows, the oppressing poverty, the frustration and the dreams.
>
>

(Introduction 8)

And, some pages later, after having begun to describe what her people experienced as "a miserable life of poverty which held no hope for the future" (13) she adds: "I am not bitter. I have passed that stage. I only want to say: this is what it was like, this is what it is still like" (13).

The book, which covers the period 1940–66 and primarily documents the problems of native people in an urban environment, is essentially the story of Campbell's own life of poverty, racial discrimination and sexual abuse resulting in alcoholism, drug addiction and prostitution. At the same time, however, it is an uplifting story of a healing process which has much to teach about how this was accomplished. The first-person narrative gives the text immediacy and, one might argue, lends it the character of an oral narrative.

From her traditional upbringing to her commitment as an adult to the native movement in Alberta, Campbell's story begins and ends with the culture of her people, the Métis. From the start, she presents herself as very much grounded in the oral tradition. As she has recalled in a later interview, in her community everyone was "a different kind of storyteller":

> My dad was a storyteller. There was a young man when I was growing up, and he was a hunting-story teller. Then there were particular stories that were told only by certain people and at certain times of the year. . . . My great auntie and my grandmother were midwives, so there were certain kinds of stories they told. And then there was the fiddle player who was a story teller. There was a sort of village fool or idiot . . . who was also a storyteller.
>
> *(Lutz 54)*

Accordingly, in *Halfbreed*, she recalls how her parents "told the stories of our people – who they were, where they came from, and what they had done. Many were legends handed down from father to son" (20); she recalls how her great grandmother Cheechum "often told me stories of the [1884] Rebellion [by Louis Riel] and of the Halfbreed people" (15), how on summer evenings the families would gather around the campfire and tell stories, and the children "would creep out to sit in the background and listen" (34). This practice was interrupted when she was sent to residential school and found that she was not allowed to even speak Cree (44).

Interrupted, but not broken, for Campbell is sustained throughout her early life by the figure of her great grandmother, Cheechum, who lives to the age of 104. It is she who ensures the influence of native culture in Campbell's life and in the book. "Cheechum speaks only Cree, eschews Christianity and practises her Cree spiritual traditions and is able to live off the land" (Episkenew, *Taking Back Our Spirits* 82). She becomes Campbell's role model: she tells her stories, instils native wisdom and a philosophy of self-reliance into her (72–3), and teaches her to use her time on Earth constructively. It is the memory of Cheechum's teaching that gets Campbell through some of the darkest moments of her difficult life when, for example, she suffers withdrawal symptoms from drug addiction (124).

★★★

As Episkenew reminds us, Campbell's autobiography, *Halfbreed*, "is credited with giving birth to contemporary Indigenous literature in Canada . . . [and] has inspired other Indigenous people to tell their stories" (*Taking Back Our Spirits* 76, 77). One such person was Beatrice Culleton, like Campbell, a Métis. Her book, *In Search of April Raintree*, differs from Campbell's in that it is fiction rather than autobiography, but it nevertheless relies heavily on aspects of Culleton's own life. Her parents were alcoholics, she was brought up in a foster-home and both of her sisters committed suicide. For the author, writing the book was therapeutic.[13] It has also proved so for others. The book is a powerful social document. In a letter to the author, Campbell described it as

> a powerful story because, with gentleness, it deals with the sickness in our society and our people. It is the kind of writing that will begin the healing of our people and help a dominant white society understand and feel the lives of a people it almost destroyed.
>
> *(prefaced to Culleton,* In Search of April Raintree 7*)*[14]

In Search of April Raintree is an account of the lives of two sisters, April and Cheryl, who are forcibly removed from their alcoholic parents and placed first in an orphanage run by nuns and then in a series of separate foster homes. The novel traces the identity struggle and the traumatic experiences of both sisters: they are exploited by foster parents, their mother commits suicide, April is gang-raped, Cheryl succumbs to alcoholism and prostitution, and eventually commits suicide herself. Faced with this tragedy, April, who is lighter of skin colour, has sought advancement through assimilation into white society, and has long been in denial about the plight of the Métis, resolves to struggle for the betterment of her own people, with whom she finally identifies (228).

Although this novel does not foreground oral culture as such, it is, like *Halfbreed*, told with the authenticity of the first-person voice; it engages with the standard narrative of Canadian history, which Cheryl furiously disputes as false since it distorts the role of the Métis (57–8); and it shows how April only succeeds in gaining some understanding for her situation in the DeRosier foster home when she decides to actually tell her story (82–3). The scene in which Cheryl and April attend an "Indian Pow Wow" is particularly significant.[15] For both of them, participation in the event raises the issue of their attitudes towards Indians and of their identification with their own people. Cheryl delivers an emotional oral narrative, condemning whites for the evils they have wrought, extolling native wisdom, and mourning the dying of the land and the people (168–70), while the more sober April, listening "to the songs and tales of Indian singers" crucially recognizes that "for the first time in my life, I felt as if all of that was part of me, as if I was a part of it" (166).

In Search of April Raintree thus ends, as does *Halfbreed*, with the narrator identifying with her culture and her people, and finding her mission in life.

★★★

Joseph Boyden's novel *Three Day Road* is important in the present context both because it demonstrates how oral narrative may be integrated into a written text and because it illustrates how, in the manner described by Episkenew, indigenous storytelling may be used as a means of healing historical trauma – in this case, the trauma of war.

The novel, which has bilingual chapter titles in Cree and English, and frequently has recourse to Cree language, is structured around two parallel, alternating narratives told by two native voices. The first narrative, that of Xavier, tells of two childhood friends, Xavier himself and Elijah, Cree natives who volunteer to serve in World War I and fight with the Canadian forces in the major campaigns on the Somme at Vimy Ridge and Passchendaele. The second narrative, that of Xavier's Aunt Niska, tells of how after the war she transports him, wounded and with his supply of morphine running out, by canoe back towards his home country in Northern Ontario where, the reader assumes, he has come to die.

The account of Xavier's experiences takes the form of the memories which go through his mind as he lies for three days in Aunt Niska's canoe. He recalls the trench warfare in Flanders in all its terrible reality, sparing the reader none of the horrors of war. He remembers how, as accomplished hunters and marksmen, he and Elijah were deployed as snipers, using the skills acquired in the Canadian bush to survive in no-man's land. He records his own growing revulsion at the number of kills they were notching up, while Elijah, increasingly dependent on drugs, came to love killing and indulged in ever greater brutality, even to the extent of murdering two of his fellow soldiers. Elijah's moral decline leads to a final struggle to his death at the hands of Xavier, after which Xavier himself lost a leg in a shelling.

Throughout the novel, this narrative is counterpointed by that of Aunt Niska, a native diviner who still lives in the bush, following the traditional way of life. We learn how during Xavier's youth and in resistance to what was being drummed into him at a Catholic residential school, she had taken it upon herself to teach him indigenous knowledge. It is on such knowledge that she now has to rely in attempting to save his life by bringing him back spiritually into the world he left when he went off to the war. Not fully understanding what he has gone through, and knowing nothing of the place where his suffering was inflicted, she decides to try to heal him by telling him stories. By the end of the novel, after a ritual of healing, Xavier is restored and can return to his people.

Interpolated between the episodes Xavier remembers from the war, Aunt Niska's stories are intended to heal him. Since Xavier cannot yet speak to her, she decides to speak to him in the belief that "maybe some of the poison that courses through him might be released in this way" (88). When he initially cannot take food, she resolves to "feed him with my story instead" (130). So she tells him stories of the history of the Cree, of her own childhood growing up in the traditional manner, of their earlier nomadic life together, of his first hunting expedition, of the residential schools and of how she stole him back from the nuns so that he could be raised "in the old ways" (216), and of how she was unable to prevent him from volunteering for the war. *Three Day Road* is remarkable for the storytelling techniques Boyden adopts. Not only does he integrate traditional oral narrative into the novel, he also departs from the strict chronology which he had adhered to in the first draft of the story. His dissatisfaction with that draft lay in the fact that he felt he was inappropriately "applying a Western style of storytelling to an aboriginal story."[16] So he chose a less linear, more circular mode of narration which would take account of the Cree notion that life is "an endless circle of birth and life and death and rebirth,"[17] and would reflect the Cree manner of storytelling.[18] Thus, the novel with its twin narrative strands, now begins near the end of the story when the war is already over and Xavier is back in Canada, and it then goes back over earlier events until it again reaches its starting point in the present. It thus takes Xavier – and the reader – full circle.

★★★

The final work I wish to discuss briefly is Tomson Highway's novel *Kiss of the Fur Queen*. This is a work which was greatly inspired by his own life: his birth in 1951 in a tent on a trap-line in remote northern Manitoba, where his father made a living hunting, fishing and trapping; the first six years of his life spent living in the traditional nomadic way, speaking only Cree; the period he spent, pursuant to the Canadian government's then policy of forced assimilation of natives, at a residential school run by the Roman Catholic Church; his experience of sexual abuse by priests; the musical training he received which started him off on a career which would take him to the Royal Academy of Music in England and would see him envisaging a career as a concert pianist; his success as a dramatist with plays such as *The Rez Sisters* and *Dry Lips Oughta Move to Kapuskasing*; the collaboration on the choreography of the plays of his brother, the dancer René Highway; and the latter's death from AIDS in 1990 at the age of 36. Writing the novel was an act of healing for Highway, who "wrote the work to purge anger and bitterness over the abuse he and his brother Rene suffered at the residential schools"[19] and in an effort to come to terms with his brother's early death.

Kiss of the Fur Queen is a highly innovative work. It tells the story of two brothers, born Champion and Ooneemeetoo but re-baptized by Catholic priests as Jeremiah and Gabriel, who grow up in northern Manitoba, are sent to residential school where they are sexually abused by priests, study in Winnipeg and later become artists – the former a pianist, the latter a dancer. The novel ends with their joint work for the theatre and with the death of Gabriel.

At the core of the novel is severe criticism of the residential schools maintained by the Roman Catholic Church, particularly of the sexual abuse to which native children were subjected, which is graphically described (72). Highway is also critical of the brutal methods used to acculturate the children to the norms of Western society – denying them their native names (53), forbidding them use of their own languages (70) and cutting off their long hair (51), for example. Although the brothers do acquire English and later practice Western art forms, they continue to communicate with one another in Cree and, as artists, maintain their native culture.

Highway's desire to preserve native heritage is apparent in this novel in his recourse to mythology, his use of Cree language, his integration of traditional storytelling and his concept of narrative structure. As in his plays, Highway introduces the figure of the native trickster, without whose "continued presence" he asserts, "the core of Indian culture would be gone forever" ("A Note on the Trickster" in *Kiss of the Fur Queen*, ii). For the non-native reader, he explains that this figure is "essentially a comic, clownish sort of character, his role is to teach us about the nature and the meaning of existence on the planet Earth; he straddles the consciousness of man and that of God, the Great Spirit." "Neither exclusively male nor exclusively female, or . . . both simultaneously," the trickster appears here in the guise of the Fur Queen. She exercises many functions: celebrating Abraham's victory in the dog-sled race, watching over the births of the brothers (21), inspiring Jeremiah in the piano competition (214), accompanying the death of the brothers' father (228) and later of Gabriel himself (306).

As Thomas King has reminded us: "Many [Native people] no longer speak their Native language, a gift of colonialism" (*The Truth about Stories* 55). Highway's use of the language, and it is of course his own first language, is therefore, as in the case of Boyden, an act of preservation, which makes the reader aware of the living reality of the language.[20] There are numerous examples in the novel of Highway's delight in the possibilities and ambiguities of multiple language use: native incomprehension of "babbling" in English (6); Jeremiah's inability to understand the "meaningless" Latin of the Church (37); Gabriel's comic attempts to interpret "the nonsensical syllables" of prayers (71); their mother's fluency in three native languages, but not at all in English (92); and Jeremiah's relishing "of the taste of Cree on his tongue" when he returns to his community (88).

It is soon clear in this novel that Highway intends to celebrate the art of storytelling. In the "Acknowledgements" he expresses

> heartfelt thanks . . . to the storytellers of my people, the myth-makers, the weavers of dreams. For it is on their shoulders that we, the current and upcoming generation of native writers, stand. Without them, we would have no way of telling our stories and, ultimately, no stories to tell.
>
> *(iv)*

And indeed, in the novel there is much evidence of the extent of this debt. From the very beginning, it is clear that Highway does not intend to confine himself to a realist narrative style. Opening with the dog-sled race, which the brothers' father Abraham wins as the first native person to do so, and with the crowning of the Fur Queen at the Beauty Pageant, which likewise forms part of the 1951 Oopaskooyak Trappers Festival, the narrative is soon transformed into an account of the fabulous birth of baby Champion (Jeremiah). The Fur Queen floats up to the sky, the stars of her tiara become the seven stars of the Great Bear and from them emerges a human foetus who tumbles to Earth as "ghost baby" (12) and "star-born child" (17) before landing in the snow and running through the forest to finally leap on to the belly of its mother to be born. Three years later, Ooneemeetoo (Gabriel) arrives in similar fashion. And in both cases, of course, the process is overseen by the Fur Queen waving her magic wand (21, 35). Or so, at least, will Abraham tell his sons in the story of their birth years later (12). He is a traditional storyteller, who will tell his children

> of arguments he had had with the fierce north wind, of how a young pine tree had corrected his direction on his homeward journey and thus saved all their lives, [and] of how the northern lights had whispered truth into his dreams.
>
> *(104)*

And when they grow up, they, who have inherited his storytelling ability, will "never tire of telling . . . yarn[s], which, as the years progressed became ever more outrageous, exaggerated, as is the Cree way of telling stories, of making myth" (38).

The author's adoption of a circular structure is a feature of the narrative which this novel shares with *Three Day Road*. Denis Johnston has shown how in his plays Highway used "cyclical character journeys" to "signal redemption" (Johnston, "Lines and Circles" 255, 256). Something similar happens here, most significantly at the death of Gabriel, where sections of the opening chapter of the novel describing his father Abraham reaching the end of the sled race and encountering the Fur Queen are taken up once again to depict Gabriel's own final meeting with her, where she accompanies him to his death (10, 11; 303, 305, 306).

One final point should be made about this remarkable novel, and that is the innovative use the story of Jeremiah and Gabriel makes of both Tomson and René's Highway's own experience as artists. The novel traces both their artistic careers, beginning with early childhood, when Gabriel is given the native name Ooneemeetoo, which means "dancer" (35), and when the three-year old Jeremiah is given a miniature accordion (23); it then goes on to depict their first encounters with Western art forms, when Jeremiah first hears the piano at residential school (56) and Gabriel first sees a performance by the Royal Winnipeg Ballet (142). As a pianist and a dancer, it is through their art that the brothers are able to devise a syncretic form based on traditional Cree storytelling culture and Western classical music. The best example of this is the play "Ulysses Thunderchild," which Jeremiah writes and Gabriel directs. Inspired by Joyce's *Ulysses*, the play is a modern version of the Cree story of the Son of Ayash, which, Jeremiah asserts, is the "closest thing the Cree have to their own Ulysses." "If James Joyce can do 'one day in the life of an Irishman in Dublin, 1903'," he asks "why can't I do 'one day in the life of a Cree man in Toronto, 1984'?" (277). The success of this play and of the subsequent "Chachagathoo, the Shaman," both of which blend traditional native and modern Western cultural practice, recalls

Highway's own highly innovative contribution to modern Canadian theatrical performance with his award-winning plays *The Rez Sisters* and *Dry Lips Oughta Move to Kapuskasing*.

★★★

The texts I have been discussing constitute a reinterpretation of oral tradition. Through their innovative use of orality and indigenous culture they demonstrate that the oral tradition is a living tradition. They show how in various ways a native universe can be created in fiction. They perform a social and pedagogical function for their readers, native and non-native. They point the way to healing for those who have suffered trauma through oppression and discrimination. And in the words of the ever-perceptive Thomas King, they show that "the truth about stories is that that is all we are" (*The Truth about Stories* 32).

Notes

1 I have borrowed the useful phrase "how to write an oral culture" from Abiola Irele, who used it to refer to the problem of African authors writing in a European language. It applies equally well to Canadian native writers like Tomson Highway, whose first language is Cree rather than English. Cf. Abiola Irele, "The African Imagination," in *Research in African Literatures*, 21, 1 (Spring 1990): 61.

2 The interview took place at the conference "On whose terms: Critical Negotiations in Black Culture and the Arts," which was held at Goldsmiths College, University of London, 13–14 March 2008.

3 Duncan Brown, who laments the lack of critical discussion of the oral tradition in South Africa, has published an illuminating essay on both poets. See "South African Oral Performance Poetry of the 1980s. Mzwakhe Mbuli and Alfred Qabula," in *New Writing from South Africa*, ed. Emmanuel Ngara (London: James Currey, 1996): 120–48. Brown also refers us to the historical examples of writers such as S. Mqhayi, A.C. Jordan, H.I.E. Dhlomo, Mazisi Kunene and B.W. Vilakazi.

4 These are: G. N. Devy, Geoffrey V. Davis and K.K. Chakravarty (ed.). *Indigeneity, Culture and Representation* (New Delhi: Orient Blackswan, 2009); G. N. Devy, Geoffrey V. Davis and K.K. Chakravarty (eds.). *Voice and Memory. Indigenous Imagination and Expression* (New Delhi: Orient Blackswan, 2011). Three more volumes are forthcoming.

5 This paper is to be found in G. N. Devy, Geoffrey V. Davis and K.K. Chakravarty (ed.). *Indigeneity. Culture and Representation* (New Delhi: Orient Blackswan, 2009): 75–86. Episkenew's ideas were later elaborated in her doctoral thesis entitled *Taking Back Our Spirits. Indigenous Literature, Public Policy, and Healing* (Winnipeg: University of Manitoba Press, 2009).

6 *Paperbark: A Collection of Black Australian Writings,* ed. Jack Davis, Mudrooroo Narogin, Stephen Muecke and Adam Shoemaker (St. Lucia: University of Queensland Press, 1990). See also anthologies published later such as *Those Who Remain Will Always Remember. An Anthology of Aboriginal*, ed. Ann Brewster, Angeline O'Neill and Rosemary van den Berg (Fremantle, WA: Fremantle Arts Centre Press, 2000) and *Indigenous Australian Voices. A Reader,* ed. Jennifer Sabbioni, Kay Schaffer and Sidonie Smith (New Brunswick, NJ & London: Rutgers University Press, 1998).

7 Daniel David Moses and Terry Goldie (eds.). *An Anthology of Canadian Native Literature in English* (Toronto. Oxford University Press, 1992). See also volumes published later such as *Native Canadian Fiction and Drama*, ed. Daniel David Moses (Holstein, ON: Exile editions, 2010); Tantoo Cardinal et al., *Our Story. Aboriginal Voices on Canada's*

      Past (Toronto: Anchor Canada, 2005); Thomas King, *All My Relations. An Anthology of Contemporary Canadian Native Fiction* (Toronto: McClelland & Stewart 1990).

8 *Te Ao marama* / selected and edited by Witi Ihimaera (Auckland: Reed 1992–96). 5 vols.

9 See also Thomas King, who emphasizes the importance of the influence of the oral tradition on many native writers in his Introduction to *All My Relations*, xii.

10 This is particularly true of the issue of residential schools. Just how important it still remains is shown by Prime Minister Stephen Harper's statement of apology (11 June 2008) and by the visit of indigenous leaders to the Pope, who prayed for healing (Communiqué, Holy See Press Office, 29 April 2009).

11 Grossman is also the editor of *Blacklines: Contemporary Critical Writing by Indigenous Australians* (see References).

12 Episkenew is the author of the first doctoral thesis on Canadian native writing by a Canadian native person (see References).

13 See Culleton, quoted in Episkenew, *Taking Back Our Spirits*, 113.

14 There are two versions of this text. The original is *In Search of April Raintree* (1983); the edition revised for school use is *April Raintree* (1984).

15 The event depicted is Indian rather than Métis.

16 "An Interview with Joseph Boyden," in *Penguin Reading Guides: Three Day Road.* http://us.penguingroup.com/static/rguides/us/three_day_road.html.

17 Tomson Highway, *Comparing Mythologies*. The Charles R. Bronfman Lecture in Canadian Studies 2002 (Ottawa: University of Ottawa Press, 2003): 44.

18 Kovach explains: "it is the nature and structure of story that causes difficulties for non-tribal systems due to its divergence from the temporal narrative structure of Western culture. For tribal stories are not meant to be oriented within the linearity of time" (95–6).

19 Linda Morra, "Tomson Highway," in *Dictionary of Literary Biography. Twenty-first Century Canadian Writers* 334 (Detroit, MI: Gale, 2007): 100–4.

20 *Kiss of the Fur Queen* includes a Cree glossary (307–10).

References

Achebe, Chinua. *Things Fall Apart* (London: Heinemann, 1958).

Armstrong, Jeannette (ed.). *Looking at the Words of Our People: First Nations Analysis of Literature* (Penticton, B.C.: Theytus Books, 1993).

Bear Nicholas, Andrea. "The Assault on Aboriginal Oral Traditions: Past and Present," in Hulan and Eigenbrod (eds.), *Aboriginal Oral Traditions*, 13–43.

Boyden, Joseph. *Three Day Road* (2005; Toronto: Penguin, 2006).

———. "Interview," in *Penguin Reading Guides: Three Day Road.* http://us.penguingroup.com/static/rguides/us/three_day_road.html.

Brewster, Ann, Angeline O'Neill and Rosemary van den Berg (eds.). *Those Who Remain Will Always Remember. An Anthology of Aboriginal Writing* (Fremantle, WA: Fremantle Arts Centre Press, 2000).

Brown, Duncan. "South African Oral Performance Poetry of the 1980s: Mzwakhe Mbuli and Alfred Qabula," in Emmanuel Ngara (ed.), *New Writing from South Africa* (London: James Currey, 1996): 120–148.

Campbell, Maria. *Halfbreed* (1973; Lincoln & London: University of Nebraska Press, 1982).

Cardinal, Tantoo et al. *Our Story. Aboriginal Voices on Canada's Past* (Toronto: Anchor Canada, 2005).

Culleton, Bertrice. *April Raintree* (Winnipeg, MB: Peguis Publishers, 1984), revised edition.

———. *In Search of April Raintree* (Winnipeg, MB: Peguis Publishers, 1983).

Davis, Jack. *The Dreamers* (Sydney: Currency Press, 1982).

Devy, G. N., Geoffrey V. Davis and K.K. Chakravarty (eds.). *Voice and Memory. Indigenous Imagination and Expression* (New Delhi: Orient Blackswan, 2011).

———. *Indigeneity. Culture and Representation* (New Delhi: Orient Blackswan, 2009).

Driskill, Qwo-Li. "Theatre as Suture: Grassroots Performance, Decolonization and Healing," in Hulan and Eigenbrod (eds.), *Aboriginal Oral Traditions*, 155–168.

Episkenew, Jo-Ann. "Contemporary Indigenous Literatures in Canada: Healing from Historical Trauma," in Devy et al. (eds.), *Indigeneity. Culture and Representation* (New Delhi: Orient Blackswan, 2009): 75–86.

———. *Taking Back Our Spirits. Indigenous Literature, Public Policy, and Healing* (Winnipeg: University of Manitoba Press, 2009).

Gingell, Susan. "Teaching the Talk That Walks on Paper: Oral Traditions and Textualized Orature in the Canadian Literature Classroom," in Cynthia Sugars (ed.), *Home-work: Postcolonialism, Pedagogy and Canadian Literature* (Ottawa: University of Ottawa Press): 285–300.

Grossman, Michèle. *Blacklines. Contemporary Critical Writing by Indigenous Australians* (Melbourne, VIC: Melbourne University Press, 2003).

———. "Fighting with our Tongues, Fighting for our Lives: Talk, Text and Amodernity in *Warlpirli Women's Voices: Our Lives, Our History*," in Hulan and Eigenbrod (eds.), *Aboriginal Oral Traditions*, 113–137.

Highway, Tomson. *Comparing Mythologies*. The Charles R. Bronfman Lecture in Canadian Studies 2002 (Ottawa: University of Ottawa Press, 2003).

———. *Kiss of the Fur Queen* (Toronto: Doubleday Canada, 1998).

———. *Dry Lips Oughta Move to Kapuskasing* (Saskatoon: Fifth House, 1989).

———. *The Rez Sisters* (Saskatoon: Fifth House, 1988).

Hove, Chenjerai. *Bones* (Harare: Baobab, 1988).

Hubbard, Tasha. "Voices Heard in the Silence, History Held in the Memory: Ways of Knowing Jeannette Armstrong's 'Threads of Old Memory'," in Hulan and Eigenbrod (eds.), *Aboriginal Oral Traditions*, 139–153.

Hulan, Renée and Renate Eigenbrod (eds.). *Aboriginal Oral Traditions. Theory, Practice, Ethics* (Halifax & Winnipeg: Fernwood Publishing with the Gorsebrook Research Institute, 2008).

Ihimaera, Witi. *The Whale Rider* (Rosedale, North Shore, New Zealand: Penguin, 2008).

——— (ed.). *Te Ao marama* (Auckland: Reed, 1992–1996), 5 vols.

Irele, Abiola. "The African Imagination," in *Research in African Literatures*, 21, 1 (Spring 1990): 49–67.

Johnston, Denis W. "Lines and Circles. The 'Rez' Plays of Tomson Highway," in *Canadian Literature*, 124 & 125 (Spring–Summer 1990): 254–264.

King, Thomas. *The Truth about Stories. A Native Narrative* (Toronto: Anansi, 2003). CBC Massey lectures series.

——— (ed.). *All My Relations. An Anthology of Contemporary Canadian Native Fiction* (Toronto: McClelland & Stewart, 1990).

Kovach, Margaret. *Indigenous Methodologies: Characteristics, Conversations and Contexts* (Toronto: University of Toronto Press, 2009).

Lutz, Hartmut. *Contemporary Challenges: Conversations with Canadian Native Authors* (Saskatoon: Fifth House, 1991).

Martin, Catherine. "The Little Boy Who Lived with Muini'skw (Bear Woman)," in Hulan and Eigenbrod (eds.), *Aboriginal Oral Traditions*, 53–59.

Mildon, Drew. "A Bad Connection: First Nations Oral Histories in the Canadian Courts," in Hulan and Eigenbrod (eds.), *Aboriginal Oral Traditions*, 79–97.

Morgan, Sally. *My Place* (1987; New York: Little, Brown, 1990).

Moses, Daniel David (ed.). *The Exile Book of Native Canadian Fiction and Drama* (Holstein, ON: Exile Editions, 2010).

Moses, Daniel David and Terry Goldie (eds.). *An Anthology of Canadian Native Literature in English* (Toronto: Oxford University Press, 1992).

Sabbioni, Jennifer, Kay Schaffer and Sidonie Smith (eds.). *Indigenous Australian Voices. A Reader* (New Brunswick, NJ & London: Rutgers University Press, 1998).

6

INDIGENOUS LANGUAGES IN CANADA

Darin Flynn

Five or six dozen indigenous languages are spoken or signed in Canada, representing over a dozen language families. Their status is briefly described in the following, after some important context.

The context of indigenous languages in Canada

This first major section sketches the geopolitical and historical context of indigenous languages in Canada, their importance to indigenous peoples, and efforts at documenting and revitalizing them.

Ô Canada! Terre de nos Aïeux! Our home and native land!

Canada is world-renowned for its official bilingualism, whereby English and French "have equality of status and equal rights and privileges as to their use in all institutions of the Parliament and Government of Canada" (Constitution Act, 1982, ss. 16 [1]). More broadly,

> the Government of Canada is committed to enhancing the vitality and supporting the development of English and French linguistic minority communities, as an integral part of the two official language communities of Canada, and to fostering full recognition and use of English and French in Canadian society.
>
> *(Official Languages Act, 1988, c. 38)*

This official language policy is a point of pride for most Canadians (Parkin and Turcotte 2004: 12–13), but it is a sore point for many indigenous people. Many dozens of indigenous languages are spoken or signed in Canada, typically by direct descendants of the diverse peoples who inhabited the land for many thousands of years before Europeans arrived.[1] Some of these languages extend beyond Canada's borders (which are recent and problematic from an indigenous perspective), but each is more tightly bound with the physical country than the twin official languages are. The latter are colonial-European, as well as international. By contrast, consider only this brief report:

> "The voice of the land is our language" was the theme of the National Elders' Gathering on Manitoulin Island in 1993. Throughout this week-long meeting, Elders from hundreds of communities across Canada told us that Aboriginal languages are spiritually interconnected with the land.
>
> *(Fettes and Norton 2000: 29)*

The understanding "that you can't separate land from language" (R. Z. Smith, personal communication in Parker 2012: 1) is well-documented for indigenous peoples in Canada. Jeanette Armstrong, famed director of the En'owkin Centre, explains it this way: "Language itself comes from how the land expresses itself. Every language comes from the different interactions we have with the land" (Armstrong 2012). The American linguist and anthropologist Edward Sapir realized the same, a century earlier, shortly after he had begun working with some Nuučaaṅułʔatḥ (Nuu-chah-nulth)[2] people and their language:

> [S]o far as language is concerned, all environmental influence reduces at last analysis to the influence of social environment. . . . In the case of the specialized vocabularies of the Nootka [Nuučaaṅuł] . . . it is important to note that it is not merely the fauna or topographical features of the country as such that are reflected, but rather the interest of the people in such environmental features.
>
> *(Sapir 1912: 228–9)*

Recently, Green (2014) was able to pick up this discussion with direct descendants of Sapir's Nuučaaṅułʔatḥ consultants. They confirmed and emphasized that their language reflects what dozens upon dozens of generations have noticed, thought about and related to in their environment. Elements and features of their traditional territory are in their ancestral language precisely "because they have social, economic, ceremonial *and* spiritual significance" (Green 2014: 9, her emphasis). The same is apparently true of all indigenous languages in Canada, as Lil'wat scholar Lorna Wanosts'a7 Williams remarks: "with each one, the language comes and emerges from the land, and we have to respect that" (personal communication to Dupuis 2016). And yet, to date, not a single Indigenous language has been recognized as "official" by the government of Canada.[3]

Death and residential schools

This insult is heaped upon injury in Canadian history. The early French and British explorers and missionaries brought with them diseases which were new, and therefore deadly, to indigenous peoples. Epidemics of smallpox, typhus, cholera, tuberculosis, measles, etc., as well as confrontation, dislocation,[4] deprivation, etc., caused the indigenous population of (what is now) Canada to plummet from perhaps a half million in the late 15th century to a mere fifth of that number by the late 19th century (Royal Commission on Aboriginal Peoples 1996: 20). Entire communities were decimated, along with their distinct dialects and languages. For example, St. Lawrence Iroquoian, the provenance of "Canada" (meaning "village"), vanished with its speakers in the late 16th century (Mithun 1982). The last of the Beothuk, who originally inhabited the island of Newfoundland, passed away in the early 19th century, along with their unique language (Marshall 1996).

Between the 1880s and the 1980s, the indigenous population bounced back, growing to a half million again (Royal Commission on Aboriginal Peoples 1996: 20). But in the same period, the government of Canada forcibly enrolled approximately 150,000 indigenous children in church-run boarding schools away from their families. The goal was to assimilate them into Euro-Canadian society. As painstakingly documented by the Truth and Reconciliation Commission of Canada (henceforth TRC) in recent years, indigenous children were forced to speak English or French, and they were shamed and even punished for using their own languages. Here is a brief tell-tale excerpt from the 528-page summary of the TRC final report:

> Michael Sillett, a former student at the North West River residential school in Newfoundland and Labrador, told the Commission, "Children at the dorm were not allowed to speak their mother tongue. I remember several times when other children were slapped or had their mouths washed out for speaking their mother tongue; whether it was Inuktitut or Innu-aimun. Residents were admonished for just being Native." As late as the 1970s, students at schools in northwestern Ontario were not allowed to speak their language if they were in the presence of a staff member who could not understand that language.
>
> *(TRC 2015a: 153)*

Most were deeply affected by these and other experiences, and many eventually became unable to communicate with their own parents and other relatives who did not speak English or French. Some also came to disavow indigeneity in general, further disaffecting them from their families and communities. In the end, the residential school system succeeded at teaching Canada's official languages to indigenous children, and to a lesser extent, at assimilating them into Euro-Canadian culture (if not society) by suppressing their own ancestral languages, cultures and identities.

A sacred trust

Unsurprisingly, indigenous languages in Canada are currently "endangered" (Moseley 2010), but in consideration of what generations of their speakers have endured, they can only be admired for their remarkable resilience and relative vitality. "Some of the earliest language activists," Pine and Turin (2017: §3) remind us, "were the children and students who, risking corporal or psychological punishment, continued to speak their languages in residential and boarding schools and at home with their families." It is indeed remarkable that in spite of the distress associated with using indigenous languages, so many former students of residential schools succeeded in transmitting their linguistic heritage to their children and grandchildren.

Former students of residential schools who have become language activists give credit to their own forebears, many of whom were themselves former students of residential schools. For example, Nora Wedzin is a cultural coordinator who is charged with advising three levels of government – the Tłı̨chǫ government, the Northwest Territories and Canada – "on how to use their respective powers in ways that respect and promote Tłı̨chǫ language, culture and way of life" (www. research.tlicho.ca/culture/cultural-coordinator, accessed on 20 April 2017). Language is central to her work, e.g., in recent months she has led the training of 25 Tłı̨chǫ language interpreters, and called on women at a National Indigenous Women's Summit to safeguard their languages. At a meeting with peers a few years ago, she shared how she managed and continues to reclaim her language in spite of spending 18 long and challenging years in residential school:

> Seta eyıts'ǫ semo elaka Tłı̨chǫ agııtee xe nezı sı Tłı̨chǫ Yatıì eyıts'ǫ dǫ nàowoò hoghàsıgetǫ masì gıwhǫ. Setsı eyıts'ǫ sehtèe tsı masì ts'ı̨ı̨hwhǫ masì gewho, ekıı tso hasıgedı ı̨lè Tłı̨chǫ neyatıì goh ezhıı lı le. Masì dıı hanı seyatıì ılaa wegho hogah sı too hanı nedı nezı denak'e wek'e hozhǫǫ ade ha.
>
> *(Nora Wedzin, personal communication, 16 July 2014)*[5]

Many younger indigenous people, in turn, have come to view their heritage tongue as a sacred trust – their forebears' will and testament of cultural and historical survival. For instance, consider how Iinohsokaki (Sandra Manyfeathers-O'Hara), who is the Blackfoot language teacher at Tatsikiisaapo'p Middle School on the Kainai Nation in Alberta, describes her sense of duty and indignation in the Blackfoot language rap song, "We're still here" (Prairie Chicken et al. 2016): "In the past our grandparents were beaten for speaking their language, and to honour them, I will continue speaking in the Blackfoot language, so that our youth in the future will speak in the Blackfoot language."

Perhaps even more compelling are indigenous activists who did not learn their heritage language as children, because it was all too effectively extinguished in their parents or grandparents by the residential school system. In *First and Second Language Acquisition: Parallels and Differences*, Meisel (2011: 2) reminds us that "second language acquisition . . . appears to be mission impossible for most teenagers and adults":

> Infants and very young children develop almost miraculously the ability of speech, without apparent effort, without even being taught – as opposed to the teenager or the adult struggling in language classrooms without, it seems, ever being able to reach the same level of proficiency as five-year olds in their first language. . . . [L]earners in a naturalistic setting do not fare much better, frequently even worse, in fact, as is demonstrated by the limited success of many immigrants who have acquired their knowledge of their new linguistic environment in the process of everyday communication, without ever attending classes.
>
> *(1–2)*

Activists who have learned, and who continue to learn, their indigenous languages as teenagers or adults are thus uniquely dedicated individuals. For example, Karahkwenhá:wi (Zoe Hopkins), a language teacher[6] at Six Nations (the largest reserve in Canada), described her own experience learning Kanyen'kéha (Mohawk) at the age of 35, essentially from scratch: "I studied the language in an immersion setting for two years of full-time study. It was the hardest thing I've ever done. It was more arduous than earning my degree. I became an advanced-mid-level speaker" (CBC 2017).[7]

According to a recent survey, second-language speakers at Six Nations (like Karahkwenhá:wi) are driven by the same family honour as native speakers (like Iinohsokaki), and this sense of duty is evidently strong enough to sustain their language learning efforts:

> One hundred percent of language learners who have become speakers indicated that they remember someone in their families who spoke Onkwehonwehnéha and that this was a source of great pride for them. Informants stated that they that they wanted to honor, respect and or continue on the tradition throughout their family line of speaking Onkwehonwehnéha.
>
> *(Tehota'kerá:tonh 2017: 34)*

That drive is described as follows by Susan Blight, an Anishinaabe artist and language activist from Couchiching First Nation in Ontario: "There was a time when our people were criminalized, abused and ridiculed when speaking Anishinaabemowin but our language survived. We shouldn't forget that. Use it as strength to go forward" (Government of Ontario 2016: 36).

The necessity of language

Another galvanizing belief, which is less obvious and therefore more interesting, is that indigenous peoples cannot survive without their languages. "We either bring our languages back, or we die," says Khelsílem, a language reclamation activist from the Sḵwx̱wú7mesh (Squamish) Nation, who himself began learning Sḵwx̱wú7mesh sníchim at age 19 from Vanessa Campbell, a fluent elder in his community. This dramatic statement can be understood in a variety ways (Khelsílem 2017), the simplest being that indigenous languages represent a crucial requirement of being indigenous. As one speaker of Sm'algya̱x put it, *Sm'algya̱x int ma̱goonda wila dildu-ulsa Ts'msyen* "Sm'algya̱x defines who we are as Ts'msyen" (FPCC 2014: 10). It follows that if one ceases speaking Sm'algya̱x, one ceases being Ts'msyen.[8]

Indigenous peoples' language-based definition of themselves is not fully appreciated or understood by most Euro-Canadians. Canadians generally identify with particular symbols, such as the Canadian Charter of Rights and Freedoms and the national flag, and with particular values, such as gender equality and human rights (Sinha 2015). Canadians also value language as part of their identity, but many – even native speakers of French – see it as less integral than symbols, values and other points of pride (*ibid.*). As Shaw (2001: 40) remarks: "Certainly, many independent physical, social, economic, cultural, and ideological attributes would rank high above Language itself in a native English speaker's definition of his or her identity." This may be because Canadians who are native speakers of English, in particular, have a rather utilitarian view of their language:

> English may be a *vehicle* for the expression of spirituality, of attitudes, beliefs, values, and perceptions of truth, of culture, of self-identification, but English is seldom considered by its speakers to be the *essence* of either their individual or collective identity.
>
> *(Shaw 2001: 39)*

By contrast, many indigenous citizens tend to regard their ancestral languages not only as integral but as core to their identities, as illustrated by Khelsílem's and others' statements, shown previously. Another good illustration is the motto "We Are Our Language," which is ubiquitous in Canada's Yukon Territory (Meek 2010). This phrase is commonly found in all eight indigenous languages of that territory, notably in a circular logo that is used by the Aboriginal Language Services and the Yukon Native Language Centre. An even better illustration is the following official statement by the Assembly of First Nations, a national advocacy organization that represents 634 First Nations communities ("reserves") across Canada:

> Language is our unique relationship to the Creator, our attitudes beliefs, values, and fundamental notions of what is truth. Our languages are the cornerstone of who we are as a People. Without our languages we cannot survive.
>
> *(Assembly of First Nations 1990: 39)*

As this statement implies, indigenous peoples in Canada are passionate about their heritage languages for many reasons, including their lived experiences – "people who lose their language often speak of a deep sense of loss of self, of loss of identity" (Grenoble 2011: 36).

The understanding that languages are vital – literally – to indigenous peoples is reaffirmed by the First Peoples' Cultural Council (FPCC) in a scrupulous report on the status of indigenous languages in British Columbia, where the majority of languages happen to be spoken in Canada:

> There is growing evidence of the link between a strong linguistic and cultural identity and wellbeing in other areas including social, mental and physical health, a reduction in harmful behaviours (such as alcohol and drug abuse and suicide), an increase in high school graduation rates and other positive educational outcomes, and higher employment rates. The discrimination that First Nations continue to face in the outside world is more tolerable when they have a strong connection to their language, history and lands.
>
> *(10)*

Especially compelling in this regard is a demonstration by Hallett, Chandler and Lalonde (2007) that an indigenous youth's likelihood of committing suicide in British Columbia is inversely correlated to their use of indigenous languages. The study authors conclude more generally that "indigenous language use . . . is a strong predictor of health and wellbeing in Canada's Aboriginal communities" (p. 398).

Nora Wedzin, already cited previously, explains how knowledge of indigenous languages helps the individual and the community:

> Goyatìı gohneetoo gıde nedı degıdı agıde dewho ʝlè dedzee koa ta wekehozha xe wenıede seyatìı weghǫneètǫ xe weke dıı ha dewho. Neyatıì hanı le nıde dǫ yatıì weghǫneètǫ xe nezı weke dıı nedı wate amìı at'ee, a dıı_nèk'e dǫ nelı̧, necho gıgodıì eyıts'ǫ wet'à nını, nedzeè (heart) nàtso xe nenàowoò dè k'èhǫǫzǫ ha. Weta dǫ loo chekoa, ohda hotıı getsedıı ha eyıts'ǫ hogahgetoo ha dıı le genı eyıts'ǫ gedzee eyıts'ǫ gotso ını natsoo ha ne eyıts'ǫ dǫ nàke làanì sìı nàtso ha.
>
> *(Nora Wedzin, personal communication, 16 July 2014)*[9]

Her explanation ends in the Tłıchǫ motto, *Dǫ Nàke Làanì Nàts'etso* "Be strong like two people." It urges indigenous people to double-up their inner resources by drawing on their traditional ways of knowing, being, speaking, signing and listening, as well as on Western ways.

Revitalization and documentation

The importance of indigenous languages to both individuals and communities is reflected by countless revitalization and documentation efforts across Canada. Language revitalization is led by individuals at home (e.g., Noori 2009), at school (e.g., Ferguson 2010), at play (e.g., Tulloch 2014), and so on. Community-level endeavours include immersion nests; junior youth language and culture camps; language study circles for youth, adults and parents; home visits with elders; mentor-apprentice pairings; meetings and gatherings in the indigenous language; and so on (e.g., FPCC 2010). Revitalization activities are generally positive and constructive for individuals and communities (Meek 2010), so much so that they are deemed worthwhile even in cases where they are unlikely to succeed at returning a very critically endangered language to everyday use (FPCC 2014: 10).

Language revitalization also engages indigenous institutions, such as language institutes, indigenous educational institutions, as well as local, regional and national political organizations. For example, in December 2016, the Anishinabek Nation, which comprises 40 communities across Ontario, voted to move forward with a new jurisdictional and fiscal Education Agreement with Canada, the largest proposal of its kind. A central goal of the new self-government agreement is to better provide Anishinaabemowin (Anishinaabe language) to students, both on- and off-reserve (http://sayyestoaes.ca/why-ratify/benefits-of-ratification/, accessed 13 April 2017). Moreover, Anishinabek Nation communities are currently voting (mostly in favour, as of July 2017) to move a related Master Education Agreement forward with the province of Ontario, which will also stress the use of Anishinaabemowin.

By contrast, the documentation of indigenous languages in Canada (dictionaries, grammars, texts, recordings, corpora, archives, etc.) tends to be led by research institutions which are largely non-indigenous, though usually in collaboration with indigenous peoples, and often in tandem with revitalization efforts. For instance, Innu-speaking communities and their institutions (notably Mamu Tshishkutamashutau and l'Institut Tshakapesh) have collaborated with linguists at Memorial University and Carleton University in documenting how their particular dialect of Cree is acquired and used in Labrador and Quebec. This collaboration is funded by the Social Sciences and Humanities Research Council, like most documentation work in Canada, and it has resulted in revitalization activities and tools: training workshops, language curriculum development, Innu-English-French dictionaries, mobile apps for smartphones and tablets, children's books and online resources (www.innu-aimun.ca/ accessed on 13 June 2017).

Unsurprisingly, language projects at research institutions derive particular benefit from indigenous faculty who are also integrated as local community members. For example, Peter Jacobs, an accomplished linguist at the University of Victoria, was recently pursued and hired by Simon Fraser University, which is located on the shared traditional territories of the Sḵwx̱wú7mesh (Squamish), Tsleil-Waututh and xʷməθkʷəy̓əm (Musqueam). As an active member of the local Sḵwx̱wú7mesh Nation and a fluent speaker of its official language, Dr. Jacobs is now able to work intensely and effectively on the documentation and revitalization of the Sḵwx̱wú7mesh snichim. Similarly, Freda Ahenakew (1932–2011) was a professor of native studies at the University of Saskatchewan and the University of Manitoba who is celebrated for her analysis, documentation and revitalization of a regional language, nēhiyawēwin (Plains Cree). A branch of the Saskatoon Public Library was recently renamed after her. Her legacy also lives on through her many books (such as *Cree Language Structures: A Cree Approach* [Ahenakew 1987], which has been reprinted 18 times), through her many children (such as Dolores Sand, a famed teacher of nēhiyawēwin), and through her many former students and trainees.

This brings us to the role of post-secondary institutions in facilitating capacity building in indigenous communities. Certain programs in language documentation and revitalization are decades old, such as the Yukon Native Language Centre at Yukon College, the First Nations and Endangered Languages program at the University of British Columbia and the Canadian Indigenous Languages and Literacy Development Institute at the University of Alberta. Pertinent diploma and certificate programs are also offered at a dozen smaller colleges around the country. Such training programs have multiplied more recently in response to the TRC's Call to Action: "We call upon post-secondary institutions to create university and college degree and diploma programs in Aboriginal languages" (TRC 2015b: 2). Thus, Georgian College has a new diploma program in Anishnaabemowin revitalization, Six Nations Polytechnic has new programs in Goyogohó:nǫ' (Cayuga) and Kanyen'kéha (Mohawk), and the University of Saskatchewan has new certificate and master's degree programs in indigenous language revitalization (in collaboration with the University of Victoria).

Families and status of indigenous languages in Canada

This second major section lists the many families of indigenous languages in Canada. The smallest families – those with a single member – are listed first. The larger families are then listed in ascending order of speakers or signers. Mixed indigenous languages – those belonging to more than one family – are described last.

As in genetics, linguistic families are established on the basis of shared traits across languages. For example, Na-Dene languages are notorious for having "classificatory verb stems" (Rice 1998: 110). In particular, verbs that refer to entities being at rest (e.g., "stand," "sit," "lie"), in motion (e.g., "throw," "drop," "fall") or manipulated (e.g., "take," "give," "handle") vary conspicuously according to the physical attributes and relations of the entities under discussion. The Sahtúgot'ıné sentences in example 1 illustrate how various verb stems are used to express "hand me the tea" (*lit.* tea me-to-you-give), depending on the situational context. (The verb stem is at the end of the verb, which itself is at the end of sentences – these are other Na-Dene hallmarks.)

1   "Hand me the tea" in Sahtúgot'ıné (Sahtu/Bearlake Dene) (Rushforth 1991: 254)

   lidí seghánįchu (the tea is in a single box or bag)
   lidí seghánįwa (the tea is in two or more boxes or bags)
   lidí seghánįhge (the tea is in a shallow or open container)
   lidí seghánįhxe (the tea is in a deep or closed container)
   lidí seghánįhxo (some loose tea, e.g., a handful)

As another example, animate entities – animals and spirits – receive a different treatment than inanimate entities in Algonquian languages. This treatment is grammatical, rather than strictly semantic. So, for instance, apples are treated as animate (like animals and spirits) in Blackfoot grammar, whereas bananas are (expectedly) treated as inanimate. Thus in example 2, observe how the first word (meaning "I disliked") has a different verb form depending on whether the direct object is animate ("that apple") or inanimate ("that banana"). Note, too, how the words of the demonstrative phrase end in *-a* or *-i*, depending on whether the noun is animate or inanimate. Such overt and pervasive grammatical agreement in terms of animacy is a hallmark of Algonquian languages.

2   "I disliked that apple/banana" in Blackfoot (Frantz and Russell 1995; Frantz 2009)

   a   *nitsííkaimmaawa anna aipastáamiinaamma* (*lit.:* I-disliked that apple)
   b   *nitsííkai'tsii'pa anni iinááni* (*lit.:* I-disliked that banana)

Note that the figures provided in the following sections are only approximate.[10] Mother tongue and home language figures are drawn mainly from the 2016 Census (StatCan 2017). Figures concerning speakers and learners of languages in British Columbia are also informed by the First Peoples' Language Map of British Columbia (FPHLCC 2005–17) and by a recent report by the First People's Cultural Council (FPCC 2014). When no census data are available, or else when the census data are implausible, I give an estimate (marked with an asterisk) based on alternate but converging sources, including personal communications.[11]

Ktunaxa (Kutenai)

Ktunaxa is a language isolate spoken in southeastern British Columbia and in neighbouring American states (notably Montana). Only 25 elderly fluent speakers remain in Canada, but 120 others (including children) are learning Ktunaxa as a second language and are making efforts to use it at home. About a fifth of these learners are semi-fluent. (Only a handful of fluent elderly Ktunaxa speakers remain in United States, but not a few young adults are actively learning the language there, too.)

X̱aad Kil (Haida)

Another language isolate in Canada is X̱aad Kil, spoken in northwesternmost British Columbia, on the Haida Gwaii archipelago (where the language is also called X̱aaydaa Kil), as well as in adjacent Alaska. In Canada, this unique language remains the mother tongue of 23 elders (all over 80) in Skidegate (Southern dialect) and of two others in Masset (Northern dialect). However, 150 youth and adults are currently learning the language and using it regularly at home, and a dozen of these second-language learners are already semi-fluent. Especially promising is that some semi-fluent speakers are now raising their children in X̱aad Kil (Cullis-Suzuki 2017). (The situation of X̱aad Kil is similar in Alaska.)

Sign languages

Inuit Sign Language (abbreviated IUR, from Inuktitut Inuit Uukturausin-git [ᐃᓄᒃ ᑐᓯᐅᕆ ᖕᒋᑦ]; MacDougall 2001) represents yet another isolate in Canada. Though its linguistic documentation is only recent (Schuit 2015 and references therein), IUR has been in use for centuries among the Inuit – the indigenous people of the Canadian Arctic. It is currently a mother tongue to fewer than 40 Deaf Inuit who are widely dispersed across Nunavut, the newest, largest and most northerly territory in Canada, where congenital deafness happens to be relatively frequent. The language is also known by perhaps 80 hearing Inuit (Schuit 2012).

Other sign language isolates were mother tongues to Deaf indigenous peoples in Canada in the past. Notably, Plains Sign Language (Hand Talk) was apparently developed by Deaf individuals and their families on the Great Plains, and its use spread as a lingua franca as far north as the North Saskatchewan River in Canada, and as far South as the Rio Grande in Mexico (Davis 2015 and references therein). Today, Plains Sign Language is rarely if ever used as a full-fledged first language by Deaf people in Canada, but some hearing elders (e.g., in Treaty 7 Territory in Alberta) still know it to some extent.

Yet another sign language was indigenous to the Northwest Plateau, including Central and Southeastern British Columbia (cf. Davis 2015: 920). Plateau Sign Language was once presumably a mother tongue to Deaf Plateau peoples, but it is now only partially known to a few hearing elders (e.g., Ktunaxa).

Wakashan

This family consists of a handful of languages in coastal British Columbia, as well as qʷi·qʷi·diččaq (Makah) on the adjacent American Olympic Peninsula.[12] As shown in Table 6.1, the most endangered is 'Uik̓ala (Oowekyala). Eighty-eight-year-old Evelyn Windsor (Nuwaqawa) is currently the only fluent mother-tongue speaker, but ten members of the small Wuikinuxv Nation are learning their heritage language from her, and half of them already consider themselves fluent. Moreover, 'Uik̓ala is supported by forming a single language with Hailhzaqvla (also Híɫzaqv or Heiltsuk), though many community members consider it to be separate. Hailhzaqvla is taught rather intensively by the Heiltsuk Nation, in a language nest immersion program for pre-schoolers, and in a 40-hour/week language program at its school (FPCC 2014: 53).

The most vigorous Wakashan languages are Kwak̓wala and Nuučaańuɫ, though in practice each of these subsumes numerous dialects which vary in terms of their degree of endangerment. Moreover, Table 6.1 shows that a majority of those who report Nuučaańuɫ or Kwak̓wala as their mother tongue are not necessarily fluent speakers. Some of them have grown up to be semi-speakers, or even non-speakers.

TABLE 6.1   Wakashan languages in Canada

Languages	Mother tongue	Fluent	Semi-fluent	Learners	Main home language	Secondary home language
'Uiḵala (Oowekyala)	1★	6	5	10	1★	5★
Diitiidʔaatx̣ (Ditidaht)	10★	7	6	55	2★	8★
Hailhzaqvla (Híłzaqv)	125	60	45	247	10	50
Xenaksialaḵala-Xa"islaḵala	145	242	21	80	70	65
Nuučaańuł (Nuu-chah-nulth)	355	134	197	422	85	260
Kwak̓wala	430	165	499	775	75	300

Sources: FPCC 2014; FPHLCC 2005–17; StatCan 2017

On the other hand, Table 6.1 also reveals that learners of the closely related dialects Xenaksialaḵala-Xa"islaḵala (Henaksiala-Haisla) are particularly likely to describe themselves as fluent speakers.

Iroquoian

The Iroquoian family is represented in Canada by a handful of languages jointly called Hodinohso:ni (Haudenosaunee), or Iroquois (an Algonquin exonym), spoken by 1,490 in southwestern Quebec and southern Ontario (and by 1,992 others in adjacent parts of the United States).

Table 6.2 focuses on mother-tongue speakers, so it excludes a sixth, rather distinct Northern Iroquoian language called Huron-Wendat. The last mother-tongue speakers of Huron-Wendat in Canada passed away a century ago, but dozens of new speakers – a few of whom claim fluency – were created in Wendake, Quebec as part of a million-dollar project titled Yawenda ("Voice") in 2007–13 (Dorais 2015). Table 6.2 also excludes a seventh, even more distinct Northern Iroquoian language called Skarù·rę'/Sgaroore̲h̲' (Tuscarora). It was a mother tongue to some Six Nations members until the late 20th century. The handful of remaining native speakers in New York have since passed away, too. Today, there are only a few semi-speakers of Skarù·rę', as well as some learners.

Kanien'kéha is the most widely spoken Haudenosaunee language, as shown in Table 6.2. Its prospects are good, as hundreds continue to learn it as a second language, and many of these learners are committed to raising bilingual children. For instance, the Six Nations Reserve in Ontario counts only six native speakers of Kanien'kéha, but it has 45 intermediate-to-high second-language speakers, as well as ten bilingual children (Tehota'kerá:tonh 2017). Similarly, there are relatively few native speakers of Goyogo̲hó:nǫ' (Cayuga), but there are 200 second-language learners at Six Nations, and 15 of their children are growing up bilingual (*ibid.*).

TABLE 6.2 Iroquoian languages in Canada

Languages	Mother tongue	Main home language	Secondary home language	Speakers in US
Onöndowá'ga:' (Seneca)	2–3★			30★
Onǫda'géga'/ Onoñda'géga' (Onondaga)	7★			2★
Goyogǫhó:nǫ' (Cayuga)	55	35	70	3★
Onʌyota'a:ka/ Onʌyotaʔa·ka (Oneida)	90	55	125	12★
Kanien'kéha/ Kanyen'kéha (Mohawk)	1,295[13]	570	1,145	1,945

Sources: StatCan 2017; p.c. Craig Kopris, 10 July 2017

Tsimshianic

This family, which gets its name from the Ts'msyan people, is located in northwestern British Columbia, except for about 40 speakers of Sm'algyax (Coast Tsimshian) in southeasternmost Alaska.

The two most widely spoken languages, Nisga'a and Gitsenimx (Table 6.3), are treated as separate for political reasons, though most linguists consider them to be distinct dialects of a single language, called Nass-Gitksan. Much attention is given to teaching these languages to children at school. For example, pre-schoolers learn Nisga'a or Gitsenimx about 14 hours per week (FPCC 2014: 51).

Salish

Ten Salish languages are currently spoken in British Columbia. Table 6.4 presents them in ascending order of speakers in Canada. Only Nsyilxcən has a community of speakers outside British Columbia: 230 Native Americans claim to speak it under the name Colville in Washington State.

The Coast Salish language Nəxʷsƛ̓ay̓əmúcən (Klallam) is not listed in Table 6.4. The last native speaker, Hazel Sampson, passed away in 2014 at age 103, but the language continues to be spoken with varying degrees of fluency by six younger Klallam as a second language on several reserves in Washington State. There may also be one or two learners of Nəxʷsƛ̓ay̓əmúcən at the Scia'new First Nation in British Columbia.

As shown in Table 6.4, the most endangered Salish language (aside from Nəxʷsƛ̓ay̓əmúcən) is shashishalhem. Only four elderly fluent speakers of she shashishalhem remain, and apparently no shishalh is currently learning it, so it risks

TABLE 6.3 Tsimshianic languages in Canada

Languages	Mother tongue	Fluent	Semi	Learners	Main home	Secondary home language
Tsimshian: Ski:xs (South Ts.)	1★	0	1	90	0	0★
Sm'algyax (Coast Ts.)	235	106	685	248	160	220
Nisg̱a'a	465	857	1,866	478	115	585
Gitsenimx̱ (Gitksan)	1020	350[14]	486	638	430	540

Sources: FPCC 2014; FPHLCC 2005–17; StatCan 2017

TABLE 6.4 Salish languages in Canada

Languages	Mother tongue	Fluent	Semi	Lear-ners	Main home	Secondary language
she shashishalhem (Seshelt)	10★	4	34	0	4★	6★
Nuxalk (Bella Coola)	20★	17	505	261	17★	100★
Skwx̱wú7mesh sníchim (Squamish)	60	21	34	204	21★	34★
Éy7á7juuthem (Ayeahjuthum, or Comox)	90	36	705	353	36★	350★
SENĆOŦEN/Malchosen/ Lekwungen/etc.	170	7	103	251	45	235
Nsyilxcən (Nsilxcín, or Okanagan)	340	194	165	295	150	340
nɬeʔkèpmxcín (Nlaka'pamux, or Thompson)	380	127	339	405	50	245
Sƛ́átimcets (Lillooet)	360	137	692	1140	60	465
hən̓q̓əmin̓əm̓/Halq'eméylem/ Hul'q'umi'num'	585	263	992	2067	105	580
Secwepemctsin (Shuswap)	640	197	1187	1134	210	625

Sources: FPCC 2014; FPHLCC 2005–17; StatCan 2017

being lost, like other Coast Salish languages before it (such as Pentlatch). But hope remains even in this case: 34 shishalh identify as semi-speakers around Sechelt. More than a few of them may actually have some proficiency in the language, but they stopped using it at some point in their lives. Such individuals hold potential for near-future efforts at language reclamation, as Grinevald and Bert (2011: 51) discuss:

> [S]uch speakers may regain or reacquire some partial active use of the language. They could be inhibited at first, or unwilling to participate, but they might join a documentation and/or revitalization project at a later point.

They should not be overlooked . . . since they can always help reconstitute or even reinvent a sense of community at organized gatherings and contribute efforts at language revitalization.

Dakotan

Dakotan is a branch of a larger family that includes the Missouri Valley and Ohio Valley languages in the United States. This grouping is named after its largest language, Dakota, which has 17,855 mother-tongue speakers in the United States. This language is represented in Canada by a continuum of Titoŋwaŋ Lakota and Ihaŋktoŋwaŋ/Isaŋti Dakota dialects in Saskatchewan and Manitoba (Table 6.5). A distinct Dakotan language, called Hohe Nakoda (Assiniboine), has just a few dozen speakers in Saskatchewan. The largest Dakotan language in Canada is Iyethka/Isga, with 3,200 mother-tongue speakers in Alberta. It is the language spoken most often at home for 2,145 Albertans, and it is spoken regularly at home by 1,140 others. The Iyethka dialect in particular has many young speakers at Morley, Big Horn and Eden Valley, and many children at these reserves continue to learn it as a first language.

Na-Dene

At least eighteen Na-Dene languages are spoken in Canada (Table 6.6). The most distinct, Łingít, is the mother tongue of 120 people in Canada, mainly in the Yukon Territory, and of another 500 or so in Alaska. The other Na-Dene languages are more closely related; they form a subfamily called Dene or Athabaskan.

The most critically endangered Dene/Athabaskan languages are Tagish and Hän in the Yukon Territory. Łingít peoples migrated and married into the Tagish speaking area, such that the Tagish people eventually became biethnic and bilingual. Though some semi-speakers remain, a few of whom continue to use Tagish at home, the last fluent Łingít-Tagish bilingual, Lucy Wren (Ghùch Tlâ/Agaymā),

TABLE 6.5 Dakotan languages in Canada

Languages	Mother tongue	Language spoken most often at home	Other language spoken regularly at home
Titoŋwaŋ Lakota (Dakota)	10*	3*	3*
Hohe Nakoda (Assiniboine)	34*	10*	10*
Ihaŋktoŋwaŋ/Isaŋti Dakota	1,325	360	835
Iyethka/Isga (Stoney Nakoda/Nakota)	3,215	2,150	1,160

Source: StatCan 2017

TABLE 6.6 Na-Dene languages in Canada

Languages	Mother tongue	Language spoken most often at home	Other language spoken regularly at home
Łingít	120	10	155
Dene/Athabaskan:			
Tagish	0★	0★	3★
Hän	2★	1★	1★
Upper Tanana	10★	3★	7★
Tsuut'ina (formerly Sarcee)	35★	15	20★
Tse'khene (Sekani)	95	25	80
Tāłtān (Tahltan)	105	20	160
Witsuwet'en/Nedut'en	135	35	100
Southern Tutchone	85	15	70
Northern Tutchone	285	45	100
Danezāgé' (Kaska)	195	45	195
Dane-zaa (Beaver)	225	85	105
Gwich'in	290	65	230
Tsilhqot'in (Chilcotin)	795	390	430
Dakelh (Carrier)	1,225	475	810
Tłıchǫ Yatıì (formerly Dogrib)	1,740	1,135	925
Slavey	2,120	955	1,255
– Dene Dháh/ Zhatié	995	425	685
– Shıh/Sahtú/ K'áshogot'ıné	815	405	395
Dënesųłiné	11,325	8,315	3,470

Sources: FPCC 2014; FPHLCC 2005–17; StatCan 2017

passed away in 2008 at the age of 91. Hän is also critically endangered, with only two elderly native speakers in Dawson City in the Yukon, and perhaps only a half dozen more in Eagle in Alaska (Willem de Reuse, personal communication, 29 September 2014).

By contrast, Dënesųłiné is very widely spoken across the Northwest Territories, Alberta, Saskatchewan and Manitoba. It currently has 11,325 mother tongue speakers, the vast majority of whom continue to use it as their main home language. It also continues to be acquired as a first language, particularly in a half-dozen northern Saskatchewan communities, where nine out of ten residents speak it fluently. Finally, some 460 second-language speakers also report using Dënesųłiné regularly at home, in addition to their mother tongue.

To give an idea of proficiency and acquisition of Na-Dene languages in Canada, Table 6.7 lists the number of fluent speakers, semi-speakers and learners in British

TABLE 6.7 Na-Dene languages/dialects in British Columbia

Languages/Dialects	Fluent speakers	Semi-speakers	Learners
Łingít (Taku River Tlingit)	2	7	53
Danezāgé' (Kaska)	16	62	60
Tāłtān (Tahltan)	45	60	113
Dene K'e (Fort Nelson Slavey)	58	128	154
Tse'khene (Sekani)	30	243	164
Dane-ẕaa (Beaver)	156	454	73
Witsuwit'en/Nedut'en	434	295	406
Tsilhqot'in (Chilcotin)	864	763	574
Dakelh (Carrier)	680	1380	767

Sources: FPCC 2014; FPHLCC 2005–17; StatCan 2017

Columbia. At present, most learners acquire their knowledge of indigenous languages through school. At Fort Nelson First Nation, for instance, Dene K'e (South Slavey) is taught to pre-schoolers for five hours per week, and to school-aged children for 18 hours per week (FPCC 2014: 40).

Inuit languages

Uummarmiutun (Canadian Iñupiaq), Siglitun (Inuvialuktun proper), Inuinnaqtun, Natsilingmiutut and Inuktitut (including Inuttitut/Inuttut) represent a dialect continuum spoken by over 40,000 Inuvialuit and Inuit, mainly in the Arctic territory of Nunavut (which is the size of Western Europe), but also the Inuvialuit Settlement Region of the Western Arctic, as well as in Eastern Subarctic regions of Quebec (Nunavik) and Labrador (Nunatsiavut and NunatuKavut). This dialect continuum is the largest in the world. It extends eastward into the American state of Alaska, where 2,583 Iñupiat speak various dialects of Iñupiaq. It also extends westward into Greenland, where approximately 800 Inughuit continue to speak the Inuktun dialect of Inuktitut. Greenlandic, the sole official language of that country, is yet another extension of the Inuit dialect continuum; it is spoken by 61,932 in Greenland and Denmark. (Speaker figures outside Canada, and those for Uummarmiutun and Natsilingmiutut in Table 6.8 – omitted by StatCan 2017 – are from Dorais 2010: 236, 243, 293.)

The Western dialects Uummarmiutun, Siglitun, Inuinnaqtun and Natsilingmiutut are endangered, whereas Inuktitut is largely safe (aside from the Inuttitut/Inuttut dialect in Labrador). The number of mother-tongue speakers of Inuktitut is actually up from 34,110 in 2011. This is not surprising: the vast majority of its speakers use it as their main home language, and many thousands more – including 2,845 second-language speakers – report speaking Inuktitut regularly at home. Inuktitut is also widely used at work, in education, in government, in technology, in media, on the web and in entertainment (notably in movies and in rap music).

TABLE 6.8 Inuit languages in Canada

Languages/dialects	Mother tongue	Language spoken most often at home	Other language spoken regularly at home
Inuit languages	39,652	31,415	11,295★
- Uummarmiutun (Iñupiaq)	122	20	100★
- Siglitun (Inuvialuktun proper)	475	70	350
- Inuinnaqtun (Inuvialuktun)	675	155	905
- Natsilingmiutut (Inuvialuktun)	1,815	785	1,000★
- Inuktitut (also Inuttitut/Inuttut)	36,185	30,240	8,790

Source: StatCan 2017

Algonquian languages

Algonquian languages represent the largest family in Canada in terms of geo-graphical distribution and in terms of speakers. In particular, the Cree language forms a dialect continuum all across the country, from Labrador on the Atlantic Ocean (Naskapi and Innu dialects), to British Columbia on the Pacific Ocean (nēhiyawēwin dialect). 96,260 report a Cree dialect as their mother tongue in Canada, as shown in Table 6.9. By contrast, 870 across the United States report being able to speak Cree, as shown in Table 6.10. One could say, then, that Cree is a de facto national language in Canada.

Nine out of ten people speak a dialect of Cree in many reserves, notably in Quebec (Atikamekw and Innu dialects). In these communities, some speakers of Cree are monolingual and many children continue to learn it as a first language. Moreover, tens of thousands across Canada have learned or are learning Cree as a second (or third) language. 14,630 of these second-language speakers report using Cree at home. One out of every four of them claim to speak Cree more than any other language at home, and three out of every four claim to speak it at home on a regular basis, alongside another home language.

Another important Algonquian language is Anishinaabemowin (Ojibwe). It has 35,870 mother tongue speakers, in far-flung communities from Quebec (Algon-quin dialect) to British Columbia (Nakawēmowin/Saulteaux dialect). As shown in Table 6.10, it is also the mother tongue of 10,700 Native Americans, which represent about 6% of ethnic Anishinaabeg in the United States. By contrast, a fifth of ethnic Anishinaabeg/Nakawēk in Canada report a dialect of Anishinaabemowin as their mother tongue. Certain dialects in Canada even retain monolingual speak-ers (180 Algonquin, for instance). Anishinaabemowin also has many second (and third) language speakers, 7,030 of whom report using it as a home language in Canada.

TABLE 6.9 Inuit languages in Canada

Languages	Mother tongue	Language spoken most often at home	Other language spoken regularly at home
Western Abenaki	2★	1★	1★
Munsee Delaware	3★	1★	2★
Neshnabémwen (Potawatomi)	4★	2★	2★
Maliseet-Passamaquoddy	360	115	380
Blackfoot	3,465	1,855	3,090
Mi'kmaq	7,140	4,225	3,505
Anishinaabemowin	35,870	18,755	18,825
- Ottawa (Odawa)	170	120	65
- Algonquin	1,595	840	895
- Oji-Cree	13,635	8,800	5,060
- Ojibway	20,475	9,000	12,805
Cree	96,260	64,825	37,950
- Southern East Cree	50	30	10
- Moose Cree	125	45	70
- Northern East Cree	365	210	165
- Swampy Cree	1,810	915	840
- Woods Cree	2,040	1,110	945
- Plains Cree	3,655	2,165	2,125
- Atikamekw	6,295	5,810	580
- Naskapi	1,230	1,210	135
- Innu (Montagnais)	10,710	9,500	1,480

Source: StatCan 2017

TABLE 6.10 Algonquian languages in Canada

Languages	Mother-tongue speakers in Canada	Mother-tongue speakers in the US
Western Abenaki	2★	2–3
Munsee Delaware	3★	–
Neshnabémwen (Potawatomi)	4★	3–4
Maliseet-Passamaquoddy	360	845
Blackfoot	3,465	1,450
Mi'kmaq	7,140	205
Anishinaabemowin	35,870	10,700
Cree (Atikamekw-Innu-aimun-Naskapi- . . .)	96,260	870

Source: StatCan 2017

Michif

The Métis are a racially mixed European-indigenous population, many of whom can trace their ancestry back to marriages between Frenchmen and Cree women during the fur trade, particularly in the early 19th century, and particularly in the

Red River region of present-day Manitoba. The Métis offspring of these marriages were bilingual in French and Cree, and interestingly, some of them developed a new mixed Cree-French language, called Michif, which spread to numerous Métis settlements across the Canadian Prairies and in North Dakota. Eventually, Michif came to be the mother tongue of hundreds of Métis in Manitoba, Saskatchewan, Alberta, the Northwest Territories and North Dakota. Its use has diminished since the late 19th century, but it remains the mother tongue of 725 Métis in Canada, and of 75 others in the United States. 280 individuals report Michif as their main home language in Canada, and 365 others report it as a secondary home language.

Bakker (1997: 119) reports that "[d]espite the geographical spread, the language is remarkably uniform among the settlements." Its extraordinary make-up is as follows (*ibid.*; Bakker 2012: 172). On the one hand, between 83% and 94% of Michif nouns are French (the rest are Cree, Ojibwe and English). On the other hand, between 88% and 99% of its verbs (including copulas) are Cree (the rest are French or mixed Cree-French). The rest of Michif grammar is similarly segregated. On the one hand, the numerals are all French, the prepositions are 70–100% French (the rest are Cree), and negation is 70% French (30% Cree). On the other hand, personal pronouns, question words and demonstratives are almost all Cree, and the adverbial particles are 70% Cree (30% French). Finally, the coordinate conjunctions are 55% Cree, 40% French and 5% English.

Bakker suggests that

> The newly emerged Métis identity and the new language symbolized a break with their parents and parent cultures. . . . The linguistic act of identity was the creation of a new language, which expressed both a connection with the ancestral cultures and, at the same time, a form of resistance against them.
>
> *(Bakker 2012: 180)*

Interestingly, Bakker (1997: 158) remarks that "some two-thirds of the Michif speakers I interviewed do not speak or understand Cree or French, which confirms the status of Michif as a separate language." Moreover, Michif can be a native language to a Métis who has no Cree ancestry. As Bakker (1997: 50) writes: "Most of the partners [of the Europeans] came from the Cree, Assiniboine [Hohe Nakota], Ojibwe, and Chipewyan [Sayisi Dene] nations. . . . Their offspring would ultimately become the Métis Nation: la Nouvelle Nation." Although Michif was created by children from French-Cree families, it was also acquired and used by children whose mothers did not necessarily know Cree. This, too, confirms that Michif is an independent language.

On the other hand, "French ancestry seems to be a condition for Métis identity" according to Bakker (1997: 62), who cites this anecdote: "I met a man in northern Manitoba who said that he was not a real Métis because he also had Irish and Scottish ancestors" (*ibid.*). But it is easy enough to find proud Métis individuals without French ancestry. For instance, consider this excerpt of an interview by Peters and Lafond (2013: 119, 123) of a 48-year-old Métis man who lives in Saskatoon, Saskatchewan:

> I'm from a place called Île-à-la-Crosse . . . and I'm Métis. My grandma was full-blooded Cree and my grandfather was English so that makes me a half-breed and I speak my language very fluently and I understand the language. So . . . in regards to cultural identity I identify myself as a Métis. . . . I'm excited to tell people I'm Métis, that I can speak my Michif language . . . I'm proud of it, proud of where I come from because . . . we're the second oldest settlement in Saskatchewan.

This man proudly identifies as Métis in multiple ways: he is racially mixed indigenous-European, he comes from an old Métis settlement and he speaks a Métis language. Crucially, his English background does not quite square with his home community or with his language if we think of the latter two as (even partly) "French." If we think of Île-à-la-Crosse and of his Michif language as simply "Métis," then there is no contradiction.

Other mixed varieties

Historically, Canada also had its share of trade jargons or pidgins, characterized by rudimentary grammars and limited vocabularies. The largest and most elaborate mixed language, Chinook Jargon, originated as a lingua franca in the Pacific Northwest. It drew many basic words from Nuučaańuł and from Canadian French. Its use peaked in the 19th century with an estimated 100,000 speakers representing more than 100 mother tongues. There are now probably no more than a dozen speakers of Chinook Jargon in Canada, mostly in British Columbia. This is not a full-fledged language (hence "jargon"), but some indigenous children in what is today British Columbia may have acquired it as one of their mother tongues in the past, particularly if their parents had different mother tongues and used Chinook Jargon at home. (This happened at Grande Ronde in neighbouring Oregon.)

Notes

1 To give just two examples, Europeans settled in British Columbia (a colonial place name if ever there was one; Pine and Turin 2017: §2.1) in the late 18th century, and in the Yukon in the 19th century, but there is archaeological evidence that indigenous peoples already inhabited these territories 14,000 years ago (McLaren and Gauvreau 2017) and 24,000 years ago (Bourgeon, Burke and Higham 2017), respectively.
2 This chapter uses endonyms to refer to indigenous peoples and their languages and dialects, particularly when these terms are favoured by many community members, even when they are speaking English. When there exists an English approximation of the sound (or meaning) of the endonym, it is given in parentheses, e.g., Nuučaańuł (Nuu-chah-nulth). Exonyms are avoided in this chapter when they are erroneous (such as Nootka for Nuučaańuł).

3   The territorial governments of the Northwest Territories and Nunavut have passed and enacted Official Languages Acts that encompass indigenous languages in those territories, alongside English and French.

4   Indigenous peoples were displaced by the tide of Euro-Canadian settlers, but this was not the only reason for their dislocation. Pine and Turin (2017: §2.1) allege that "in Canada, settler-colonial authorities observed the unique relationship that existed between a language and the land on which it was spoken and focused their attention on breaking this apart by destroying the language and forcibly relocating communities far away from their traditional territories." The authorities, for their part, claimed to relocate communities "for their own good," but in reality, relocation was typically disastrous for indigenous peoples (e.g., Petch 1998 and references therein). Incidentally, and regrettably, calls for such relocation continue until present-day (e.g., Gilmore 2016a, 2016b, 2016c; cf. Rice 2016).

5   "Both my father and mother are Tłįchǫ and they both taught me my Tłįchǫ language and way of life. I'm very thankful for their teaching. I'm also thankful to my grandfather and grandmother. They always told me not to be ashamed to speak my Tłįchǫ language. I'm thankful and it's good that I'm still learning my language because it will help me to understand my language better." (Translated from audio recording at http://ucalgary.ca/dflynn/nora, accessed on 29 April 2017.)

6   Karahkwenhá:wi also writes and directs films that showcase her heritage language Kanyen'kéha as well as other indigenous languages in Canada. For instance, she has made documentary shorts on Hailhzaqvla, which is another heritage language for her (Karahkwenhá:wi 2010c), on Ktunaxa (Karahkwenhá:wi 2010b), and on nłeʔkèpmxcín, Státimcets and Nisga'a (Karahkwenhá:wi 2010a).

7   This quote is from a news story about one of Karahkwenhá:wi's more famous students, Marc Miller, a non-indigenous member of parliament who recently addressed the House of Commons in Kanyen'kéha, a first in the 150-year history of the Parliament of Canada. On National Indigenous Peoples Day in the same month, Romeo Saganash, an indigenous member of parliament, asked a question of the Prime Minister in Iyiniw-Ayamiwin (Southern Inland East Cree), to protest a ruling that the House of Commons would not provide translations of indigenous languages into English and French. This translation request had come from Robert-Falcon Ouellette, another indigenous member of parliament, after he addressed the House in nēhiyawēwin (Plains Cree) in the previous month. Such linguistic activism at the highest level of government is mostly symbolic, but it is significant in the context of Canadian history (e.g., Saganash is a former residential school student) and politics (e.g., the Prime Minister recently promised to develop an Indigenous Languages Act).

8   A literal interpretation of this statement is challenging, as only 4–8% of ethnic Ts'msyen speak Sm'algyax (FPCC 2014; StatCan 2017). Alexa Manuel (p.c., 24 July 2017) remarks that after making the same point regarding Hodinohso:ni languages, Chief Jake Thomas went so far as to cite former Canadian Prime Minister Pierre Trudeau at a First Ministers conference in 1983: "if you no longer speak your language and no longer practice your culture, then you have no right to demand aboriginal rights or claim land from the Canadian government, because you are assimilated with the ruling power" (Thomas and Boyle 1994: 141–2).

9   "When I was told to love my language and preserve it, I didn't understand the meaning of it. Today I understand. When you love and preserve your native language, you will know your identity, place of birth, your ancestors' history and stories and their connection, you will be strong emotionally and mentally, and you will know your traditional way of life. You can then teach and help your people, young and old, to love and to preserve their native language, so they will become strong mentally, emotionally and spiritually, and be 'strong like two people.'" (Translated from audio recording at http://ucalgary.ca/dflynn/nora, accessed on 29 April 2017.)

10 It is notoriously difficult to count speakers of indigenous languages; see, e.g., Grenoble (2011), Grinevald and Bert (2011), Ouellette (2013), FPCC (2014), Norris (2016) and Boltokova (2017).

11 E.g., Craig Kopris (10 July 2017) regarding Iroquoian languages.

12 Ruth E. Claplanhoo, the last fluent mother-tongue speaker of qʷi·qʷi·diččaq, passed away in 2002, but 150 members of the Makah Tribe claim to be second-language speakers.

13 This figure is possibly inflated (as the US figure probably is), as it represents an increase of 750 from the mother-tongue figure in the 2011 Census (545), which was itself an increase of 250 over the figures in the 2006 Census (295) and in the 1996 Census (290). These increases may be ascribed to recent changes in self-reporting, but also to the fact that ever more children are learning Kanien'kéha as one of their mother tongues, at home (with parents who may be semi-speakers) and in language immersion nests (which were pioneered by the Kanien'kehá:ka in Canada).

14 This low figure from FPCC (2014) is possibly a self-reporting error. Crystal Azak (p.c., 26 July 2017) reports that speakers may deny their fluency for a number of reasons, such as not being able to read or write in their language.

References

Ahenakew, Freda. 1987. *Cree Language Structures: A Cree Approach*. Winnipeg, MB: Pemmican.

Armstrong, Jeanette. 2012. 'Recovery of Everyday Language Use: Adult Fluency Building'. Paper presented at the *19th Annual Stabilizing Indigenous Languages Symposium*, Thompson Rivers University, Kamloops, BC, 17–19 May 2012.

Assembly of First Nations, Education Secretariat. 1990. *Towards Linguistic Justice for First Nations*. Ottawa, ON: Assembly of First Nations.

Bakker, Peter. 1997. *'A Language of Our Own'. The Genesis of Michif, the Mixed Cree-French Language of the Canadian Metis*. New York: Oxford University Press.

Bakker, Peter. 2012. 'Ethnogenesis, Language and Identity: The Genesis of Michif and Other Mixed Languages', in Carolyn Podruchny, Nicole St-Onge and Brenda McDougall (eds), *Contours of Métis Landscapes: Family, Mobility, and History in Northwestern North America*, pp. 169–193. Norman, OK: University of Oklahoma Press.

Boltokova, Daria. 2017. ' "Will the Real Semi-Speaker Please Stand Up?": Language Vitality, Semi-Speakers, and Problems of Enumeration in the Canadian North'. *Anthropologica*, 59(1): 12–27.

Bourgeon, Lauriane, Ariane Burke and Thomas Higham. 2017. 'Earliest Human Presence in North America Dated to the Last Glacial Maximum: New Radiocarbon Dates from Bluefish Caves, Canada'. *PLoS ONE*, 12(1): e0169486.

CBC, the Canadian Broadcasting Corporation. 2017. ' "Like Being Inside a Heritage Moment!" On Hearing My Student Speak Mohawk in Parliament'. *CBC News*, 2 June 2017. www.cbc.ca/2017/like-being-inside-a-heritage-moment-on-hearing-my-student-speak-mohawk-in-parliament-1.4143131 (accessed on 3 June 2017).

Cullis-Suzuki, Severn. 2017. 'Learning the Ancestral Language of My Children'. *PhDs Go Public Research Talk Series*, 23 March 2017 [video]. www.youtube.com/watch?v=7_QxY-A6bNg (accessed on 12 June 2017).

Davis, Jeffrey. 2015. 'North American Indian Sign Language', in Julie Bakken Jepsen, Goedele De Clerck, Sam Lutalo-Kiingi and William B. McGregor (eds), *Sign Languages of the World: A Comparative Handbook*, pp. 911–932. Berlin: Mouton de Gruyter.

Dorais, Louis-Jacques. 2010. *The Language of the Inuit: Syntax, Semantics, and Society in the Arctic*. Montreal: McGill-Queen's University Press.

Dorais, Louis-Jacques. 2015. 'Le Projet Yawenda De revitalisation De la Langue Huronne-Wendat: Une Alliance De Recherche Entre Communauté Et université'. *Projectics/Proyéctica/Projectique*, 15(3): 129–144.

Dupuis, Braden. 2016. 'Language of the Land: With Fluent Speakers Declining, First Nations across B.C. And Canada Fight to Save Their Traditional Tongues'. *Pique Magazine*, 1 July 2016. www.piquenewsmagazine.com/whistler/language-of-the-land/ Content?oid=2795558 (accessed on 17 September 2016).

Ferguson, Jehanne. 2010. 'Shäwthän Dän, Shäwthän Kwänjè: Good People, Good Words: Creating a Dän K'è Speech Community in an Elementary School'. *Current Issues in Language Planning*, 11(2): 152–172.

Fettes, Mark and Ruth Norton. 2000. 'Voices of Winter: Aboriginal Languages and Public Policy in Canada', in Marlene Brant Castellano, Lynne Davis and Louise Lahache (eds), *Aboriginal Education: Fulfilling the Promise*, pp. 23–54. Vancouver, BC: UBC Press.

FPCC, the First People's Cultural Council. 2010. *Report on the Status of Bc First Nations Languages*. Brentwood Bay, BC: First People's Cultural Council, Language Programs.

FPCC, the First People's Cultural Council. 2014. *Report on the Status of B.C. First Nations Languages*. Brentwood Bay, BC: First People's Cultural Council, Language Programs.

FPHLCC, the First Peoples' Heritage, Language and Culture Council. 2005–17. *First Peoples' Language Map of British Columbia*. Brentwood Bay, BC: First Peoples' Cultural Council. http://maps.fpcc.ca/ (accessed on 10 June 2017).

Frantz, Donald. 2009. *Blackfoot Grammar*, 2nd edn. Toronto, ON: University of Toronto Press.

Frantz, Donald and Norma Jean Russell. 1995. *Blackfoot Dictionary of Stems, Roots, and Affixes*, 2nd edn. Toronto: University of Toronto Press.

Gilmore, Scott. 2016a. 'La Loche Shows Us It's Time to Help People Escape the North'. *Maclean's Magazine*, 27 January 2016 [Article]. www.macleans.ca/news/canada/la-loche-shows-us-its-time-to-help-people-escape/ (accessed on 2 June 2017).

Gilmore, Scott. 2016b. 'The Hard Truth About Remote Communities'. *Maclean's Magazine*, 9 February 2016 [Article]. www.macleans.ca/news/canada/scott-gilmore-the-hard-truth-about-remote-communities/ (accessed on 2 June 2017).

Gilmore, Scott. 2016c. 'The Unasked Question About Attawapiskat'. *Maclean's Magazine*, 13 April 2016 [Article]. www.macleans.ca/news/canada/the-unasked-question-about-attawapiskat/ (accessed on 2 June 2017).

Government of Ontario, The. 2016. *The Journey Together: Ontario's Commitment to Reconciliation with Indigenous Peoples*. Toronto: Queen's Printer for Ontario. https://files.ontario.ca/progress_report1_en_web.pdf (accessed on 9 June 2017).

Green, Denise. 2014. 'Producing Materials, Places and Identities: A Study of Encounters in the Alberni Valley'. Unpublished Ph.D. dissertation, University of British Columbia.

Grenoble, Lenore A. 2011. 'Language Ecology and Endangerment', in Peter K. Austin and Julia Sallabank (eds), *The Cambridge Handbook of Endangered Languages*, pp. 27–44. Oxford, UK: Cambridge University Press.

Grinevald, Colette and Michel Bert. 2011. 'Speakers and Communities', in Peter K. Austin and Julia Sallabank (eds), *The Cambridge Handbook of Endangered Languages*, pp. 45–65. Oxford, UK: Cambridge University Press.

Hallett, Darcy, Michael J. Chandler and Christopher E. Lalonde. 2007. 'Aboriginal Language Knowledge and Youth Suicide'. *Cognitive Development*, 22: 392–399.

Karahkwenhá:wi, Zoe Hopkins. 2010a. *Spelling Bee*. Vancouver, BC: Knowledge Network. www.knowledge.ca/program/our-first-voices (accessed on 3 June 2017).

Karahkwenhá:wi, Zoe Hopkins. 2010b. *Ktunaxa*. Vancouver, BC: Knowledge Network. www.knowledge.ca/program/our-first-voices (accessed on 3 June 2017).

Karahkwenhá:wi, Zoe Hopkins. 2010c. *Airplane*. Vancouver, BC: Knowledge Network. www.knowledge.ca/program/our-first-voices (accessed on 3 June 2017).

Khelsílem, Tłakwasikan. 2017. 'Truth and Reclamation: A 1000 Hours of Teaching Squamish Language at Sfu'. *Kwi Awt Stelmexw*, 26 April 2017. https://vimeo.com/218629038 (accessed on 30 May 2017).

MacDougall, James. 2001. 'Access to Justice for Deaf Inuit in Nunavut: The Role of Inuit Sign Language'. *Canadian Psychology/Psychologie canadienne*, 42(1): 61–73.

Marshall, Ingeborg. 1996. *A History and Ethnography of the Beothuk*. Montreal: McGill-Queen's University Press.

McLaren, Duncan and Alisha Gauvreau. 2017. 'Long-Term Culture Landscape Development at (Ektb-9) Triquet Island, British Columbia, Canada'. Paper presented at the *82nd Annual Meeting of the Society for American Archaeology*, Vancouver, BC, 30 March 2017.

Meek, Barbra A. 2010. *We Are Our Language: An Ethnography of Language Revitalization in a Northern Athabaskan Community*. Tucson, AZ: University of Arizona Press.

Meisel, Jürgen M. 2011. *First and Second Language Acquisition: Parallels and Differences*. Cambridge, UK: Cambridge University Press.

Mithun, Marianne. 1982. 'The Mystery of the Vanished Laurentians', in Anders Ahlqvist (ed.), *Papers from the 5th International Conference on Historical Linguistics*, pp. 230–242. Amsterdam: John Benjamins.

Moseley, Christopher (ed.). 2010. *Atlas of the World's Languages in Danger*, 3rd edn. Paris: UNESCO Publishing.

Noori, Margaret. 2009. 'Wenesh Waa Oshkii-Bmaadizijig Noondamowaad? What Will the Young Children Hear?', in Jon Reyhner and Louise Lockard (eds), *Indigenous Language Revitalization: Encouragement, Guidance and Lessons Learned*, pp. 11–22. Flagstaff, AZ: Northern Arizona University.

Norris, Mary Jane. 2016. *Report and Reference Manual on Documentation and Classification of Aboriginal Languages in Canada*. Ottawa: Norris Research.

Ouellette, Robert-Falcon. 2013. *Michif: A Language Born and near Death on Our Native Land*. Winnipeg: University of Manitoba. https://attheedgeofcanada.blogspot.ca/2013/01/michif-language-born-and-near-death-on.html (accessed on 2 July 2016).

Parker, Aliana. 2012. 'Learning the Language of the Land'. Unpublished M.A. thesis, University of Victoria.

Parkin, Andrew and André Turcotte. 2004. *Bilingualism: Part of Our Past or Part of Our Future?* Ottawa: Centre for Research and Information on Canada.

Petch, Virginia Phyllis. 1998. 'Relocation and Loss of Homeland: The Story of the Sayisi Dene of Northern Manitoba'. Unpublished Ph.D. dissertation, University of Manitoba.

Peters, Evelyn and Carol Lafond. 2013. '"I Basically Mostly Stick with My Own Kind": First Nations Appropriation of Urban Space in Saskatoon, Saskatchewan', in Evelyn Peters and Chris Andersen (eds), *Indigenous in the City: Contemporary Identities and Cultural Innovation*, pp. 88–109. Vancouver, BC: UBC Press.

Pine, Aidan and Mark Turin. 2017. 'Language Revitalization', in Mark Aronoff (ed.), *Oxford Research Encyclopedia of Linguistics*. New York: Oxford University Press, Online Publication Date: March 2017. DOI: 10.1093/acrefore/9780199384655.013.8.

Prairie Chicken, Brent, Sandra Manyfeathers-O'Hara, Noah Wings and Sage Manyfeathers-O'Hara. 2016. 'We're Still Here', in Karim Rushdy and Darin Flynn (eds), *Blackfoot Language Junior Youth Rap Camp*. Calgary: University of Calgary.

Rice, Sally. 1998. 'Giving and Taking in Chipewyan: The Semantics of Thing-Marking Classificatory Verbs', in John Newman (ed.), *Linguistics of Giving*, pp. 97–134. Amsterdam: John Benjamins.

Rice, Waubgeshig. 2016. 'Walking in 2 Worlds: Indigenous Ottawans Reflect on Leaving Home'. *CBC News*, 11 May 2016 [Article]. www.cbc.ca/news/canada/ottawa/walking-in-2-worlds-indigenous-ottawans-reflect-on-leaving-home-1.3568401 (accessed on 2 June 2017).

Royal Commission on Aboriginal Peoples, Canada. 1996. *Report of the Royal Commission on Aboriginal Peoples*. Ottawa: Royal Commission on Aboriginal Peoples.

Rushforth, Scott. 1991. 'Use of Bearlake and Mescalero (Athapaskan) Classificatory Verbs'. *International Journal of American Linguistics*, 57(2): 251–266.

Sapir, Edward. 1912. 'Language and Environment'. *American Anthropologist*, 14(2): 226–242.

Schuit, Joke. 2012. 'Signing in the Arctic: External Influences on Inuit Sign Language', in Ulrike Zeshan, Connie de Vos and Marie Coppola (eds), *Sign Languages in Village Communities: Anthropological and Linguistic Insights*, pp. 181–208. Berlin: Mouton de Gruyter.

Schuit, Joke. 2015. 'Inuit Sign Language', in Julie Bakken Jepsen, Goedele De Clerck, Sam Lutalo-Kiingi and William B. McGregor (eds), *Sign Languages of the World: A Comparative Handbook*, pp. 431–448. Berlin: Mouton de Gruyter.

Shaw, Patricia A. 2001. 'Language and Identity, Language and the Land'. *BC Studies*, 131 (Autumn): 39–55.

Sinha, Maire. 2015. *Spotlight on Canadians: Results from the General Social Survey: Canadian Identity, 2013*. Ottawa, ON: Statistics Canada. www.statcan.gc.ca/pub/89-652-x/89-652-x2015005-eng.pdf (accessed on 13 November 2016).

StatCan, Statistics Canada. 2017. *2016 Census Topic: Language*. Ottawa: Statistics Canada. http://www12.statcan.gc.ca/census-recensement/2016/rt-td/lang-eng.cfm (accessed on 2 August 2017).

Tehota'kerá:tonh, Jeremy Green. 2017. *Pathways to Creating Onkwehonwehnéha Speakers at Six Nations of the Grand River Territory*. Ohsweken, ON: Six Nations Polytechnic.

Thomas, Chief Jacob and Terry Boyle. 1994. *Teachings from the Longhouse*. Toronto: Stoddart.

TRC, the Truth and Reconciliation Commission of Canada. 2015a. *Honouring the Truth, Reconciling for the Future: Summary of the Final Report of the Truth and Reconciliation of Canada*. Winnipeg, University of Manitoba: National Centre for Truth and Reconciliation. http://nctr.ca/reports.php (accessed on 15 March 2017).

TRC, the Truth and Reconciliation Commission of Canada. 2015b. *Calls to Action*. Winnipeg, University of Manitoba: National Centre for Truth and Reconciliation. http://nctr.ca/reports.php (accessed on 15 March 2017).

Tulloch, Shelley R. 2014. 'Igniting a Youth Language Movement: Inuit Youth as Agents of Circumpolar Language Planning', in Leisy T. Wyman, Teresa L. McCarty and Sheilah E. Nicholas (eds), *Indigenous Youth and Multilingualism: Language Identity, Ideology, and Practice in Dynamic Cultural Worlds*, pp. 149–167. New York, NY: Routledge.

INDEX

Printed in the United States
By Bookmasters